Bringing Business Ethics to Life

Achieving Corporate Social Responsibility

Also available from ASQ Quality Press:

Business Process Improvement Toolbox
Bjørn Andersen

Root Cause Analysis: Simplified Tools and Techniques
Bjørn Andersen and Tom Fagerhaug

Performance Measurement Explained: Designing and Implementing Your State-of-the-Art System
Bjørn Andersen and Tom Fagerhaug

Transformational Leadership: Creating Organizations of Meaning
Stephen Hacker and Tammy Roberts

The Trust Imperative: Performance Improvement through Productive Relationships
Stephen Hacker and Marsha Willard

The Change Agents' Handbook: A Survival Guide for Quality Improvement Champions
David W. Hutton

Making Change Work: Practical Tools for Overcoming Human Resistance to Change
Brien Palmer

The Recipe for Simple Business Improvement
David W. Till

The Change Agent's Guide to Radical Improvement
Ken Miller

The Synergy of One: Creating High-Performing Sustainable Organizations through Integrated Performance Leadership
Michael J. Dreikorn

To request a complimentary catalog of ASQ Quality Press publications, call 800-248-1946, or visit our Web site at http://qualitypress.asq.org.

Bringing Business Ethics to Life

Achieving Corporate Social Responsibility

Bjørn Andersen

ASQ Quality Press
Milwaukee, Wisconsin

American Society for Quality, Quality Press, Milwaukee 53203
© 2004 by ASQ
All rights reserved. Published 2004
Printed in the United States of America

12 11 10 09 08 07 06 05 04   5 4 3 2 1

Library of Congress Cataloging-in-Publication Data

Andersen, Bjørn.
  Bringing business ethics to life : achieving corporate social
responsibility / Bjørn Andersen.
    p. cm.
  Includes bibliographical references and index.
  ISBN 0-87389-621-1 (pbk. : alk. paper)
  1. Social responsibility of busines. 2. Business ethics. I. Title.

HD60.A42 2004
174'.4—dc22   2004000117

Publisher: William A. Tony
Acquisitions Editor: Annemieke Hytinen
Project Editor: Paul O'Mara
Production Administrator: Randall Benson
Special Marketing Representative: David Luth

ASQ Mission: The American Society for Quality advances individual,
organizational, and community excellence worldwide through learning,
quality improvement, and knowledge exchange.

Attention Bookstores, Wholesalers, Schools, and Corporations: ASQ Quality
Press books, videotapes, audiotapes, and software are available at quantity
discounts with bulk purchases for business, educational, or instructional use.
For information, please contact ASQ Quality Press at 800-248-1946, or write to
ASQ Quality Press, P.O. Box 3005, Milwaukee, WI 53201-3005.

To place orders or to request a free copy of the ASQ Quality Press Publications
Catalog, including ASQ membership information, call 800-248-1946. Visit our
Web site at www.asq.org or http://qualitypress.asq.org.

 Printed on acid-free paper

Quality Press
600 N. Plankinton Avenue
Milwaukee, Wisconsin 53203
Call toll free 800-248-1946
Fax 414-272-1734
www.asq.org
http://qualitypress.asq.org
http://standardsgroup.asq.org
E-mail: authors@asq.org

Good people do not need laws to tell them to act responsibly, while bad people will find a way around the laws.

—Plato

When I do good, I feel good; when I do bad, I feel bad. That's my religion.

—Abraham Lincoln

A man's ethical behavior should be based effectually on sympathy, education, and social ties; no religious basis is necessary. Man would indeed be in a poor way if he had to be restrained by fear of punishment and hope of reward after death.

—Albert Einstein

Ethics, too, are nothing but reverence for life. This is what gives me the fundamental principle of morality, namely, that good consists in maintaining, promoting, and enhancing life, and that destroying, injuring, and limiting life are evil.

—Albert Schweitzer

Table of Contents

List of Figures and Tables

Preface

Iam not sure, but I assume normal practice is to first write a book, then backtrack and fill in the preface. This is what I have done, which means that at the time of this writing, I have put behind me a process lasting close to a year. Paradoxically, this book has been both the hardest one I have ever written and the most motivating. Hardest in that it has required extensive investigation of relevant literature, Web sites, and news coverage of current cases; motivating in that the topic is fascinating and different from previous things I have written. Looking back, I cannot deny the fact that I am glad it is done, but it has been a true learning experience for me.

Whether you are already well versed in the field of business ethics or not, I hope this book turns out to be a learning experience for you as well. As you will see in the first chapter, my discovery of this field had been a long time coming, and I hope this book will inspire you to explore it further. You should also realize that this is not primarily an academic book, written for university students or academic peers. During my research for this book, I found more than enough literature of this type, reinforcing my belief in the need for a more down-to-earth book on ethics. My main intention has therefore been to translate philosophical debate and esoteric definitions of corporate social responsibility into an operational manifestation that can be applied in your organization tomorrow.

The book is structured around what I call the *business ethics framework*. This framework is presented in the introductory chapter outlining benefits to be achieved by basing business on ethical values and practices. The framework is divided along the dimensions of strategic versus operational issues, internal versus external focus, and remedial versus philanthropic intentions, all in all eight distinct areas of ethical application. Following chapter 3 and its roadmap for implementation of an ethical approach to business in an organization, these eight areas are covered one by one in chapters 4 to 11. Building on the implementation principles outlined in chapter 2, some additional advice has been included at the end of each chapter dealing with specific areas of the business ethics framework.

The final chapter looks more critically at the ethics concept and any potential negative effects.

From this focus, it follows that individuals are not the main "unit of analysis". Organizations and their collective behavior are of course the result of decisions and actions of individuals, but this book deals with individuals as representatives of organizations. I should also point out that the organizations I refer to are "normal" organizations, that is, not criminal organizations or government dictatorships. The latter example is pertinent, though, as I clearly target both private sector enterprises and public sector organizations. Business ethics are just as relevant for the public sector, and in many cases, actually more of interest to public sector monopolies or authorities with strained budgets than private companies.

In writing a practically oriented book, I have been obliged to include real-world examples from industry and the public sector. Although these might appear to be unevenly distributed, I have always tried to illustrate key concepts or discussions through the use of a case reference. I have also tried to provide sufficiently extensive descriptions of such cases to allow you to grasp their background and meaning. Where such case descriptions are longer than merely a line or two, they have been highlighted in shaded sidebars. You will also notice that in many examples the organization in question has been identified by name. There are, however, many descriptions where this is not the case. These are either cases where the organization or individuals prefer to remain unidentified or simply where the example has been related to me without any names attached. At any rate, the case descriptions are only included as illustrations.

Finally, I must acknowledge that I could not have written this book without help from many people. A year ago, the executive group and the director of our research unit decided to support a small study on a more operational approach to business ethics by earmarking some funding to such work. This was really the start of a more systematic adaptation of general ethical principles to a more hands-on approach. My colleagues Bjørnar Henriksen, Lars Onsøyen, and I had a few good discussions and talked to some interesting people. When the funding ran out, I decided to see if I could structure my thinking on the topic into a book. Annemieke Hytinen at ASQ Quality Press was responsive to the idea and did a great job of having the proposal reviewed by experts. After some tweaking of the concept, she gave me the green light in March 2003. Since then, the book and its subtopics were with me day and night until the last word was written that following September. As always, my dear wife Hilde has been most supportive and helpful in reading and commenting on the manuscript.

I will put down my pen now (or rather push the keyboard back) and let you get on with your reading. If you have comments on the book in general, ideas for changes in future editions, or real-world examples that should have been included, please let me know.

Bjørn Andersen
Trondheim, September 2003
authors@asq.org

1

Introduction to Business Ethics and Its Benefits (or Disadvantages?)

This introductory chapter is supposed to be the only chapter of a "missionary" nature, where the merits of ethics and business ethics are argued. Some of the primary benefits that can be achieved through an ethical approach to business are presented and discussed briefly. Even though chapter 11 elaborates further on the criticisms of corporate social responsibility and its possible disadvantages, it also includes a brief balancing view of the concept. At the end, the business ethics framework is introduced. This separates chapter 11 from the rest of the book, which is much more focused on providing practical, hands-on advice on how to compose and pursue such an ethical approach. If you are already convinced of the benefits of business ethics, you might even skip the first part of this chapter and move on to the business ethics framework.

FACTORS DETERMINING COMPETITIVENESS AND LONG-TERM VIABILITY

If you're reading this book, you are probably involved in running an organization of some sort, plan to be so, work for an organization, are a student striving to belong to one of these categories in the future, or buy products and services from one or more companies. No matter which of these apply to your specific situation, the first point in this context is that all of us are engaged in some type of relationship with professional organizations. Thus, every one of us are in a position to have an opinion as to what predicts the competitiveness and long-term viability of such organizations, be they commercial companies, schools, public sector institutions, nonprofit organizations, or sports teams. It is very easy to generate a list of at least five factors that create competitive edge, (there are most likely many more), typically containing elements such as the following:

- Product or service design and performance

- Quality and reliability

- Lowest manufacturing or service delivery costs

- The ability to innovate

- Shorter lead times and more reliable delivery performance

- Superior customer service

These six were taken from Todd (1995) simply as an example. If these would be on your list—congratulations, that is commendable! These are no doubt very important areas to master if you want to be a successful manufacturing or service company.

However, an increasing number of people claim that this and similar lists are not exhaustive as long as they lack the aspect of ethics (or professional integrity, social responsibility, honesty, or whichever term you prefer). In this first chapter of the book, some reasons why this might be the case will be reviewed.

"THE STATE OF THE REALM"

Open one arbitrarily chosen newspaper, tune in a radio news channel, or switch the TV to your news station of choice—it is easy to get depressed by what you see and hear. Of course there have always been war, crime, poverty, disease, dishonesty, but it seems that all of these have both increased in magnitude and decided to occur simultaneously. Arguably, the number of news sources and their global reach and ability to transmit news instantly have exploded, but it still seems that the occurrence of "negative news" has increased. There are numerous reasons why—issues related to morality, religion, politics, societal values, world economy, and globalization. However, as this is not a history, philosophy, or sociology book, the argument will not be taken any further here. Suffice it to say that society seems to have grown colder.

It might seem as if personal and corporate greed have become a prominent feature of today's society, at least if you take a pessimistic view of the world: Individuals spend more and more time working to earn more money to pay for more, larger, and better homes, cars, appliances, clothes, and travel. Traditional family values are deteriorating, resulting in broken homes, single-parent families, which only increase the pressure to keep working longer hours to compensate for the reduced household income. Singer Shania Twain put this observation into words in her 2003 hit song "Ka-Ching!" (the title of course mimicking the sound of a cash register ringing up a sale). The results can be seen in terms of increased drug abuse, higher crime levels, and serious juvenile problems. For the parents, and indeed lately all kinds of employees, the time bind of interesting, seductive jobs with long hours coupled with busy personal lives leaves a trail of professional burnout in all age, gender, and professional groups.

Correspondingly, the governmental part of society has grown more concerned with financial resources, having to make more with less money. Again, the results manifest themselves in a colder society offering less "positive" services to its citizens and spending ever more on "negative" services like judicial, police, and corrections systems. In sync with the diminishing visible, tangible signs of positive returns from government, people stop caring about politics and public debate. Record low levels of election participation are observed in almost every democracy around the world. The same trend holds true for religious institutions, at least in the Western world; all the traditional churches struggle to maintain people's interest and commitment.

Turning to the area of society of most interest to the subject matter of this book, the corporate world, we see similar signs of this coldness and greed. The foremost objective for any commercial organization is of course to maximize its profits. Most modern organizations realize that in order to survive in today's competitive arena, customers have to be satisfied. However, the more money that can be charged for less value, the higher the profits. Anyone who has bought something that has broken within the warranty period knows what a struggle it can be to have it repaired or replaced at no extra cost. Much more serious than this are full-blown news scandals involving large grocery store chains systematically relabeling meat and other products that have passed their expiry date in order to sell them, insurance companies with double sets of claims-handling protocols, and public transportation companies that deliberately delay preventive maintenance of vehicles to save money, fully aware that this jeopardizes passenger safety.

Furthermore, most people know that some CEOs and high-level managers make extraordinary amounts of money, both in direct salaries and in terms of bonuses and stock options. In addition, scandals are disclosed weekly about inside stock trading, overly generous compensation schemes, "golden parachute" retirement plans, all while the very same executives continuously advocate downsizing and fight the unions over any pay raise, however minute. The latest icing on this bitter cake has been the revelations of how the constant pressure CEOs and other high-level managers of industrial companies are under to maximize short-term profits and stock levels has led them to commit fraud and felonies. Maximizing profits becomes so important that people one would assume should know the difference between right and wrong deliberately falsify accounts, claim fictitious income levels, appraise assets at ridiculously inflated values, to boost earnings figures, share prices, and ultimately their own personal standing and rewards, financial and otherwise.

One could fill entire chapters of this book with in-depth coverage of the large number of other cases from around the world where a lack of integrity, morals, or ethics have caused scandal, disgrace, bankruptcy, and other misery. However, from this rather brief introduction and the massive exposure to news about such cases that you no doubt have sustained lately, you are probably quite familiar with these already and perhaps even agree that there is a need for a new approach. Although the vast majority of business leaders and employees are "good people" and do nothing wrong, there

---

The Enron and WorldCom scandals provide excellent examples of financial pressures leading to criminal behavior. These two cases in particular prompted a response from the U.S. government—President George W. Bush's Wall Street speech to industrial leaders on July 9, 2002. Bush suggested that leaders found guilty of this kind of fraud should be liable to up to ten years imprisonment. Legislation that will hold CEOs personally responsible for the accounts of their companies is on the way, and the SEC (Securities and Exchange Commission) will be furnished with generous additional funding to finance new recruitment and technological aids in the fight against financial crime.

On the other side of the Atlantic, Margaret Beckett, the UK secretary of state for the environment, food, and rural affairs, in a speech on February 6, 2003, hardened her stance on corporate ethics. She especially criticized the "produce, use, and discard" mentality of manufacturers and consumers alike and called for a fundamental shift in the way businesses operate to make consumption more sustainable. Ms. Beckett argued the need for regulation and legislation and promised to introduce new laws and regulations shortly.

is sufficient evidence on the table that many certainly do need a new set of tools. We all can benefit from changing our ways. For some, this means mainly minor adjustments, for others it is truly turning a new leaf.

WHY DID I CHANGE MY WAYS?

My greatest fear in writing this book has been to come across as a deeply religious, perhaps fanatical, do-gooder who cannot stand the thought that some make more money than others, evade a few tax dollars, or fail to return the ten bucks received as erroneously calculated change. Let me tell you a little about my own motivation for starting to work with this topic and ultimately coming to promote business ethics through this book. In my career so far, I have devoted much of my time and energy (and will continue to do so) into understanding what creates a competitive edge and how organizations can improve it. In my quest to continuously uncover another piece of the extremely complex jigsaw puzzle constituting competitiveness, I have studied business process orientation, performance measurement, strategy development, process reengineering, balanced scorecards, just-in-time production, project-oriented business, time-based management, human resource management, professional burnout, and many other fragments of what is popularly termed management literature. Together with colleagues, I have been engaged in a large number of projects for all kinds of organizations analyzing their needs, preparing for the application of some approach, implementing new solutions, and studying their effects.

Gradually, I have become more and more convinced that the question of competitiveness is one interrelated complex of principles, thinking, approaches, and tools that fit together, impact each other (positively or negatively), and thus must be understood as a whole. The tendency of academics and consultants, as well as industrial practitioners, to mark off a minute fragment of this whole and delve deep down into it is to some extent counterproductive. Of course there is a need for someone to understand the nitty-gritty details of the different topics that make up the larger picture, but someone also must devote attention to the larger picture. Only then is it possible to identify shortcomings on a higher level. This might sound pompous and arrogant, even an excuse for not being able to excel within subareas where my peers do create significant results and insight. That might even be true to some extent, but in having covered quite a lot of this ground in depth already, I might have been able to develop some of this overall understanding as well.

Anyway, it is from this quest for the key to competitiveness that I have come to focus my attention on *ethics*. For one, besides all the other ways organizations create their competitive edge, ethics stands out as one additional approach that many organizations can benefit from by including it in the overall image they attempt to achieve and their organizational design. In addition, it seems quite clear that some of the current ways organizations achieve their competitiveness (at least in the short term) do not support a long-term viable development (for example, pushing employees so hard that burnout spreads throughout the organization; conducting sufficiently shady transactions to attract attention from the legal system or activist groups). Thus, an ethics approach might very well be required simply to ensure that the other approaches balance out and the organization stays afloat. This has led me to realize that it does no longer suffice to keep working on productivity-enhancing tools and new competitive approaches as long as these might induce a backlash of negative consequences somewhere down the road. These are the reasons why I changed my ways and started working on this aspect of competitiveness in addition to the other fields I study. And just for the record, I am not particularly philosophically inclined, nor am I a "prude" or a religious person—thus, the remainder of this book has been written with the perspective of a hands-on, tangible, and implementable approach to industrial ethics and integrity.

WHY SHOULD YOU CHANGE YOUR WAYS?

Now you know what pushed me in this particular direction, but the much more important question remains: Why should you, and your organization, go in this direction? There are many reasons, of which a few that should carry some weight are:

- Improved employee and organizational morale
- Customer loyalty and the ability to attract new customers
- Financial performance
- Negative exposure and backlashes under a nonethical approach
- Attracting other stakeholders
- Making the world a better place

Over the next few pages, these will be elaborated on. First, however, please consider the diagram in Figure 1.1, developed by Ferrell, Fraedrich, and Ferrell (2000). It demonstrates quite clearly the compounded effects of an ethical climate in an organization. By contributing to several key aspects

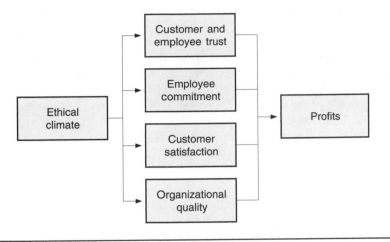

Figure 1.1　The link between an ethical climate and profits.

of an organization's internal life and commitment, it ultimately impacts profit levels. Keep this mutual reinforcement effect in mind when the individual relationships between business ethics and each of these elements are described in the following pages.

Improved Employee and Organizational Motivation and Morale

Conducting business in an ethical manner does produce a feeling of doing things right. Initially, perhaps, this is strongest at the individual level. As this feeling spreads and multiplies, it can become an almost tangible positive ambience within the entire organization, a strong sense of community and belonging.

This is a powerful force that constitutes an invaluable asset to any organization. In addition, this force is powerful in attracting future employees, another strong advantage in a world where access to the best people is becoming more and more important. Business ethics is a field of study and practice so deeply connected to the feeling of doing good, of contributing something to others, that people who become enticed by the concept often become highly enthusiastic about it and can sometimes make it a personal crusade to proliferate these ideas. This has a strong motivational effect that can spur individuals and indeed entire organizations to unheard-of peaks of performance. The other concept that perhaps has had some of the same power and lure is quality. Perhaps not in every shade that quality comes, but in the true sense of dedication to delivering the best products or services to

Some twenty years ago, a group of students at a polytechnic university shared their frustrations with each other over the cost of a decent stereo system. Even though different chain stores were competing fiercely, it was almost as if they had agreed on a bottom price threshold that would not be crossed. In addition, they found that most salesclerks knew much less than their customers about stereo systems in general and the products they sold in particular. Whether their mounting frustration, a spark of inspiration, or both, led them on is unclear, but the idea of a new type of stereo store was born and developed during the next few weeks. While maintaining their full-time studies, the students started looking for a suitable store location, talking with suppliers, and developing a marketing image. A few months down the road, their first "Hi-Fi Source" store opened. The primary factors distinguishing it from traditional stores were:

- Carrying brands of exceptional quality, but often less well known than the mass brands sold in other stores

- Lower prices through direct import and low markups

- Personnel extremely knowledgable about their products, usually due to having tested them personally at home

- Repackaging of products where necessary to include decent cables (quality cables often being the difference between good and great sound).

From a slow start, business soon picked up. Stereo-interested students got very competent equipment at great prices, word-of-mouth started spreading, and customers other than students began coming to the store. After a few weeks, more and more people were equipped with high-quality stereos that matched their needs and homes. Many of them even came back to thank them for their excellent advice. The students started feeling as if on a mission: to give people good stereo at reasonable prices.

New employees were hired and more stores opened, but always with the key goal of giving people good stereos. Though difficult to describe, the sense of shared goals these students and their employees developed could be sensed by their customers. Many of them refuse to buy stereo or home entertainment equipment anywhere else. Even today, it is hard to tell who has the bigger smile when a new customer has been educated about stereos and sold the right system at the right price, but one might actually suspect the sales representative.

create satisfaction and delight, quality ignites some of the same "internal glow" in its followers. Indeed ethics and quality share many common traits, a fact that will be addressed later in the book, especially when talking about product and service safety and quality in chapter 6.

There is truly a connection between the ethical position and practices of an organization and the feeling of well-being, motivation, and inspiration among its employees. This has been documented in numerous studies; see for example Loe (1996) and Maignan (1997). There are several ways this result can be interpreted, but the most apparent one is as follows: an organization that consistently demonstrates that it is unwilling to sacrifice its ethical values develops an image as trustworthy, both toward its external contacts and its employees. In such an organization, the employees expect, rightfully so, to be treated with respect, have their rights acknowledged, and be compensated fairly. As a result, levels of intrafirm trust, both within departments, across departments, and between managers and their subordinates are higher than in organizations with a less clear ethical stance.

Companies that succeed in building high levels of intrafirm trust are normally also much more successful in retaining their employees. Covey (1998) found that the average corporation loses half of its employees within four years, and the costs of recruiting, training, and getting new ones up to speed can be detrimental to an organization. The consequences of loss of employees are getting even direr as the average organization comes to rely more and more on the tacit knowledge of the individual and the organization.

Furthermore, in seeing that external stakeholders, customers, and others alike are being treated fairly and equally and thus being satisfied, most people will feel pride in their organization. It is rewarding to be part of a team that manages to create satisfied customers or other stakeholders, and this is a self-reinforcing effect that quite often turns into a virtuous circle. More satisfied customers inspire the organization to go that extra mile, which leads to even higher contentment on the part of the customers. Having a clear ethical position has been found to be one way of achieving this development.

Customer Loyalty and the Ability to Attract New Customers

As these ripples of positive and good feelings continue to spread, they extend even to the organization's external network, not in the least to its customers, where the most successful cases have managed to create something close to a constituency of extremely loyal customers. This can in some ways be compared to the "delight" the forerunners in the field of quality were able to create for their customers, but goes above and beyond this. There is also a clear link between the treatment of and the attitudes among your "internal" organization, that is, the employees and managers, and the treatment of and attitudes toward your organization among your "external" organization, that is, its stakeholders. These affect each other in both directions, thus constituting both an opportunity and a threat.

Some companies succeed in positioning themselves as the *only* choice for their customers when buying a certain type of product or service. This position goes beyond simply shopping at the same store out of habit or because it has managed to keep reasonable prices for years. It is not a question of convenience, but rather that their customers will accept even inconvenience to stay loyal. There are several ways to achieve such a position, from delivering consistent quality over many years to implementing loyalty programs to always being cheapest, and probably many more. However, it seems the organizations that get to this position by appealing to something more "noble" than the price consciousness or taste for quality in their customers manage to stay there even longer.

When customers understand and see tangible evidence that their patronage contributes to something beyond the profits of the company and the owners of the company that they do business with, this is an extremely strong motivator for continuing to take their custom there. Think of companies like Ben & Jerry's, The Body Shop, or LensCrafters: part of your dollar for ice cream goes to charity; a fair share of the price of cosmetics is channeled to the original producer of the raw materials; or part of your dollars spent on glasses gives free eye care to less fortunate people. Finding that your specific needs are fulfilled and that your business contributes to a greater good in the process is one quite easy way each of us can do something for more worthy causes. Most people complain that even if they want to, it is very difficult to make a difference in this world. This way, everyone can, and that produces a positive feeling that keeps these customers coming back.

A less altruistic motive for staying with ethically oriented suppliers of products and services is that you, as a customer, can expect to be treated fairly. If the organization is consistent in its dealings, chances are that their prices reflect the actual value of what you buy, that any claims you might bring forward will be taken seriously, that a product breaking down during the warranty period will be repaired or replaced without any hassle. All together, the case should be convincing; a well-defined and communicated ethical position is a good way of ensuring customer loyalty.

As for attracting new customers (who will later on be your loyal customers), the traditional business objective of corporate and personal profit maximization is not always such a good approach. Consumers and other stakeholders of today are exposed to such a massive amount of marketing and attempts at influencing them that many have become wary of whom they can and cannot trust.

This can lead to the *marketing uncertainty paradox* (Fagerhaug and Andersen, 1998), which in the end dissuades a potential customer from becoming a real customer. In order to present a competitive offer, a company must offer high value at a low price. At the same time, this company must charge as high a price as it can for as little material and effort put into the product or service as possible. As the customer cannot know which of these conflicting pressures is dominating a given situation, a customer cannot feel certain if the deal made was good: "Did I pay too much? Is the quality poor? Did the manufacturer use inferior components to shave off a few dollars of the cost? Am I paying for the CEO's next Mercedes? Will my money in turn be used to clear-cut endangered rain forest for the next project the company gets engaged in"? And so on. . . .

In marketing terms, this marketing uncertainty paradox constitutes a problem. A company may spend millions of dollars trying to create a positive image in the market. Still, the customers' uncertainty, induced by the general culture of greed in modern society and by revelations about the specific company's greedy behavior, could prevent purchase. The crux of this argumentation is that under the current marketing and business philosophy paradigm, to which almost every single company subscribes, a truly convincing marketing message cannot be conveyed to potential customers. The core of this paradox is depicted in Figure 1.2.

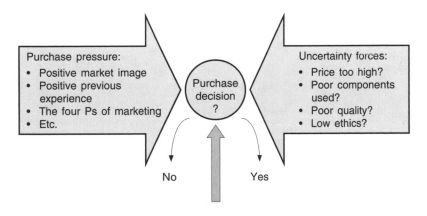

Figure 1.2   The marketing uncertainty paradox.

However, when an organization has managed to position itself in such a way that their general image in the marketplace is that of a company with integrity, potential customers will be less afraid of committing to a purchase from this company. The uncertainty is reduced and people will find it less "frightening" to become a customer based on their belief that this is a trustworthy organization. This has also been documented in several empirical studies, for example a study conducted by Cone Communications and Roger Starch Worldwide in 1995, which found that 31 percent of respondents viewed a company's sense of social responsibility as a key factor in their purchasing decisions (Kurschner, 1996). Furthermore, large percentages of the surveyed adults said they would pay more for products, brands, and retailers that supported a cause they cared about (respectively 54, 66, and 62 percent). In another study conducted in New York in 1995, close to 90 percent claimed that in a case where quality, service, and price were equal, the best reputation for social responsibility would likely determine their decision to buy (see Figure 1.3 for a graphical representation of these findings). All in all, the evidence to support this relationship is becoming overwhelming.

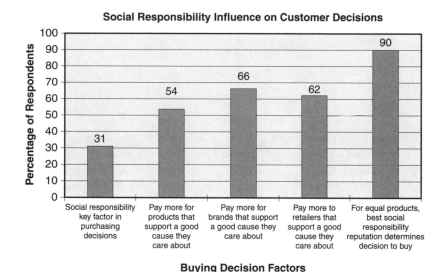

Figure 1.3   Findings in different studies about the influence of social responsibility on customer buying decisions.

Financial Performance

One juicy carrot to tempt you down the ethics path should be several studies that report a link between corporate social responsibility (CSR) and profitability. While this might seem too good to be true, there is some evidence indicating that there exists a positive relationship between corporate social responsibility and improved financial performance.

In studies of corporate citizenship, another term for business ethics, and past and future business performance alike, both Graves and Waddock (1993) and Taylor (1987) found such evidence. The same was true in a study by Maignan (1997), where a positive relationship was found between CSR and return on investment, sales growth, and profit growth. These findings were based on information given by respondents in a survey. In their treatment of this crucial question of a link between CSR and financial performance, Ferrell, Maignan, and Loe attempt to explain this relationship by looking at the aspect of reputation. *Fortune* magazine annually examines the performance of the most admired companies, where admiration is determined from criteria that do seem to correlate closely with how corporate citizenship is defined; overall reputation, quality of management, quality of products, innovativeness, and responsibility to the community (Stewart, 1999). At the time of this investigation, the ten most admired companies were General Electric, Coca-Cola, Hewlett-Packard, Microsoft, Intel, Southwest Airlines, Berkshire Hathaway, Disney, Johnson & Johnson, and Merck. Comparing the financial performance of these with some kind of average, an investment of $1000.00 ten years ago in each of these companies would have given a return nearly three times that of a $10,000.00 investment in the Standard & Poor's 500 index. Although some of these companies have, either previous to this ranking or afterwards, been exposed to negative publicity due to various issues, these numbers are quite convincing. To what extent the admiration assessment is due to an ethics approach can of course be questioned, but the premise of Ferrell, Maignan, and Loe is that companies that are perceived positively in the marketplace perform better than others. If anything, an ethical approach to business contributes to such a perception, and should thus also support financial performance.

Another contribution to the empirical data on this issue came from Verschoor (1998), who reported a study of the 500 largest corporations in the United States. One of the findings stated that those who commit to ethical behavior or emphasize compliance with their code of conduct have better financial performance.

The most recent research on this topic was reported by Ruf, Muralidhar, Brown, Janney, and Paul (2001). These researchers set out to look for a link between corporate social performance (CSP) and financial performance. As the measure of financial performance, the two indicators of growth in sales and return on equity were used, while corporate social performance was determined using an aggregate measure developed by Ruf, Muralidhar, and Paul (1998). The hypothesis developed was: change in CSP is positively related to current and future changes in financial performance, after controlling for size, industry, and prior year's financial performance. The analysis did support the hypothesis, albeit with reservations regarding its applicability to other time periods and the types of stakeholders surveyed.

All of these studies can probably be critiqued for various elements of their approach, data material, analysis, and it seems clear that still further research is required to be able to determine beyond doubt that there is a link, especially a clear causal relationship. As is discussed toward the end of this chapter, there are also those that claim CSR mainly drives up costs while not contributing equally to positive effects. Still, there seem to be quite a few studies providing evidence to support the belief that corporate social responsibility can have a positive effect on financial performance. And if this comes as icing on the cake, in addition to all the other benefits, it is a tough case to argue against the merits of an ethical approach to business.

Negative Exposure and Performance Backlashes

If you are not convinced of the merits of these studies, consider the other side of the coin. If one assumes that an ethical standpoint does not in itself contribute to higher profits, it should be sufficient to browse the list of companies involved in scandals lately stemming from poor ethics, and their fate in the aftermath of these. Going bankrupt is diametrically opposed to increased profits. The point is that there are so many eyes and ears on high alert looking for any sign of something going on that does not hold up to scrutiny that chances are you will be caught red-handed if you stray too far from the straight and narrow, with all the ensuing negative consequences.

Consider all the "watchdogs" on the alert for organizations committing less-then-ethical deeds or conducting their business in unacceptable ways. For example:

• Perhaps the most damaging of these are the law firms that have specialized in so-called mass tort litigation. (For a grim inside look into this particular branch of the practice of law, you should read the entertaining and terrifying book *The King of Torts* by John Grisham.) These are firms that constantly look for products that have caused injuries, illnesses, product problems incurring costs for customers. Typical examples are drugs with side effects, vehicles with faults that lead to fatal accidents, or poor mortar causing houses to crumble. Especially in the United States, this branch of the law has become so profitable for the lawyers that there is a whole industry specializing in this kind of pursuit of large manufacturers. Typically, they assemble large portfolios of thousands of plaintiffs, through mass advertising across the country, and file so-called class-action suits against the manufacturer of the product. Often, these cases never go to trial, as juries have been known to award gigantic sums to victims in punitive damages and other compensation, in the most horrendous cases in the area of hundreds of million dollars. In such cases, a landslide will follow based on the precedent set by the first case; thus, settling all claims in one agreement is typically less expensive. Even when these cases are settled outside the courtroom, the total costs for the manufacturer often reach billions of dollars, in many cases pushing the companies into bankruptcy or at least damaging them seriously. As the lawyers representing the plaintiffs usually take 25 to 40 percent off the top of the settlements in fees, this is a hugely profitable industry, attracting thousands of law firms. The result is that the scrutiny of potentially "sueable" products is so close that chances are very small someone will get away with a product with dangerous or questionable characteristics. As concerns grow over the horrendous figures involved and the time these cases consume in the judicial system, there have been attempts at curbing mass tort litigation practices, but so far the lawyers are prevailing.

• Another group is made up of all the different legal and judicial bodies that in one way or another can detect misdoings on your part and follow these up. Some are obvious, for example, various financial crime squads, fraud units of the police, typically units that pursue legal retribution if they detect irregularities. There are, however, many additional instances as well, ranging from antitrust authorities to competition monitoring bodies to the tax system, and so on. Varying from country to country, these can be more or less equipped to do their job and the form of retribution can vary widely. In some cases, there are even super-national bodies like various EU units, global trade organizations. The common denominator for all of these is that they can seriously harm your organization if they find you guilty of any wrongdoings, deliberate or not.

• There have always been a number of various pressure groups around, watching out for their special interests, some with more power and clout than others. What is interesting to note these days is the sheer proliferation of such groups and organizations and how they have succeeded in becoming global entities. The Internet is surely one important factor in bringing about this dramatic growth, and the result is that there exist an unbelievable number of special interest groups that use a variety of means to achieve their goals. Some are concerned with the environment, others with the rights of the physically impaired, some fight third-world poverty, while others have launched their crusade against telephone marketing after six P.M. The most extreme groups stage demonstrations and rallies; others hold peaceful membership meetings. One of the more damaging approaches to businesses is the practice of launching global, Internet-propelled smear campaigns against anyone found to overstep the borders these campaigns find suitable. What is beyond any doubt is that the influence of such groups is increasing fast, and the most powerful ones are able to dictate consumer behavior on a global scale. Suffice it to say; should you fall seriously out of grace with one of these, chances are that this will seriously harm your organization and its chances for survival.

• Increasingly more conscientious and aware consumers represent the last obstacle to maintaining an unethical mode of operation and getting away with it. There is no need to feed this picture to you by the spoonful; we all know that the general public has access to, and makes use of, increasingly more information on any thinkable and unthinkable subject. Besides all the kinds of pressure groups discussed above pushing their information aggressively, the newspapers, TV, the Internet, are all filled to the brim with material on products and services such as comparative tests, documentaries and exposés, updates on suppliers of products and services, general information on scientific advancements, what is good for you and what is not, and so on. Altogether, the average customer, or any other stakeholder for that matter, of your organization is so well informed and up-to-date on developments within your area of business that it is only a matter of when, not if, you will be found out if straying too far from acceptable business practices.

Summarizing, there is probably no other alternative than to clean up your act and "go ethical." . . . Well, this might be stretching it a little . . . most of us know of someone who always gets away with murder. The question is, are you willing to risk it? Certainly there are organizations operating either outright criminally or bordering on it and enjoying lucrative lives, but do you think they have lucrative lives in terms of conscience? Unless they are extremely scrupulous, they probably sleep poorly at night and are always worried that someone is after them. Still, it would be naïve to say that crime never pays—of course it does, as does sometimes cooking books, extending a pass-by date, giving poor advice, but the risk involved is increasing.

And even if you are not exposed to lawsuits, criminal prosecution, bankruptcy, from conducting shady business, even a completely legal outfit

Putnam Investments, the fifth-largest U.S. mutual fund company, encountered serious problems during the fall of 2003. Four of the company's fund managers were fired after it was discovered that they had used inappropriate market timing transactions to produce personal gains at the expense of fund shareholders. In the wake of the revelations of this scandal, a record 15 billion dollars were withdrawn from Putnam's mutual funds by customers in only seven days. The financial impact of this exodus is gigantic. Furthermore, John D. Carifa has resigned as president, chief operating officer, and director of Alliance Capital and chairman of the board of its mutual funds while Michael J. Laughlin stepped down as the chairman of the company's mutual fund distribution unit; both officials were urged to resign. Putnam Investments has also been running full-page advertisements in newspapers like *The Wall Street Journal* to announce changes in its practices, ads that are no doubt very expensive to run. All in all, the negative impact from the unethical practices followed by a small number of fund managers has been dramatic for the company.

run a little too tight and with too much pressure can experience backlashes in terms of employee turnover, absenteeism, errors due to fatigue, that ultimately cost money. Lately, it has become more and more obvious that in addition to the external reactions to a poorly managed business, the internal reactions can be severe as well. Whereas organizations with a positive ethical position have been found to have better organizational cultures and better ability to attract and retain employees, the opposite is true for companies with less pronounced views in this respect. And in this case we are not only talking about companies that behave criminally or on the edge of rules and regulations, but also companies with simply less-than-perfect approaches and ways to do things. Absenteeism is on a steady rise in all industrial countries, both short-term as well as longer-term absences. The latest trend is the proliferation of professional burnout, where some are lucky and return to work after a few weeks or months, whereas others never do.

It seems as if all our clever ways of improving productivity quite often do produce the expected immediate and significant improvements we are after, and we happily record these as successful results of our efforts. A few months or years down the line, when the 3.2 percent productivity gain is completely absorbed by the 8.2 percent increase in absenteeism and employee turnover, we are rarely there recording it with the same enthusiasm. There is undoubtedly a need for continuously improving processes and their performance, but there are different ways of doing so, some more viable long-term than others. This is, however, an aspect of improvement work and tools that has not been given much attention.

Finally, the negative impact from an unethical profile and practices does not only originate from external penalties or poor internal performance. Different costs, tangible and intangible, associated with unethical conduct at all levels in the workplace represent enormous sums of money. Considering only one of these types of unethical conduct, fraud, a 1994 survey by KPMG (1994) found annual work fraud to be $224 million, with 18 percent of the companies surveyed indicating frauds aggregating one million dollars or more.

Attracting Other Stakeholders

Investors and shareholders, especially the larger, institutional investors (which often represent the kind of attractive players with long-term focus and stamina that you want in your corner) are increasingly applying ethical standards and criteria to evaluate investments and stocks. Thus, having a favorable ethical profile can attract investors, and not having one may deter them.

The stakeholder concept, which has been around for quite some time now, has proven to be a very useful model for all kinds of analyses of the interplay between an organization and its surroundings (for a more general introduction to the stakeholder concept, see for example Freeman (1984), Donaldson and Preston (1995), or Jones (1995). Basically, the idea is that any organization exists in a network of links to other organizations, institutions, individuals, or other elements that in one way or another has a vested interest in the behavior and results of the organization. The most prominent stakeholder is the customer, but there is a whole range of others that are important to an organization. Owners, employees, suppliers, constantly play important roles, spare-parts vendors or joint venture partners come and go in terms of importance over time, and some stakeholders play very little role in the everyday life of an organization, but can sometimes become crucial, for example, the fire department or a scandal journalist. And the clear premise of the stakeholder model is that long-term survival and growth of an organization depends on its ability to maintain good relations with all or most of its stakeholders.

Covey (1998) pointed out that, in addition to losing half of its employees within four years, the average corporation also loses half of its customers within five years and half of its investors within less than one year. Reicheld (1996) suggested that these current rates of disloyalty could damage corporate performance by as much as 25 to 30 percent. Again, there is empirical evidence supporting the idea that being a good corporate citizen has a positive impact on an organization's ability to satisfy its stakeholders. Customers have been dealt with earlier, but many of the same mechanisms come into play for other types of stakeholders.

Suppliers are more susceptible to entering into favorable agreements with and going the extra mile for customers they think treat them fairly and have a reputation for treating others fairly as well. The media can very often make or break a company, and journalists often tend to fall victim to the so-called Halo effect, that is, someone who already has a bad reputation tends to be seen negatively no matter what she or he does, and vice versa. Thus, organizations who stand out as positive often continue to be portrayed this way. However, concerning the media, one warning is in order: organizations that over time come to be perceived as ethical, virtuous corporate citizens are tempting subjects for slander and scandal. A journalist can make a great story out of digging up something on such an organization, and many will direct their efforts into such pursuits.

Other investors apply ethical standards and criteria to evaluate investments and stocks. One example of this is the specifically designed subindex of the London stock exchange, the FTSE4Good (FTSE—Financial Times Stock Exchange).* To be included in this index, companies (or constituents as they are called by FTSE) must first of all not operate within industries that are automatically excluded (tobacco producers, companies manufacturing either parts for, or entire, nuclear or conventional weapons systems, owners or operators of nuclear power stations, or companies involved in the extraction of uranium). Secondly, they are screened according to the predefined criteria of the FTSE4Good (for more information on the detailed criteria, see www.FTSE4Good.com), which cover:

- Environmental sustainability

- Social issues and stakeholder relations

- Human rights

Thus, having a favorable ethical profile can attract investors and not having one can deter them. In short, several of a typical organization's stakeholders react positively to a clear ethical point of view and reputation.

---

* On the United States side, the Dow Jones Sustainability Index is similar to FTSE4Good, but perhaps not as clearly ethically focused. A total of 27 assessment criteria are weighed with factors ranging from one to 4.5 for a total of 100. These are distributed within the categories of economic, environmental, and social criteria in addition to risk and opportunity–related criteria for specific industry groups. For more details, see www.sustainability-index.com/assessment/criteria.html.

My home country, Norway, is in the fortunate position of having paid off all national debts and is now channeling huge tax profits from North Sea oil activity into what is popularly called the Oil Fund. The fund is managed by the central bank and is seen as insurance for future generations. Currently, the fund holds a staggering 100 billion dollars, being invested for maximum return. However, it has become known that the fund owns shares in both arms and tobacco companies. Many politicians and the public think this is inappropriate and new guidelines for ethical investing are now being drawn up for the fund.

Making the World a Better Place

Finally, and perhaps not to be overlooked, if we all made an effort to behave more in accordance with established ethical standards, both in our personal and professional lives, it is quite possible that the world we live in would be a better place for all of us. . . . However, this issue might not seem appropriate when targeting business practitioners as the audience. You might even laugh at the entire idea that as an employee of a company or as a company itself, you have either a duty or chance to make the world a better place. Perhaps correctly so—this has been a topic of debate for a very long time. Classic economic theory is firm in its belief that if enterprises look after their legal and economic responsibilities in a sound manner, profits are maximized more or less continuously and thus they carry out their major responsibilities to society (Steiner and Steiner, 1988).

However, inherent in running an organization is the fact that some kind of "damage" is inflicted upon the world and its society. This ranges from simply consuming natural, nonrenewable resources such as gasoline, electric power, forests, and minerals; to polluting the environment through emissions, discharges, to exploiting less favored people and countries. Expecting organizations to try and rectify some of these damages is perhaps not all that unfair. Continuing this argument, is it so unthinkable that companies can even go further than simply making up for what negative impact they might have? With the kinds of resources, in terms of manpower, money, equipment, knowledge, and know-how, that the companies and other organizations of this world have at their disposal, are they not in an ideal position to contribute beyond the areas and levels related to their own "wrongdoings"? More and more people seem to be of this belief.

While few individuals, even as members of organizations, are in a position to contribute immensely on their own to the bettering of the world, each can contribute in her or his own small ways. At this level, much of the discussion on ethics turns to the concept of virtues. The Scottish philosopher David Hume (incidentally, Adam Smith's best friend) defined a virtue as a trait that is both pleasing and useful to ourselves and pleasing and useful to others. Depending on which school one confesses adherence to, there exists a whole range of different virtues, but in this setting the most relevant ones are probably character traits like integrity, honesty, trustworthiness, punctuality, and industriousness. Aristotle identified the virtues as the basic constituents of happiness, where virtues also included nonmoral aspects like wittiness, generosity, and loyalty. And virtues were seen to be both essential aspects of the individual as well as the "excellences" that a society required to function and thrive. Despite the common understanding of modern capitalism as a society system that is based on maximizing individual and enterprise profits for the good of society as a whole, capitalism could not survive without a basic foundation of trust.

By trying in a small way to develop and abide by these valuable virtues, each and every one of us can contribute to making the workplace a better and more caring place to function in. When the workplace becomes filled with virtues, this has a tendency to extend to relationships with other organizations and individuals, and in the end the world can in fact become a better place for all. While this might seem overly naïve and in conflict with the often-used jargon of war, competition, and ruthlessness that many connect to modern business, no one seems to argue against the positive effects of better local communities, less poverty, or reduced crime levels. Doing what we inherently know is right and good, something that impacts others in a positive way, be it customers, fellow coworkers, the environment, or the local community, is a good thing to experience at work. It makes us feel good about our jobs and ourselves, and if we at the same time contribute positively in some way or another to the "state of the realm" (ref. the rather negative picture painted earlier), this is not trivial!

ANY REASONS WHY YOU SHOULD NOT CHANGE YOUR WAYS? (OR THE DISADVANTAGES OF CORPORATE SOCIAL RESPONSIBILITY)

Of course there are. If an ethics business approach were the holy grail of business success, do you not think this would be the norm rather than the exception?

There is no reason to deny the fact that trying to change to this approach has its downsides as well. For one, it is hard work just getting there, involving massive changes in practices, values, and perhaps not in the least organizational culture. And when you do get there, being a good citizen organization certainly means making some trade-offs, very likely refraining from some short-term wins for the sake of a more long-term view, both on the part of the organization and its individual employees and managers.

Although the concept of business ethics and corporate social responsibility has been warmly welcomed by large parts of both industry and academia, resulting in a steady increase in interest in and proliferation of these ideas and practices, there are certainly critics as well. While most literature on the subject tends to be positive and promoting of these ideas, this is perhaps not surprising—to take sufficient interest in such a concept to publish articles or books on it, a positive attitude is almost a prerequisite. Still, there are a certain number of publications taking a negative view of this thinking.

One of the more comprehensive and well-argued pieces of criticism against corporate social responsibility was published by David Henderson (2001) through the New Zealand Business Roundtable. In summary, Henderson's position is that corporate social responsibility as preached and practiced by many marks an acceptance and endorsement of views and demands mostly presented by anti-business groups that are hostile to the market economy and far from representing the general view of the average consumer. Henderson also questions the benefits of, and in fact claims there are serious negative effects from, the development of official or unofficial international standards for worker conditions, pay levels, environmental behavior. He claims further that many of the actions that have to be taken to implement such new practices would incur additional costs for companies that it has not been proven can be recouped through increased sales. Some of these claims are much less substantiated by any empirical evidence than many of the well-documented benefits reported earlier in this chapter, but there is merit to some of Henderson's views. By considering these, a process for implementing an ethically based approach to business can be given a better design, taking into account some of the possible downsides and avoiding some obvious pitfalls.

However, to avoid deterring you from an ethical approach altogether at this stage of the book, the in-depth discussion about negative effects and pitfalls can be found in chapter 11. Where they are relevant, these issues will of course be brought into the descriptions of the more hands-on ways to implement business ethics during the next chapters. For now, however, suffice it to say that any coin has two sides, including corporate social responsibility.

NAÏVE, REALISTIC, OR CYNICAL?

So, are you convinced yet that emphasizing a more ethical profile makes sense? The arguments for such an approach to business can (at least) be deemed naïve, realistic, or cynical (or a combination of these):

• Naïve, in the sense that it is founded on a positivistic view of the world and people. Positive and optimistic people are often accused of being blue-eyed and ready victims for anyone willing to take advantage of them. More cynically disposed, pessimists love to prove them wrong, but, sadly, pessimists only have the opportunity to gloat when things have gone wrong. Optimism and belief in a better future have for all times been the driving forces behind evolution, invention, and entrepreneurship. Call believers in ethical business naïve, but not in a negative sense. However, there is no denying the fact that some decisions and choices made in the name of business ethics or corporate social responsibility can have short-term negative impacts on sales, revenues, or profits. You might have to decline with a "thanks, but no thanks" to sales and deals that cannot be justified, accept higher prices on certain goods or parts purchased, increased costs for employee welfare, and short-term falls in stock prices. Still, the argumentation is:

• Realistic, in the sense that breaches of laws or the general understanding of acceptable behavior are almost always detected, resulting in many more negative consequences than the short-term impacts mentioned above. Thus, in the longer term, a good-citizen approach to business makes sense, including financially. This is supported by much empirical evidence and is as such a realistic claim.

• Cynical motivation. The vice president of corporate social responsibility in a large corporation recently confided to me that he considered himself the most cynical person in the entire company. Not that he doesn't believe in the concept, its positive benefits, or the obligation of such a large organization to have a powerful CSR program, he is indeed completely committed to it. But in his struggles to have the program permeate the organization and convince his colleagues of its merits, he has consistently used argumentation centered on avoidance of negative publicity and penalties and the positive publicity potential of a CSR program, sometimes in addition to, sometimes instead of focusing on the company's duties, the rewards of doing good, and similar "naïve" argumentation. In this way, pursuing an ethical business profile can certainly be grounded in cynical motivation, at least partly, but as long as the end result is ethical conduct, the result is not degraded or of less value to those it benefits.

These are some issues that point to the power and benefits of this approach to business. Call it business ethics, integrity management, corporate social responsibility, good citizenship, or whichever term suits you, the arguments and evidence available are quite convincing. The field of business ethics emerged during the 1970s, and it has been constantly gaining more and more awareness and support. This probably makes it one of longest surviving management fads, another testament to its viability.

TO REAP THE BENEFITS, YOU NEED TO MAKE IT WORK IN PRACTICE

The motivation for writing this book has not been to add to the (important, no doubt) lofty discussion of the concept of ethics in business, its virtues, and philosophical or even religious overtones. There are a multitude of sources on this topic by authors far more qualified than myself (see for example Solomon [1999]). What seems to be missing in existing literature within this field is a more down-to-earth, hands-on treatment of how to convert the well-meaning intentions of business ethics into something tangible that is communicable and implementable.

Of course many authors have dealt with issues along these lines, especially in terms of how to organize responsibilities regarding ethics in an organization and the development of ethical guidelines or codes of conduct that can help direct the behavior of individuals and groups in general and in specific situations. Others have made valuable contributions regarding the development of local community programs, fair trade schemes, environmental concern programs. There are two main shortcomings in the material available to date; there are numerous additional areas where business ethics can be converted into action that have been poorly covered, and few attempts have been made at synthesizing the various aspects of business ethics into a holistic framework. Thus, the ambition for this book has indeed been to conceive such a framework that spans as much of this field as possible and is accompanied by a practical treatment of how the different elements making up the framework can be put into action.

This ambition is based on the assumption that:

- The principles of business ethics hold the potential for numerous benefits for the organizations that adopt them, including profitability.

- Those organizations that have implemented the approach of an ethical view on business fail to achieve the full potential inherent in the concept.

- Far fewer companies and other types of organizations have adopted the ethical approach than we would like to see.

Thus, if such a tangible framework can in part induce more organizations to convert to a business ethics approach (since it can be depicted as a more manageable process) and those that do can achieve even more benefits, it is truly a worthwhile undertaking. So, let's get down to business— the next sections present an overall model of business ethics in a larger context and delineate the framework itself as well as the basis for its portrayal. Following this, each of the elements of the framework will be briefly touched upon before the subsequent chapters of the book discuss them in more detail.

A SOCIALLY RESPONSIBLE BUSINESS MANAGEMENT MODEL

The average model of management in a modern organization will typically depict elements such as stakeholder management, organizational culture development, business process orientation, continuous performance review, perhaps supply chain management. Such a model should be adjusted by putting a distinct ethical slant on these elements. In changing your approach to business to a more socially responsible one, you will of course not be forced to dramatically change everything about your organization and the way it is run. Granted, it can be a tough transformation, but that mostly applies to the values of the organization, its focus on and adherence to these, and to some extent its practices and procedures. The main "logic" of the organization and its management remain the same, thus most of the average business model elements remain unchanged.

How these elements can be tweaked to represent an approach to business management that is socially responsible is shown in Figure 1.4. It is composed primarily of the same pieces as were mentioned earlier, but adjusted in order to focus on an ethical conduct in its scope and activities.

The logic of the model is as follows: The organization's stakeholders, including both the obvious ones (customers, owners, employees) and less obvious ones (the environment, society, suppliers, even competitors) form the very basis for its existence. The more trust you can build into the relationship with these, and the more the organization is able to satisfy the stakeholders, the more viable it is in the long run. Empirical data clearly shows that ethically founded businesses maintain higher levels of stakeholder satisfaction than those with a weaker ethical basis. Consequently, converting the stakeholders' needs and expectations into an ethical strategy is an excellent starting point for growing a healthy business.

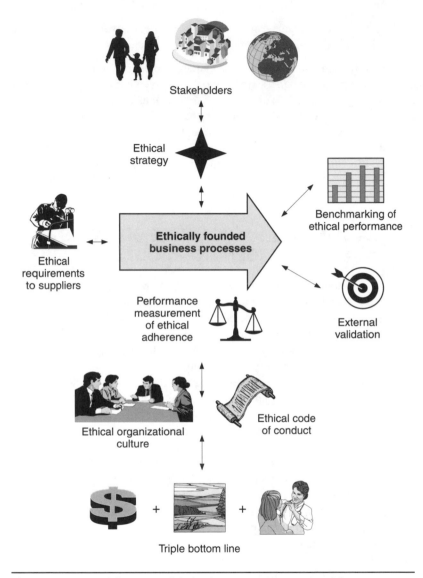

Figure 1.4 A socially responsible business management model.

Strategies need to be implemented to make an impact, so the ethical strategy must be converted into a set of operational business practices—ethically founded business processes. These must include practices that make good on the strategy and bring its ideal to life (determining which practices should be employed is the main purpose of the business ethics framework presented shortly). To develop and ensure that these ethically founded business processes are performed consistently and in accordance with the spirit of the overlying strategy, an organizational culture that appreciates and holds dear an ethical stance must be developed and continuously maintained, along with a strong set of ethically based guidelines for the organization's conduct.

As every organization is part of a larger supply chain or network of suppliers, partners, their suppliers and partners, imposing strict requirements on its own strategy and operations is not sufficient to come across as a credible good citizen organization. The same strict requirements must be transmitted backward (and very often also forward) to these actors in the organization's network. Claiming to be socially responsible very often means sticking "the organizational neck" out and exposing it to scrutiny and attacks from media, interest groups, and competition. Being able to document the level of integrity in the organization's strategy and business practices is therefore a vital part of a socially responsible management model. Undertaking external benchmarking of ethical performance is one approach to achieving this; another is subjecting the organization and its operations to various forms of external validation. Such approaches often take the form of third-party assessments where the results are communicated to the public. Finally, as a basis for both benchmarking and external assessments, as well as the organization's interaction with the public and media regarding its ethical performance and adherence to the standards it has set for itself, keeping accounts over the triple bottom line (financial, environmental, and ethical performance) constitutes an important element in the model.

Altogether, this is a synthesis of proven elements in a corporate social responsibility approach to business that should provide a clearer picture of what is involved in "going ethical." Organizations considering changing their ways are not deterred by the prospect of having to alter their organizational culture, introduce triple book-keeping, or set ethical standards for their suppliers. What most organizations struggle with is figuring out how to convert a well-intended desire to change their approach into hands-on business practices. Simply issuing a press release stating "we are from now on an ethical company" will certainly not do. From this struggle came the idea of the business ethics framework.

THE BUSINESS ETHICS FRAMEWORK

Frequently, when discussing ethics or CSR with organizations considering "implementing it," the problem is they have no idea where to start. They have usually read up on the topic and have an idea that this is about appointing a

CSR manager, selecting a pet charity to donate money to, perhaps even establishing a local community development program, but there is no structure to these ideas. When designing the business ethics framework of this book, the main motivation has been to create a structure within which all of these different elements that are part of an ethical approach can be placed. The framework can take on the format of a "menu" from which a transformation toward an ethical business approach can be more easily designed and planned.

There are probably a number of dimensions that can be used to span this framework, but the following three are excellent starting points:

• *Internal versus external focus.* Where are the ethics components directed, internally or externally, and who benefits from them, the organization and its members or the organization's external stakeholders? This is generally not an either/or situation for many of the elements that comprise business ethics, but to some extent a defining characteristic. We have already discussed briefly the fact that there is a clear bidirectional link and interaction between the way an organization treats its employees and its internal life versus the organization's environment and its many stakeholders. Focusing on merely one of them will constitute an imbalance and likely not be viable in the long run, thus, striking a balance between the internal and external focus is essential.

• *Strategic versus operational.* Are the components of the ethics approach mainly related to strategic aspects of the organization and its operations or focused more on operational levels? As you will see later on, this is certainly an area where there is a continuous scale and individual elements can be hard to assign to one or the other, but again, this is not the point of these dimensions. Typically, strategic elements will be geared toward policy setting, overall image creation, and pointing out direction for the organization's ethics endeavor. To put these into practice, operational, hands-on approaches are required to achieve what the policies dictate. Again there is a need for balance and progression, that is, putting the strategic elements in place before populating the strategies with operational practices.

• *Remedial versus philanthropic impact.* Do the various activities and actions undertaken under the ethics approach merely minimize or compensate for any negative impact the organization and its operations have had on the "world" (that is, local community, the environment, and stakeholders) or do they go even further, to give contributions beyond any "damage" the organization itself has inflicted? There are probably many gray areas here as well, but this stands out as another pivotal distinction between CSR elements. In this case as well, a balance is important, but there is also some

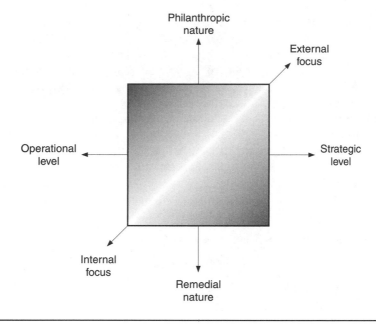

Figure 1.5 Dimensions spanning the business ethics framework.

kind of logical progression between the two. Before initiating philanthropic activities, with the image these carry along, it is essential to have "cleaned up your own house" or any positive impact from the philanthropic side will quickly be overshadowed by any revelations of "damage" inflicted by the organization.

Presenting these as polar entities is not suggesting that everything is black-and-white and that different ways of achieving an ethical position fall into one or the other. There is a continuous scale where elements can be a mixture of the two, as is hopefully apparent when these dimensions are used to construct a three-dimensional matrix along these axes (see Figure 1.5).

THE DIFFERENT AREAS AND ELEMENTS OF THE BUSINESS ETHICS FRAMEWORK

The framework spanned by these axes attempts to illustrate that initiatives, actions, programs, and organizational design elements that contribute to an ethical business approach can be structured inside the space of these dimensions. It is not the intention to present this as a geometrically correct representation of this thinking—it is clearly not. You cannot "calculate" the ethical coordinates of an ethics program based on this diagram. Rather, it is intended as an aid in trying to get your arms around all of the different "tools" that are available in the process of constructing an ethical business approach. As you will see, this framework is used to structure these "tools" according to these three bipolar dimensions, thus hopefully making it easier for you as a reader to assess them and consider which ones to implement yourself. You will also notice that no attempt has been made at actually depicting the various business ethics elements graphically in this framework. Perhaps it is feasible, but the sheer number of them is too large for this approach. Instead, the bulk of the book is sectioned into parts reflecting the eight combinations of classifications:

- Remedial, internal, and strategic

- Remedial, internal, and operational

- Remedial, external, and strategic

- Remedial, external, and operational

- Philanthropic, internal, and strategic

- Philanthropic, internal, and operational

- Philanthropic, external, and strategic

- Philanthropic, external, and operational

Some of these combinations are of course more extensive than others in the selection of approaches available, but all show some merit. You might also argue that some of the approaches have been pigeonholed inaccurately, which can certainly be a valid observation. However, the actual placement of an approach inside these dimensions is not of great importance in itself, as long as the approach is presented and made available to you on the "menu." Over the next eight chapters, each area of the framework will be presented in more detail, focusing on the specific elements belonging to each area.

At first glance, these chapters might look like a very helter-skelter mess of all kinds of different activities, but that is to some extent the point. You should view this as a menu of possible courses to choose from, and, as with a restaurant menu, selecting too many or indeed all of them will likely have you biting off more than you can chew. As each of these different elements of the framework will be presented in more detail over the next chapters, you will later on be better equipped to make qualified choices as to where to start

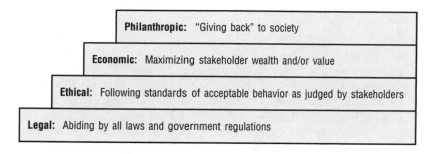

Philanthropic: "Giving back" to society

Economic: Maximizing stakeholder wealth and/or value

Ethical: Following standards of acceptable behavior as judged by stakeholders

Legal: Abiding by all laws and government regulations

Figure 1.6 Progression through the steps of social responsibility.

on your "ethics journey." In line with the brief discussion earlier about there being some progression among the dimensions of the business ethics framework, please consider an illustration of this progression adapted by Ferrell, Fraedrich, and Ferrell (2000) from the original contribution by Carroll (1991) (see Figure 1.6).

This figure underlines the message that there is indeed a way to go before an organization will be taken seriously as an ethical and socially responsible actor. Cleaning up any legally questionable issues must precede the same cleanup of ethical issues, though ethical norms and standards often are stricter than legislation. Only then is the organization ready to be perceived as a good citizen corporation with the well-being and value of all its stakeholders in mind, before finally making the step toward a philanthropic organization. This is not to say that it should be the goal of any organization to reach this latter stage—many of the benefits described in the previous chapter start materializing long before then.

BASIC ETHICS CONCEPTS DEFINITIONS

Before concluding this chapter and moving on to the more operational descriptions of each of the elements of the business ethics framework, a few core definitions are in order. Particularly in this field, a number of terms have developed that may be confusing, although they are basically different ways of saying pretty much the same things. The key terms you have likely come across, both in general and in the imprecise usage of them so far in this book, are:

• *Business ethics,* which is perhaps the broadest of these concepts, denoting the general inclusion of ethical considerations into business thinking and practices.

• *Corporate social responsibility (CSR),* which can be seen as an attempt to define business ethics more precisely (and perhaps to give the concept a "brand name"). CSRWire defines CSR as follows: "Corporate social responsibility (CSR) is the alignment of business operations with social values. CSR consists of integrating the interests of stakeholders—all those affected by a company's conduct—into the company's business policies and actions. CSR focuses on the social, environmental, and financial success of a company—the so-called triple bottom line—with the goal being to positively impact society while achieving business success" (Connolly, 2002).

• *Integrity,* another ambiguous term, not unlike virtue. Both are mainly used in connection with individuals, but lately also with organizations as units of reference. To adopt a business ethics approach or CSR, it seems inevitable that an organization and its individual members must possess both integrity ("complete honesty and goodness" as defined in the Collins dictionary) and virtue ("goodness of character" by the same dictionary).

• *Good citizen corporation,* another term for the ethically conscientious corporation, not unlike CSR. As defined by Ferrell, Maignan, and Loe (unpublished working paper), "the good corporate citizen offers superior value to customers by embracing economic and social responsibilities. Customers enjoy the benefits of this commitment directly because the good citizen corporation treats them fairly and continuously strives to satisfy their changing needs. Customers also enjoy the fruits of corporate citizenship indirectly: as social actors, they enjoy the efforts organizations undertake to generate revenues, respect established regulations, adopt modes of conduct considered morally right, and help their community."

Hopefully these definitions have helped demystify some of the previously mentioned concepts, certainly sufficiently so to make you keep reading on for the more operational treatment of the business ethics framework and its implementation in the next chapter!

2

Bringing the Ethical Business Approach to Life—An Implementation Road Map

Before presenting the detailed aspects of each area of the business ethics framework, this chapter presents a sort of road map for implementing an ethical approach to business and raises some implementation issues. During my years of research and being involved in projects with industrial enterprises or public sector organizations, I have been unfortunate enough to witness closely how often the mistake is made of deciding on a change and then not seeing it through to real implementation. During the last couple of decades, companies have spent a lot of time and money assessing concepts like just-in-time manufacturing approaches, total quality management, business process orientation, balanced scorecard, and every management fad you can think of. If they finally make it to deciding that one of these is right for their organization, big plans are made, project organizations staffed, and steering groups assembled. Very often, such initiatives die after some time, either upon encountering resistance throughout the organization, not finding any enthusiasm among the employees, or simply out of loss of momentum and poor follow-up.

Despite a rather extensive effort invested in finding a source of some wisdom about implementation, no reference has been found, but I have seen it written somewhere that:

- Achieving fundamental changes in an organization's basic thinking and reflex behavior takes two years.

- Implementing practical elements of a typical management fad takes eight months.

It is common in most change processes that when starting to make the transition, the organization experiences a dip in performance as old ways are abandoned and time is taken to hone the new ways. Depending on the extent of the change, putting this dip behind you and starting to reap the benefits can take months and even years. This is part of the reason why many implementation attempts, despite all good intentions, are stopped prematurely. The problem is, by staying abreast of "fashion" and embracing all new concepts, the disadvantages of each concept are experienced while the benefits are rarely achieved. In the end, the organization becomes a collection of residual practices from old implementation of new concepts. For well-intentioned projects to avoid this fate, stamina is required to see the change process through.

This is really only one nugget of wisdom that can be gleamed from the mounting body of literature on change management. Two quite different books that are useful on the subject are *Who Moved My Cheese* (Johnson, 1998) and *Successful Change Management* (Pendlebury, Grouard, and Meston, 1998). As change management in general will not be covered in this book, you should consider looking up these or other relevant sources for more specific change management information.

Suffice it to say that if you are considering an adjustment of the course of your organization to some degree of business ethics, this is not merely a management decision. The new approach must permeate the organization like a breath of fresh air, bringing it to life. People must be motivated for the new way of doing things and enthusiasm must be created. Like most other business concepts, an ethical business approach is a question of not going for it at all or doing it wholeheartedly. As you will soon see, though, there are different degrees of business ethics and deciding on the suitable level of ambition and staying true to the decision is a crucial part of the implementation decision and process.

THE BUSINESS ETHICS IMPLEMENTATION PROCESS

Bringing an ethical approach to business to life in an organization is a task that consists of many different elements and activities. A streamlined implementation process of clear-cut steps in a logical sequence that will lead you to the desired state would of course be beneficial. This is, however, virtually impossible to develop. Depending on characteristics of the organization, prior levels of awareness and training, organizational culture, and many other aspects, such a process can vary significantly from organization to organization. Even if the process will be different in terms

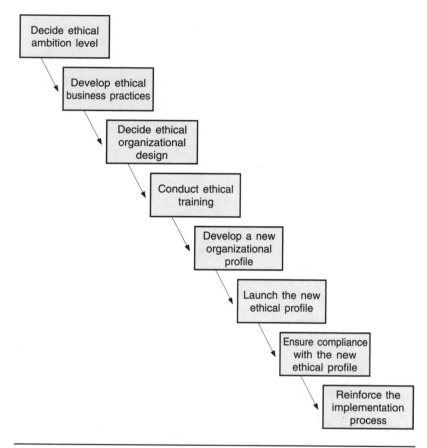

Figure 2.1 The implementation steps for a new ethical business approach.

of sequencing, duration, emphasis of certain elements, organization, and responsibilities, there are many elements that typically will be common for most such change processes. The intention is therefore to devote this section to listing some of the more important elements of such a process, and later in this chapter going into more detail on these. Schematically speaking, though, Figure 2.1 is an attempt at outlining these typical elements in a time sequence.

These key decisions or process activities are:

• *Deciding, on a strategic level, the ambition level for the ethical business approach.* This should normally be the very first consideration to be made, as this decision forms the basis for the rest of the implementation process. The time and effort required for design and training of new business practices will be more extensive if a wide-reaching philanthropic profile is the target than in the case of mere compliance with laws and industry norms.

• *Developing the required business practices to implement the chosen ethical profile and ambition level.* Once the initial decision has been made as to what level of ambition the organization will aim for, a consistent set of required business practices must be developed. In some cases, this will involve adjustments to existing practices, in others this translates into establishing whole new business processes and perhaps even organizational units.

• *Deciding on an organizational design to handle the new approach to business.* Depending on the ambition level of the ethical approach, it might suffice to extend the responsibilities of certain existing organizational functions to handle the new business practices, but in other cases, more elaborate changes may be required.

• *Conduct ethical training and awareness exercises throughout the organization.* No matter what ambition level is aimed for, training of some extent will be required when transforming the organization to a more ethically oriented entity. The extent, both in terms of who are targeted for training and how much, can vary, but this is a crucial element.

• *Developing a new organizational profile and making this known to external stakeholders.* As has been discussed earlier in the book, a "secret" ethical business approach will rarely achieve the benefits the concept has the potential for. Thus, redefining the public profile of the organization in accordance with the ethical ambition level is an important activity, as is making this profile publicly known.

• *Launching the new ethical profile and business practices.* So far, designing and developing the new organization and its business processes has been discussed. At one point, the actual transition must be made to start working according to these. This is often a milestone event, formal celebration of which may be appropriate.

• *Ensuring compliance with the new business profile and practices.* There is no point in denying the fact that the organization and its members will constantly face temptations to take shortcuts and stray from the new business practices. Implementing mechanisms for ensuring compliance is an element easily overlooked.

• *Assessing progress and reinforcing the implementation process.* In line with the discussion above about failed change processes, defining one or more milestones where the implementation progress is assessed is an important follow-up approach. It may be necessary to alter ambitions or add implementation elements to reach the set targets.

So what should be the extent of such an implementation and change process? This is a question that is impossible to give a general answer to. There are companies where the core philosophy has always been that of decency toward internal and external stakeholders, and where "going ethical" has merely been a matter of accentuating aspects of this culture, a change accomplished in a matter of a couple of months. In other cases, a high ambition level of a philanthropic profile has not been reached after two years of struggle. As always in matters of change, planning is crucial, and striking a balance between ambitious and feasible progress must accompany the planning.

DEFINING THE ETHICAL PROFILE OF YOUR ORGANIZATION

The framework in itself heralds the possibility for taking on a business ethics approach with various levels of ambition—clearly the remedial and the philanthropic halves of the framework represent two quite different levels of commitment and dedication. This is a coarse division of ambition levels; it is possible to break this down into a much finer set of steps. There are at least five such stages of ambition and corresponding levels of activity and dedication (see Figure 2.2):

• *Law-abiding,* reaching a stage where the organization and its members respect and comply with all relevant laws and regulations. This might not sound very ambitious, but most organizations still have a way to go before they can really claim to be there. This stage is not just about proclaiming to have changed to an ethical business approach and that all laws are abided by, but instilling an organizational culture that truly believes this to be important and that respects such a strategic policy. While it might not seem much of a competitive edge, in many business sectors, getting here can be a strong advantage. In the restaurant industry, often plagued with problems of cheating with food expiration dates, watered out alcohol, taxes, opening hours, and many other issues, a chain of restaurants in England has actively built an image of not trying to bend any rules. This has paid off, in terms of massive increases in turnover and high ratings in consumer confidence polls. Still, reaching this stage is usually not a strong basis for actively portraying the organization as an ethical player to the outside world, this only a first step toward higher ambitions.

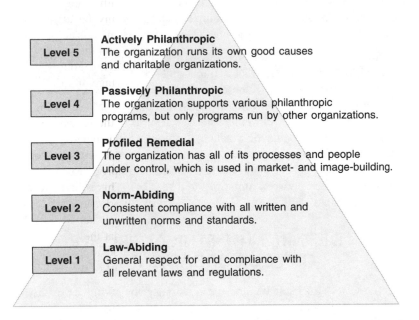

Level 5 — **Actively Philanthropic**
The organization runs its own good causes and charitable organizations.

Level 4 — **Passively Philanthropic**
The organization supports various philanthropic programs, but only programs run by other organizations.

Level 3 — **Profiled Remedial**
The organization has all of its processes and people under control, which is used in market- and image-building.

Level 2 — **Norm-Abiding**
Consistent compliance with all written and unwritten norms and standards.

Level 1 — **Law-Abiding**
General respect for and compliance with all relevant laws and regulations.

Figure 2.2   Five ambition levels of ethics.

• *Norm-abiding,* meaning going one step further than law-abiding, to consistently complying with all written and unwritten norms held by the major players in the sector in question and the general public. Norms are of course a much less defined entity than laws and regulations, but most business sectors acknowledge the existence of industry standards that usually supersede laws in terms of stringency. While it might not be illegal for a store to sell a product at full price one day to several customers even when it knows full well that the same product will be discounted 30 percent the next day, most customers would think this an unfair practice. Getting to a point where the organization truly lives up to such norms is certainly some way along the road to a full-fledged philanthropic approach. What marks the difference between norm abiding and stage three, profiled remedial, is the extent to which the organization uses this position actively as an asset in building its public image. In the norm-abiding position, this is not a pronounced trait.

• *Profiled remedial,* where the remedial half of the business ethics framework is really stretched to its limits and the organization has all of its processes and people under control and in line with a policy of committing no breaches and generally making up for any negative impact caused by its very existence. In addition, this achievement is actively used as part of the marketing strategy of the organization and the way it develops its image in the marketplace. At this stage, having gotten this far should truly represent a source of competitive advantage and this should be exploited actively.

• *Passively philanthropic,* having moved beyond the remedial boundary, an organization at this stage has introduced various philanthropic elements into its business operations. This philanthropic support is, however, offered through existing external organizations or programs where the organization itself need not take a very active part. This still represents a clear step into the philanthropic sphere of the framework and sets the organization aside from all those that merely clean up their act without contributing anything to external stakeholders beyond what they are expected to. Properly exploited, having reached this stage can be an integral part of the organization's external profile and an important part of the basis for its competitiveness.

• *Actively philanthropic,* which separates itself from passively philanthropic by the level of active involvement the organization displays in terms of the good causes it supports. At this final stage, the organization itself runs charitable programs or separate organizations or foundations that aid various groups of less fortunate stakeholders. In terms of outlays, in both money and time, this is certainly the ambition level that costs the most to the organization, but also the level that possesses the highest potential for benefits in return.

As you can see, there is a natural progression through these ambition levels. This applies to the effort they entail, usually the costs incurred, the potential for return on investment, and certainly also the potential for failing, even failing miserably. The higher in this hierarchy an organization climbs, the more susceptible it becomes to outside scrutiny, sometimes downright persecution motivated by the potential for a good story found in catching a proclaimed ethical organization red-handed doing something wrong. Staying on the straight and narrow gradually becomes more paramount in maintaining the position; this is also why it is usually recommended to progress carefully upward. Reaching for the top in one fell swoop will ordinarily be an extremely tough strategy to pull off as it leaves no time for the organization to build the moral fiber into its culture that is required to stay at the top. This is not saying you should climb one rung at a time and take years and years before you might eventually reach an ultimate target of actively philanthropic, but rather that one or two remedial levels should precede any philanthropic profiles.

Once you start to develop a credible image in the marketplace as being more ethically grounded, there is also the danger that elements in your approach that first are seen as novel and that are highly appreciated by the stakeholders they benefit come to be taken for granted and no longer are able to create the same excitement. This is part of the message conveyed by the so-called Kano model (Kano, 1984), a model that was developed to illustrate the effects of quality in terms of customer satisfaction. This model can be adapted to an ethical business setting as shown in Figure 2.3.

Customers, authorities, employees, any stakeholder really, will hold some expectations regarding the conduct of the organization it deals with and its output, be it products, services, information, payment, or whatever. In the original Kano model, these expectations relate specifically to product or service quality, but here they apply to ethical aspects of the conduct

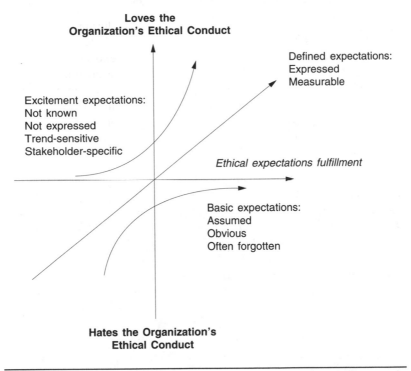

Figure 2.3   The ethics Kano model.

and output of the organization. The basic expectations are as the name implies, so basic that the stakeholder will not even mention them in communication with the organization. Tax authorities will take it for granted that a serious organization handles its accounts according to the rules and pays its taxes; you probably didn't even consider the possibility that the tumble dryer you bought the other day was stolen property fenced by the appliance store, and you clearly didn't specify in your current work contract that you would like to avoid being seriously injured in the course of doing your job. In terms of stakeholder satisfaction, fulfilling all such basic expectations contributes nothing at all; it merely avoids dissatisfaction.

The straight line in the figure represents expressed expectations or requirements, so-called defined expectations of such a nature that the more of them that are fulfilled, the higher the satisfaction. In ethical terms, an example can be environmentally minded customers in grocery stores. The more products that are available as ecologically grown alternatives, the more this is appreciated by such a group of customers. In both cases, there will typically be a minimum threshold that must be respected to get on the plus side, and anything beyond this will increase the level of satisfaction. These expectations are normally clearly communicated during negotiations, through written conditions, or well known in the marketplace.

The third set of expectations, called excitement expectations, are not voiced by the stakeholder, mostly because they are not known to the stakeholder. When shopping for ice cream, you might not know that buying a pint of Ben & Jerry's ice cream means a certain amount of money will be channeled to a charitable cause, and thus not use it as a buying criterion. Realizing after you get home and open the box that this is the case, you will probably be positively surprised by this fact and it might lead you to become a repeat customer. Since you did not know beforehand that this was an element that could be offered by the organization you were doing business with, you did not hold any expectations toward it. Consequently, not satisfying any of these potential expectations will not cause any dissatisfaction on your part, but offering them anyway can be highly effective in creating extra delight on the part of the stakeholder in question.

Beyond clarifying the existence of these three sets of expectations, the Kano model is powerful in visualizing the fact that the expectations tend to migrate downward in the diagram. Unspoken delight expectations, once having been experienced a few times, have a peculiar habit of becoming defined ones and thus expected every time. Defined expectations that are consistently satisfied are tomorrow's basic and undefined expectations, and will cause dissatisfaction when not fulfilled. This is the dilemma of always striving to offer more or better or bigger to stakeholders—you help to educate them, you spoil them, and at the same time contribute to jacking up their expectations and demands. This applies to product or service quality or features, and it applies to ethical dimensions. A customer previously used to being half-cheated now and then will initially react positively simply by being offered a fair and honest deal. As this becomes the norm, you might add a charitable element to the custom brought to you by the person and this can create delight. As this also becomes the norm, you'd better keep up the charitable aspect or you will disappoint. This might seem like a losing battle that cannot lead to anything good, and you might be right. It is, however, a fact of life and if you do not raise the stakes, someone else will. You can just as well get used to having to constantly improve and take the active role of being the one at the forefront instead of just following suit whenever your competitor moves forward.

A couple of other issues to keep in the back of your mind when pondering this decision of ethical profile are related to the ethical profile (or lack thereof) of the other players in your market segment or industry. If everybody else frequently bends a few rules, hides some profits from taxation, takes their customers by the nose, and so on, it is easy to fall into step. Clearly the most logical argument in such a case is that "as long as everybody else does so and so, there is no point in us being any different. It will cost us in lost revenues and increased costs and altogether be bad for business." Actually, this is perhaps the ideal situation in which to pursue an ethically founded business strategy! Just reaching *law-abiding* and making this known to the marketplace will set you so much apart from the rest that customers and other stakeholders will flock around you. Putting even more distance between you and the competition will just increase this tendency and is bound to pay off.

The other issue pertains to the organization's motivation for changing its ways and aiming for an ethical approach to business. This can range from an inherent desire to use its power and resources to do something good for others, to avoiding negative repercussions from having less-than-acceptable business practices exposed, to wanting to build a stronger basis for competitive advantage, and probably others. A final obvious motivation is a guilty conscience and an urge to assuage it. Feeling this way is in some ways positive as it shows that the organization can feel collective remorse over past wrongdoings and want to remedy these. It is, however, not an ideal motivation for going ethical. In this mode, you will always find yourself catching up with past "sins" and find it hard to turn the ethical approach into a positive asset. While this might partly pay off in creating a more positive attitude in stakeholders, you will probably not be able to reap the full benefits. From the very outset, you should see such a change in strategy as a vehicle for attaining a position of higher competitiveness and more attraction toward customers and other stakeholders.

DECIDING ON AND DEVELOPING ETHICAL BUSINESS PRACTICES

The business ethics framework is an extensive object encompassing a large number of possible elements to include in an ethical approach to business. For the most part, these elements are sorted according to which type of internal or external stakeholder they will benefit and they have been divided into strategic versus operational practices and into remedial versus philanthropic aspects. Having decided on the main ethical profile to start out with, the next step is to compose a suitable set of business practices to constitute the body of this profile.

There are several issues to consider when making your selection:

- Striking a suitable balance between remedial and philanthropic practices to match the chosen profile.

- Matching the ambition level of the ethical profile with the practices to be implemented, especially in terms of not stretching your resources too far by choosing too many or too costly elements.

- Considering how far a leap from current practices the chosen ethical elements will represent. The larger a change is required to move from the current state, the harder the implementation will be.

- Analyzing the needs for training and investments in equipment, new processes, or other elements that will be generated by the ethical practices you decide to implement.

All in all, it is a matter of using common sense in composing a set of ethical business practices that matches the ambition level decided on and that does not represent so gigantic a leap from today's culture and practices that it will be impossible to attain. During this process, the intention with the business ethics framework has been for it to serve as a source of ideas and inspiration for the organization. And as always in major change processes, please keep in mind that these initial decisions regarding the change to an ethical approach should be subjected to discussions throughout the organization. This will take advantage of creativity and good ideas from the employees and help make the actual implementation easier.

Once a set of ethical elements has been decided on, care must be taken to actually develop the details of the business processes and organizational mechanisms required to put these into action. In addition to training, which will be covered a little later, this can include acquiring equipment of different types, making agreements with external partners or suppliers, establishing new organizational units, detailing administrative procedures, and most often, designing new business processes. It is impossible to provide any more detailed instructions on how to accomplish this job. The best advice is to not take this task too lightly. If you simply assume that people who have not been heavily involved in the strategic deliberations about the ethical approach will easily turn around and start practicing these ideas, this can easily blindside you down the road.

ONE CHIEF EXECUTIVE OFFICER OR ALL EMPLOYEES AS CEOS?

The heading alludes to the issue of where to place the responsibilities for the ethical profile and the running of the new ethical business practices. This is a discussion that closely resembles the one that has been raging for a couple of decades concerning the role of quality in an organization, accentuated by the question of whether or not to have a separate quality manager and quality management staff. As this discussion precedes ours by perhaps twenty years, there might be some valuable lessons to learn from that field. Key aspects are (Aune, 2000):

• Organizations that have a clearly defined vision, well-documented objectives, pronounced values, and behavioral guidelines, and have taken care in making these common among all members of the organization, can manage better with flatter hierarchies than "old-fashioned" organizations. The need for top-down control is reduced and the formality of the organizational structure, responsibilities, reporting lines, and so on, can be relaxed.

• Coordination and communication take place through a network of people, not through a bureaucracy.

• Employees at all levels are trained to possess the competence and skills required to perform their job well, and as a consequence, decisions are left to be made at the level of the organization where their consequences are best known.

• All employees are themselves responsible for the quality and ethical acceptability of their work and actions. This transfers much responsibility to the individual employee, but also authority to question practices and stop business processes on suspicion of problems.

• To the extent that control personnel still exist, be they quality control operators or ethical watchdogs, their job is not as much to uncover errors and questionable behavior, but to uncover improvement potential and aid regular employees in exploiting this potential.

These bullet points are not just wishful thinking about ideal organizations of the future; more and more organizations are abandoning old staff control functions and deploying quality and performance responsibilities, along with decision-making authority, throughout the organization. In the truly excellent organizations, quality has become a way of life, part of the fiber of the individual employee and the organizational culture. As such, there is no need for dedicated quality control people, but you will often find that there is at least still a quality manager. This person plays the devil's advocate and the voice of the customer in discussions regarding product or service design, quality policies, and so on. She or he is usually the public spokesperson for the organization on matters pertaining to quality and is considered the best-qualified internal expert on quality issues. The Commission on Public Trust and Private Enterprise in the United States, which will be mentioned several times throughout the book, has made some general recommendations regarding ethics. For example, the Commission recommended the designation of a board committee to oversee ethics issues, and the designation of an officer to oversee ethics and compliance with the code of conduct, similar to the ever-more common practice of having a Chief Ethical Officer.

Translating these principles into the ethical dimension, some solutions to consider are:

• In general, avoid establishing a heavily manned staff function at a high organizational level dedicated to business ethics. Perhaps in a very early phase of a transformation to an ethically oriented business approach, such a unit can be of some use, but there are probably other ways to achieve the same effect.

• Instead, combined with the required training and awareness-building, leave the daily responsibility (and authority) for ethical aspects to the employees in charge of all the tasks and processes in the organization. If you have reached a stage where business process orientation has been implemented in your organization, this is a particularly suitable organizational mode for this type of distributed responsibility. In a process-oriented organization, there are usually so-called process owners that oversee larger or smaller business processes and their performance levels. (For a more detailed discussion of process owners, see Andersen [1998].) By including ethical performance in their sphere of command, responsibility is easily linked to the person with the best qualifications for upholding it.

• Equal to the quality manager, an ethical manager can take on the role of external figurehead for ethics, represent ethical matters in strategic discussions at the executive level, and assume the role as the foremost expert in the organization on ethics. Referring back to the heading of this section, many organizations have opted to title this position CEO for *chief ethical officer*. This is probably as good a title as any, as long as it is clear to all employees that this is one of many CEOs in the organization—within a limited sphere of command, every employee is their own CEO.

• Finally, if you have a good memory for what you have read so far, you will recall that for certain elements in the business ethics framework, it has been suggested that a dedicated committee or panel should be formed to take on certain responsibilities or tasks. For example, this has been the case for equal employment and promotion rights and organizational bullying. This recommendation is still valid—there are some areas where placing the responsibility with one person or job function is inappropriate and where a committee with some kind of proportional representation is required to command respect and make decisions that will be accepted.

Organizing the ethical responsibilities and tasks this decentralized way poses strict requirements for the levels of ethical training provided to process owners and other key people. This is the topic of the next section.

TRAINING THE ORGANIZATION IN ETHICAL MATTERS

Returning to the Commission on Public Trust and Private Enterprise, its report also focused on the need for companies to take steps to implement appropriate standards to ensure ethical conduct. It noted that a major challenge for corporations was "to create a 'tone at the top' and a corporate culture that promotes ethical conduct on the part of the organization and its employees." The Commission recommended that corporations adopt codes of conduct and policies for promoting ethical behavior and have "processes that encourage and make it safe for employees to raise ethical issues and report possible ethical violations." All of this partly addresses the question of training in ethical matters.

There is a complex dilemma facing any organization trying to make a pronounced change from a previous state of being, if not expressly unethical, at least less concerned with ethical issues and perhaps condoning some shortcuts and bent rules, to a new state of ethical compliance and even an active marketing of this to external stakeholders. The dilemma is partly that the executive level of the organization can decide to "go ethical" only to find that the bulk of the organization does not catch on to the idea. A further part of the dilemma is that the organization becomes even more vulnerable to external scrutiny and the discovery of breaches and unethical behavior. Finally, at some stage, the actual transformation must be marked and communicated externally, but you can never be sure whether the organization is ready for this and people have been trained well enough. Part of the answer to this challenge seems to be investing in sufficient amounts of suitable ethical training.

Such training must cover the following aspects of an ethical business approach:

- General principles and theories of business ethics and corporate social responsibility.

- Ethical decision making in general.

- The ethical values defined and the "ethical fiber" that the organization tries to develop as part of its organizational culture.

- Personal and organizational virtues and the part these play in an organization's ethical profile.

- The specific ethical guidelines developed for the organization.

- The specific ethical business practices developed as part of the transformation.

Without going into detail in this respect, this training will typically be included in a more holistic ethical training program. Such a program must be wide enough to cover all employees to some extent and at the same time allow for a tailored approach to the different levels and groups within the organization. The executive level typically requires training in overall understanding of ethical principles and their strategic importance, whereas a possible chief ethical officer and perhaps a small support group require in-depth training in all aspects of ethical business approaches. Middle management is a layer of the organization that plays a crucial role in any extensive change process. Very often, middle management has the power to make or break any such attempts at strategic change, thus, targeting them with pertinent and relevant training in all issues they can be questioned about by their employees is vital. For the general body of employees, it is necessary to train them in general ethical principles, the core values of the organization, and specific and relevant guidelines and business processes.

As for any training that targets adults who are out of school and holding jobs, the training must be adapted to give the best effect. Traditional school-type theoretical training will rarely be very effective in changing the attitudes and practices of such a target group. On-the-job training that is closely related to the skills required and tasks that will later be performed is an essential principle. Experience-based learning and developing a repertoire for improvisation will be dealt with later on (see chapter 3), but some other training issues include (Aune, 2000):

- All learning takes place in the individual, but collective training is linked to the team(s) the individual belongs to, and presupposes common and shared objectives and tasks.

- Adults learn based on experience and the principle of learning through imitation.

- Learning is an endless process that generates knowledge through observing and reflecting over consequences of actions—which in turn leads to new understanding.

- Learning requires time for such reflection and discussion.

Ultimately, the objective for any organization with regard to training and knowledge is to achieve a so-called learning organization, where experiences are continuously refined into new knowledge and applied to constantly improve performance, be it ethical performance or cost control performance. To arrive at this stage, a culture and tradition for learning must be stimulated and people allowed to refine their knowledge, including ethically related knowledge. This comes as a result of both formal training and an organizational culture that is positive toward individual thinking and initiative and accepts trial and error. This brings us back to the discussion in chapter 3 on what is a suitable organizational culture, closing the loop in training. Let us move on to launching the new ethical profile and start using it as a marketing element.

LAUNCH AND MARKET THE NEW GOOD CITIZEN ORGANIZATION

First, rest assured that this will be a brief section. This point in time, when the organization has probably moved all the way from an initial strategic debate about whether to emphasize business ethics more than before to having developed detailed ethically oriented business processes and conducted ethical training, is a monumental one. This is the point where the cat is officially let out of the bag and the world is told of the new business approach of the organization. It is still a minor topic to cover in this book.

Basically, any transformation of this kind, be it focusing on quality, ethics, or cost reductions, deserves lots of attention and some "pomp and circumstance" to be elevated to a state where people realize that it is truly important to the organization. This is partly achieved by internal "launches" of the new approach, but since the organization will have to go through much debate, development, and training as part of the process, it is difficult to pinpoint such a launch. It is much easier for the organization to define a date when the news is spread to the outside world. This is not suggesting that you turn such a thing into a major press event with invited media, cheering speeches, and the handing out of caps with logos, but it is often useful to mark such a launch in one way or another.

Some organizations have invited customers and suppliers, other partners, and perhaps local authorities to a small gathering to outline how the new business practices will affect them, others have quietly informed key actors of possible changes in practices, and some simply let outside players find out through changed practices and word-of-mouth.

More important than a marked launch event or communication is the use of the business ethics approach as part of the platform for the organization's public image and marketing profile. As you will hear many times throughout this book, there are very few benefits to be achieved (possibly beyond the good feeling of doing good) from business ethics if it remains a "secret" that only the organization itself is privy to. There are subtle and not-so-subtle ways of doing so, Part of the implementation job is making the change known to the outside world. The discussion will be raised in more detail in chapter 9 so it will not be foregone at this point, but it is a fact that that many organizations find it, perhaps *tasteless* is the word, to actively market that it does good to others. It might seem like a little boy who does not squash a bug and loudly proclaims this to his mother, expecting to be rewarded with an ice cream for the good deed. In this light, *marketing,* as in TV commercials or newspaper ads, is perhaps not the best word. This is rather about exploiting the new ethical profile as a means of building a public image as a caring and decent organization. This is really the job of well-paid and clever public relations people, thus this book will not give any advice on how to practically accomplish this. Suffice it to say, you will benefit much more from an ethical business approach if it becomes a well-known part of the public's image of your organization.

ENSURING COMPLIANCE WITH THE NEW ETHICAL PROFILE AND BUSINESS PRACTICES

The greatest threat to a successful change to an ethical business approach, as well as a continued successful maintenance of such an image, is the risk of minor or major breaches of the ethical standards the organization imposes on itself and by which external stakeholders will assess it. It only takes one employee breaking fundamental ethical standards to make a big dent in the organization's credibility, and more serious systemic breaches can ruin the ethical profile altogether. Thus, installing mechanisms to encourage compliance with the ethical standards and practices is paramount.

There are several mechanisms and approaches that partly support this objective, some aimed at creating positive incentives for compliance, others at follow-up and assessment, and yet others at punishment and exposure:

• Ethical compliance incentive systems, general mechanisms that link ethical behavior, compliance with ethical standards, and ethical performance to one or more types of benefits. Such benefits can be of a financial nature, promotions, time off, favorable recognition, and so on, and be bestowed upon individuals, teams, or organizational units. Such systems can either be used deliberately as part of the implementation process to foster the desired behavior and then be disbanded once the new ways of working have settled, or they can be permanent institutions. No matter how they are designed or how long they last, the point is to create knowledge in the organization that there are benefits to be achieved by following the new approach, thus hopefully enticing the members of the organization to turn around quickly. Such systems do, however, have notorious problems connected to them in terms of being perceived as unfair, or that the benefits come to be seen as something that is deserved no matter what, and so on.

• Incentive systems must use some form of evaluation criteria to determine who are entitled to the announced benefits and who are not. One common way is linking the incentives to achieved levels of performance, measured in a predefined manner. This quickly leads us to the subject of performance measurement and performance measurement systems, which is an academic and industrial field of its own. Together with a colleague of mine, I have even written a book about performance measurement systems (Andersen and Fagerhaug, 2001). A fascinating capacity of performance measurement is to impact and alter the behavior of people and organizations (see sidebar).

An acquaintance of mine had a small car without many extra features, certainly no on-board computer that would measure fuel consumption. At traffic lights, this person was a fierce competitor, always trying to win the race with the car in the next lane, never even considering how much fuel was wasted in quick accelerations. After changing cars, his new one came equipped with a gauge that would show average fuel consumption at any time. When hitching a ride with this person one day in the new car, I noticed that he would shift to neutral when going down hill, that the car would be allowed to roll slowly across a flat stretch to the next downhill, and so on. Upon reaching the final destination, one glance at the fuel consumption gauge showed that the average consumption had been reduced by a fraction, evoking boisterous cheers from my driver.

Simply by the presence of a form of performance indicator in his new car, my acquaintance's driving style had changed completely overnight from an aggressive, competitive attitude to one of maximum fuel economy driving. The same effect is seen in organizations. A purchasing department in a manufacturing company was given reduction in procurement costs as a primary performance indicator to be evaluated by. A year down the road, the costs had indeed been reduced, by as much as 15 percent on average. The only problem was that manufacturing costs had increased by 20 percent, the reason being that the purchasing department had turned to spot buying from various suppliers, many of which delivered products too late, of poor quality, and not according to specifications. Defining and following up performance indicators that assess ethical performance throughout the organization can thus be a powerful tool in changing people's behavior, regardless of whether the measurements are linked to incentive systems or not. The inherent problem of performance measurement lies in the effect seen in the case of the purchasing department, namely that indicators defined with the best of intentions turn out to motivate and encourage a behavior that has negative effects. People are ingenious in finding ways to maximize performance, often to the extent that they undermine the intentions of the system. Defining good performance indicators without any such unexpected side effects is an art in itself, so take care if attempting this.

• With the existence of performance measurements and performance data, the table is set for undertaking performance benchmarking. The core principle of benchmarking is that of comparison, internally between departments or processes, or externally with other organizations or some type of standard. In benchmarking circles, it is also common to differentiate between performance benchmarking, primarily comparing performance figures, and process benchmarking, where the focus is more on learning from other's business processes and practices. Both these latter types of benchmarking can serve a purpose in an ethical compliance setting. Performance benchmarking can be used to compare the ethical performance levels of your own organization to others. If yours is better, this is a motivation to keep up the good work; if it is poorer it indicates that higher performance levels can be reached, and it can also bring out the competitive spirit of people (nobody likes competing and coming out short). Process benchmarking can be used to learn how organizations with a higher ethical performance level achieve this.

• Related to benchmarking as a tool for assessing the performance of the organization, external (or third-party) assessments can serve much the same purpose. Such assessments are especially well known from various certification schemes, for example ISO 9000 quality management system certification or ISO 14000 environmental management system certification. The main idea is that a qualified, neutral third party performs an overall assessment of the organization, its performance, and its business processes and procedures in relation to a predefined standard. If the organization meets the standard, the certificate is maintained until the next assessment; if not, improvements must be made for a follow-up visit and a second chance to qualify. Experience shows that the first such certification process is especially useful in getting the organization on its toes and cleaning up its act; subsequent re-certification assessments are rarely as effective in bringing about useful changes. The same approach can obviously also be used for ethical system assessments, either as a separate entity or as part of a future certification scheme (which will probably be developed in the not so distant future).

• On the opposite side of incentive systems are punishment mechanisms, that is, negative incentives that are meant to keep people in line through threats of pay reductions, fines, loss of promotion opportunities, even being fired. While it is easy to agree with those who argue that positive incentive systems typically are a more effective and modern alternative to punishment systems, the latter still have a role to play. If members of the organization know they can get away with anything, respect for ethical guidelines and standards will deteriorate quickly. The point is, you should not define various types of punishment for every small breach that might occur, but rather make it clear that serious incidents and repetitive minor breaches will not be tolerated and will induce negative consequences.

• To impose punishment on someone, the organization must first become aware of a breach having been committed. In many cases, breaches are of such a nature that they will become instantly known, but more often breaches occur more silently and can go on for a long period of time before someone finds out. In such cases, people surrounding the culprit normally have either suspected or known what was going on, but hesitated to tell superiors. To make sure breaches are disclosed as soon as possible, no matter where in the organization they take place, whistleblowing must be an accepted practice. Whistleblowing is discussed in chapter 6, and can form part of the overall set of mechanisms ensuring that the organization stays in line.

• Reporting the triple bottom line is the last mechanism to be mentioned. The key of a triple bottom line is that an organization not only should report its financial results, but also societal and environmental results (Elkington, 1999). This follows as a consequence of the fact that any organization is part of society and the external environment, and its operations and very existence impact these two. To judge the results produced by a company, it is not sufficient to know only how much money it made, but how it impacted, positively or negatively, the world around it. As you will see in the next chapter, criticism has been voiced over this "obligation," but for now let us accept that this is the concept of the triple bottom line. By reporting all three results, an organization subjects its results to public scrutiny, and to dare to do so, there is a pressure to ensure that things are in order. As such, triple bottom lines are a means to enforce self-justice and adherence to set standards. The side effect is that publishing such results presents a good opportunity both to profile the organization's ethical results and document that it sticks to what it has promised (given that it has kept its house in order).

All of the above are mechanisms an organization can use to increase the likelihood that all of its members stay in line with defined standards for ethical behavior. A final issue that should not be overlooked is that of personal integrity, morality, moral fiber, virtue, or whichever term is used. They all refer to the same basic quality in a human being of trying to do the right thing. A test of moral integrity are a person's actions if given the chance to gain personal benefits (money, esteem, products or services, and so on) through an act that is objectively in breach of laws or accepted moral norms, if it very likely that such a breach would not be discovered by anyone. Most people would be tempted to charge ahead, but many will be able to resist the temptation, simply because it goes against what they believe to be right.

If all or a majority of an organization's members have strong personal moral codes, this is probably much more effective in ensuring compliance than any reward or punishment mechanism you can think of. Personal integrity is of course measured on a continuous scale, it is not a question of yes or no; part of a person's moral code is probably genetic, tied to their basic personality, and part is certainly a result of upbringing. Personal integrity can be strengthened through motivation, enlightenment, education, and training, though, and is a worthwhile investment. In fact, in the end, very much regarding an organization's collective behavior in terms of ethics comes down to such personal values and integrity. This is both frightening, as it is more or less outside the control of the organization and its management, and promising, as it means that good people will do the right thing.

This concludes the issues regarding implementation of the business ethics framework and an ethical business approach. From here on, the business ethics framework will be presented in detail.

3

Building an Ethically Founded Platform for a Sound Organizational Culture: Remedial, Internal, and Strategic Instruments

T here is some logic to the order of treatment of the different areas of the business ethics framework. The intention is to progress from "getting your act together" and cleaning up the house on the inside first to an external orientation in the second round. There is also a natural progression, starting with a remedial approach before embarking on activities of a more philanthropic nature. As such, a good starting point is focusing on developing an ambitious strategy or policy statement on the treatment of employees and defining the values on which the organization is based. This is the focus of this chapter.

KEEPING ONE HAND CLEAN IS NOT EASY IF THE OTHER IS DIRTY

The interplay between internal policies and behavior and external image and perception has already been mentioned. There are numerous examples of organizations that have tried, or even at first been successful at, building a positive image in the marketplace as a trustworthy and caring supplier or partner, but later failed. Some of these never succeeded at developing the desired image, in other cases, an actually achieved image has eroded gradually over time, while in others the façade has been instantaneously shattered. Very often, this has come as a result of a mismatch between internal attitudes and practices and the coveted external image.

The hand hygiene reference in the heading of this section is a good metaphor for this interplay. In former times, before the invention of modern

Consider what is undoubtedly one of the best-known cases of a trusted organization failing its image completely: the auditing and accounting firm of Arthur Andersen & Co. The role of an auditor is of course to be a neutral, credible third party auditing the accounts and accounting practices of companies to ensure that authorities, the stock market, and other stakeholders receive accurate and pertinent information from the company. Being one of the dominant global auditors, Arthur Andersen had built an image as a competent and reliable supplier of such services. Following the Enron disclosures, a domino effect of scandals and problems has left the former giant in a completely different state. At one time, Arthur Andersen was auditor for the following companies: Enron, WorldCom, Qwest, Global Crossing, Dynegy, CMS Energy, Halliburton, Peregrine, and Merck. Since then, these companies have all been alleged to have used questionable accounting practices at the time when their auditor was Arthur Andersen. Since then, the European branch of the auditor has been merged with Ernst & Young and the name has ceased to exist in Europe; the name Arthur Andersen has been dragged through the mud in the media; and trust in the company as an auditor has all but vanished. According to CNN's special section on the Web dedicated to corporate fraud (CNN, 2002), on June 15, 2002, a jury found the accounting firm guilty of obstructing justice when it shredded Enron documents. On October 16, a federal judge imposed the maximum sentence—a $500,000 fine and five years' probation, but that was largely a formality since the firm already had lost most of its clients. The company vowed to appeal.

hygienic principles and aids, people would often use one hand for eating and the other for things that would inherently make it dirty. Not surprisingly, life expectancy was not too much to boast about—common infections and bacteria that we never have to worry about today killed people back then. Of course it is not possible to keep your two hands so perfectly separate that one stays clean while the other is used for all sorts of tasks. Being educated in the principles of hygiene, we do not question this fact. Still, many seem to think that the way an organization treats its employees or suppliers can be kept so apart from the way it treats (or wants the world to think it treats) its customers that highly varying standards can be applied to the two areas.

It seems equally obvious to us that this is impossible. Perhaps you could get away with it in times when society and industry were not as transparent as they have become and before consumers arrived at their current level of consciousness about ethical issues. Today, however, it is highly unlikely you could maintain a practice of bullying suppliers or neglecting your employees without having this "infect" your external reputation. Thus, first defining how the organization views its employees and with what standards it will treat them, and secondly putting this into practice, are logical first steps in building a solid platform for a more conscientious approach to business.

EMPLOYEE TREATMENT AND WORK CONDITION POLICY (HUMAN RESOURCE POLICY IN OTHER WORDS)

This can be a somewhat tricky item to start the entire hands-on approach to business ethics treatment with. Many practitioners tend to be slightly skeptical whenever the word "policy" comes up, as they have seen how a policy translates in the end into nothing more than a piece of paper (or these days a page on the intranet). I need not look any further than my own organization; I manage a research unit that is part of a 1600-person-strong research organization for which a massive manual has been developed outlining policy and practices for human resource management. Even though the intentions of the policy are probably more or less adhered to throughout the organization, I dare say I believe this is due more to the fact that they represent standard, commonsense issues than that most managers have actually read and know it.

This can easily become the case with any form of policy, be it a human resource policy or an ethical stance policy. And you might recall that this is exactly the chief shortcoming of ethical business approaches this book is trying to counteract. Good intentions will not produce results unless they are also followed up in practice. However, seeing end results in terms of sound practices is more likely if these can build on a platform of good policies; thus, such policies do have a role to play.

What, then, should such a human resource policy in its broadest meaning contain? There is of course no general answer to this question. As you will see is very often the case with an ethical approach, it is to a large extent a matter of ambition and what you ultimately want to achieve through the policy. Staying within the category of "remedial," the level of ambition can range from providing a safe working environment to ensuring that your employees are among the best skilled and paid in the industry. There is, however, a thin line between the so-called remedial treatment of employees to a more philanthropic approach where employees are treated and compensated beyond what is deemed "fair." Offering more than acceptable pay levels, medical benefits, or on-site kindergarten services might be seen as part of a normal human resource policy in some cases and far into the philanthropic range in others. Fortunately, the distinction is not an important one, and the objective of this chapter is to illustrate how such a policy can be designed and what it can encompass.

You should also beware of the fact that too ambitious or generous policies can backfire. To a certain extent, very good policies will probably help the organization in attracting and retaining good human resources, keeping them motivated, and hopefully enabling them to achieve their best performance. However, "pampering" people too much can easily lead them to become complacent, lazy, and less motivated to perform. Once people become accustomed to a certain benefit, it is taken for granted and removing it will create discontentment. Again, there is a thin line between what is suitable and serves its purpose and what is too much. The key is probably to figure out what policies (and their subsequent implementation) really make a difference and are able to motivate people, and at the same time ensure that these benefits are not a given, but a reward distributed based on performance. This entire issue of keeping up motivation versus making people complacent will be revisited later on in this book (see chapter 7 about implementation).

Let us start by breaking the subject of human resource management down into some distinct areas that such a policy normally should cover (see Figure 3.1):

• *Physical work conditions,* covering issues such as work climate indoors or outdoors, space, access to facilities, light and noise, health and safety hazards, and so on. Having ambitious policies in this area could contribute to higher productivity, as work conditions allow people to perform at their best, and also support the well-being and level of contentment among employees, as they can experience every day that the organization strives to provide positive work conditions.

• *Organizational work conditions,* meaning interpersonal relationships; treatment by superiors, peers, and subordinates; access to other people in the organization; work pressure, and so on. As is the case for physical work conditions, good policies in this area should help improve productivity, ease of communication, and motivation among employees.

• *Compensation structure,* including both direct pay, other types of fiduciary compensation, for example, bonuses or stock options, indirect compensation through medical benefits, company car, free telephone, and so on. When push comes to shove, this is often the true foundation for

Figure 3.1 Human resource management broken down into subareas.

From the beginning of the more than thirty-year history of oil field development in the UK and Norwegian North Sea, many of the job functions on the platforms were highly risky, with high rates of injuries or fatal accidents, due to both operating dangerous and complicated equipment and the hazardous weather conditions. As the pioneering phase gradually was replaced by a phase of normal operations, the oil companies operating the fields put enormous resources into making the conditions safer for all involved personnel. For some, health and safety issues are even among the few fixed agenda items in senior management and board meetings. This has certainly paid off, both in terms of a dramatic reduction in injuries and a sharp increase in productivity and the attractiveness of these jobs.

employee motivation and satisfaction, and a sound policy in this area must strike a balance between attractiveness to existing and future employees and acceptable cost levels for the organization.

• *Access to information and decision-making power;* to what extent employees have access to relevant information, quality of communication, right to participation in decisions, and so on. This is again an area that typically determines motivation levels among employees at all levels of the organization and the extent to which people understand the larger picture of their jobs and thus are able to contribute beyond merely performing routine tasks.

• *Respect for laws and regulations;* to what extent the organization abides by applicable laws and regulations governing all types of work-related issues. This area is important both in terms of avoiding any repercussions from authorities of different kinds as well as demonstrating to the employees that the organization is consistent in terms of honesty and fair treatment.

• *Competence and career development;* how the organization facilitates systematic growth of its employees in terms of further education, development of skills, and opportunities for career development. As for most of these subareas, ensuring good policies in terms of continued development of human resources contributes to the general contentment of employees and helps keep them motivated, productive, and committed to the organization.

• *Concern for the 24-hour employee;* how the organization acknowledges its obligation toward (and benefits from) enabling its employees to thrive as complete human beings. Again, this demonstrates to employees that the organization is concerned about their well-being and at the same time helps reduce absenteeism from injuries or other problems encountered outside the work place.

All of these areas, which together constitute modern human resource management, should of course be well taken care of in any organization, irrespective of whether it subscribes to an ethical business perspective or not. However, the extent to which far-reaching policies are defined for these areas will probably depend on the general worldview of the organization and its possible inclination toward a business ethics standpoint.

Under the remedial heading, Table 3.1 summarizes some typical policy elements that it would be logical to include for each of these human resource management subareas. When reviewing the table, please keep in mind that this chapter deals with remedial policies, thus the intention of the different elements is to adhere to the organization's duties in a sober manner, not lavishly dote on people in every way possible. For example, physical work conditions should of course be designed to ensure that people can

Table 3.1   Remedial human resource management policies.

Human Resource Management Subarea	Policy Element
Physical work conditions	Policy for providing a physical work climate that complies with recommendations regarding working space, temperature, air quality, noise, light, and other relevant aspects to the extent possible, depending on specific characteristics of the job in question.
	Policy for providing other physical facilities that render work comfortable, for example sufficient restroom capacity, access to food and beverages, locker rooms, and so on.
	Policy for protecting employees from all types of health and safety hazards, to the extent possible.
Organizational work conditions	Policy for actively contributing to the development of a sound organizational culture.
	Policy for preventing and reprimanding bullying or unacceptable conduct among employees, both at the same hierarchical level or upward or downward in the hierarchy.
	Policy against discrimination based on gender, age, race, creed, sexual orientation, or any other traits and the promotion of equality in recruiting, compensating, and promoting.
	Policy for attempting to the extent possible to keep task complexity and work loads at levels that match the employee's abilities and capacity.
	Policy for shielding employees from unnecessary bureaucracy to the extent possible, in terms of paperwork, meetings, e-mails, and so on.
	Policy against downsizing and other types of layoffs that are solely aimed at increasing already acceptable profit levels.
Compensation structure	Policy for keeping compensation at fair levels with a match between performance, results, and compensation, and avoiding obvious under- and overpayment.
	Policy for assisting employees in designing compensation structures that maximize the employees' benefits, for example, converting parts of their pay to other types of compensation like free telephone, company car, insurance, and so on, should this be more beneficial to the employees.
	In countries where this is not covered through taxes, policy for providing adequate medical benefits in addition to other types of compensation.
Access to information and decision-making power	Policy for openness in terms of employees' access to relevant information that poses no security risk to the organization.
	Policy for high communication quality, including emphasizing important information and shielding employees from unnecessary information.

continued

continued

Human Resource Management Subarea	Policy Element
	Policy for empowerment of employees and their active participation in discussions leading up to and the making of relevant decisions.
	Policy for listening to employees and being responsive to ideas, suggestions, and complaints.
Respect for laws and regulations	Policy for the organization's adherence, in the role of employer, to applicable laws and regulations pertaining to human resource management and work-related issues.
	Policy for relevant training in and encouragement of adherence to laws and regulations relevant to the organization and its operations, for employees at all levels.
Competence and career development	Policy for systematically assessing employees' current skills and capabilities and future needs for career development and contributing to enabling employees to develop their competence in line with these needs.
	Policy for encouraging internal career development and promotion within the organization and supporting employees in their career development.
Concern for the 24-hour employee	Policy for contributing to employees' contentment as complete human beings through ensuring they have sufficient leisure time to nurture personal relationships and interests.

work comfortably, but not to such an extent that they are more comfortable at work than in their own homes. There is also a limit to what is possible to achieve; if the job takes place outdoors in areas where winter means frost and snow, warm working clothes can relieve some of the exposure to the cold, but it would be impossible to make such a job as comfortable as an indoor job.

Notice also that the area of employee treatment is one of the areas most extensively covered in the so-called Caux Round Table Business Principles of Ethics (Caux Round Table, 1994), and many of the Caux principles coincide with those of the table above.

DIFFERENTIATED VERSUS GLOBAL HUMAN RESOURCE MANAGEMENT STANDARDS

This is a good place in the text to raise the issue of international standards for work conditions and human resource management. While it might seem blatantly unfair, it is a fact that there are vast differences in standards of how employees are treated and compensated from continent to continent, country to country, and industry to industry. And while it seems equally obvious that attempting to even out these differences is a good thing to do, such an approach can also create problems. The first impulse of an organization that establishes a facility in a foreign country where employee conditions are far lower than in the organization's home country is often to transfer some of their home country practices to this facility. Two possible problematic outcomes from such an approach can be:

• If one organization introduces pay levels or work conditions that are significantly higher or better than the average in the region, this organization will usually stand out like a lighthouse. While obviously being positive for those few employed by the company, it can be negative for all those that are not. Should this practice induce other organizations in the same region to follow suit and improve their standards, this is of course a beneficial side effect, but more often than not, other organizations will not be able to do so. The result is the obvious jealousy created by learning what a few fortunate ones achieve while realizing that you will not achieve the same. In such cases, all those not employed by the organization were probably better off before.

• In many cases, such establishments in foreign countries are undertaken by a number of companies at the same time, often also in cooperation with international bodies like the United Nations, the International Labour Organisation, or other types of interest or pressure groups. In such cases, the pressure for improved work conditions comes from a broader range of sources and is more likely to have a real impact. And while such initiatives have in some cases truly contributed to an overall improvement of standards, they have also created significant problems in other instances. As an example, in many cases international pressure from global companies and pressure groups have led to the introduction of a minimum pay level in a certain region or country. While the global companies present have been able to adhere to this pay level, local companies have not been sufficiently financially viable to carry these costs. The result has often been detrimental to local industrial initiatives with the end outcome that a few jobs at higher pay levels have replaced a much higher number of jobs with lower pay.

Thus, while it seems completely logical and the right thing to do to migrate existing Western human resource management practices and standards to other parts of the world, it is worthwhile considering such an approach carefully. If the standards of industrialized democracies were to be instantly imposed globally, it would undoubtedly spell disaster for the world economy. The answer is obviously a step-by-step line of attack, but whether or not one specific individual organization in a specific situation is in a position to start such a movement is an open question and one that should be considered in each separate case. Thus, in cases of establishment in foreign countries, the recommendation is not to automatically transfer existing policies to this country, but rather make a specific judgment in each case, preferably in collaboration with interest organizations knowledgable about the country and its conditions.

SAMPLE HUMAN RESOURCE MANAGEMENT POLICY

Many of the industrial examples published in business ethics literature are from American organizations or from a small number of companies of European origin often described in such publications. When looking for a sample of this kind of policy, I have therefore deliberately looked outside the United States and beyond this small sample of non-U.S. companies and finally ended up with a set of policies from the Norwegian energy company, Statoil, where the policies have been collated under the heading "Putting People First" (see following pages). It is rather extensive and part of an even more extensive booklet titled "The Future Is Now: Statoil and Sustainable Development."

PUTTING
PEOPLE FIRST

Contributing to sustainable development is also about respecting people. We believe that corporate citizenship begins with the way we treat our own employees: how we protect their health and safety, how we reward their performance, how we seek their counsel, how we develop their potential and how we promote diversity and inclusiveness. If we cannot manage our human capital properly, we are shirking our responsibility to the individual employee, to shareholders and to society at large.

Safety and occupational health

TOTAL RECORDABLE
INJURY FREQUENCY

	1997	1998	1999	2000	2001
	12.2	8.5	10.3	10.1	6.7

Definition: The number of fatalities, lost-time injuries, cases of alternative work necessitated by an injury and other recordable injuries per million working hours

Absolute safety in oil and gas operations is essential on both humanitarian and commercial grounds. We believe that high HSE standards have a value in themselves. They are also a prerequisite for strong financial results and a good reputation. Managing HSE is about dedication, leadership and culture.

CHALLENGES

We take pride in the progress we have made over three decades in improving our safety performance. Still, we are in a business which is not without risks. People can get injured and lose their lives. Over the years, some have – much to our regret.

Concern about the risk of major accidents has focused public attention on safety conditions on NCS installations. The Norwegian Petroleum Directorate has sounded a warning against complacency and slipping performance. We have pledged to make a strong health and safety culture even stronger.

SERIOUS INCIDENT
FREQUENCY

	1997	1998	1999	2000	2001
	6.7	3.5	4.0	4.3	4.1

Definition: The number of undesirable events with a high loss potential per million working hours

Under no circumstances will we compromise our HSE standards to achieve cost reductions. As we see it, there is no acceptable trade-off between the two.

PIONEERING WORK ON SAFETY

The most extensive safety inspection in Statoil's history has just been completed. It was carried out over an 18-month period at our premier land-based and offshore installations by in-house personnel in cooperation with Det Norske Veritas (DNV). The aim was to raise the general level of safety in the company, thereby further reducing the potential for major incidents.

According to the final report, about 85 per cent of our safety systems passed the inspection without any remarks. Some deficiencies were identified, but none of the findings were so critical that they required immediate improvement or stoppage.

Says Magne Ognedal, director for supervisory activities at the Norwegian Petroleum Directorate (NPD):

"The NPD will follow up this pioneering work and apply the knowledge and insights gained to the rest of the oil industry."

Supplier or contractor involvement in oil and gas operations is continuing to grow. Strengthening collaboration between operator and contractor is a key element in achieving further improvements in our company's safety performance.

Safety incidents often involve human error. This is why awareness and training are so important. In order to improve our safety results, moreover, we seek to arrive at a better understanding of the interaction between people, facilities and management systems.

POLICIES

Zero harm to people, and zero accidents or losses. This is our ultimate goal. Striving to get to zero is what our efforts in safety and occupational health are all about. It forms part of our zero mindset for HSE, and underpins a continuous improvement process of measuring and reporting results.

The zero mindset states that no harmful incidents are acceptable. It serves as a warning against complacency. It makes us work hard – continuously – to bring the number of accidents and injuries ever closer to zero, both within Statoil and among our contractors. Because of the zero mindset, we stretch ourselves a little further.

PERFORMANCE

After several years of stagnation, we now see an improvement in our safety results. The number of recordable injuries decreased in 2001, along with the number of serious incidents.

Sickness absence in Statoil is low and declined further in 2001. In Norway, where two-thirds of our employees live, our sickness absence rate compares favourably with the national average, as recorded by the Confederation of Norwegian Business and Industry (NHO).

Some of our installations recorded a particularly notable safety performance in 2001:

- Statfjord A – our oldest production platform on the NCS – managed to reach zero by operating for a whole year with no recordable injuries.
- The Tjeldbergodden methanol plant in mid-Norway and its main contractor, Reinertsen Orkanger, won the chief executive's HSE prize for 2001 after operating for nearly two years without any lost-time injuries.

At the same time, however, we suffered two fatal accidents last year. The two people who tragically lost their lives were both working for Statoil contractors.

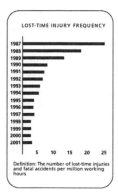

LOST-TIME INJURY FREQUENCY

Definition: The number of lost-time injuries and fatal accidents per million working hours

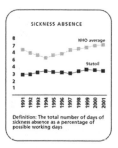

SICKNESS ABSENCE

Definition: The total number of days of sickness absence as a percentage of possible working days

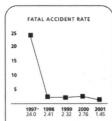

FATAL ACCIDENT RATE

	1997*	1998	1999	2000	2001
	24.0	2.41	2.32	2.76	1.45

Definition: The number of fatalities per 100 million hours worked
* Twelve people were killed in a helicopter crash

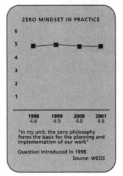

ZERO MINDSET IN PRACTICE

	1998	1999	2000	2001
	4.8	4.9	4.8	4.8

"In my unit, the zero philosophy forms the basis for the planning and implementation of our work".

Question introduced in 1998.

Source: WEOS

We annually spend in excess of NOK 200 million, or more than NOK 12 000 per employee, on HSE training with the aim of building awareness and expertise. Training is a question both of mindset and skill-set.

An important new measure for improving safety is the "open safety dialogue" conducted between an employee and their supervisor at the work site. The purpose of this discussion is to obtain an honest assessment of any potential hazards in connection with the job. The open safety dialogue approach has been developed and is being used by our Exploration & Production Norway business area.

TARGETS
- Zero harm to people, zero accidents or losses.
- We seek to improve on our performance continuously. Our goal is that safety will be better this year, even better next year, and so forth for every subsequent year.

SUPPORTING FORMER DIVERS

We decided in 2001 to provide financial support to former divers whose health had been damaged as a result of their work in the pioneering years on the NCS. Many of them have since lived in difficult circumstances, both financially and socially.

Although these divers were generally not directly employed by us, we decided to assume partial responsibility for their plight.

Divers were given the opportunity to apply for financial support to a specially appointed Statoil board. Seventy-six applicants, including five widows, have received full support, amounting to NOK 750 000 each. Eighteen applications were turned down.

Labour standards

A commitment to core labour standards promotes dialogue and cooperation between employees and employers. This helps to create a stable business environment and to secure a company's licence to operate.

CHALLENGES
We need to make sure that our commitment to high labour and social standards is not diluted as we expand our operations abroad and move into some countries where labour rights are violated and social standards are low.

In order to secure our licence to operate, we should be prepared to counter the erroneous impression created by some anti-globalisation activists that we – by expanding our operations in the developing world – are participating in a race to the bottom over labour and social standards.

POLICIES

Statoil is committed to a set of core labour standards which we believe should be universally applied, regardless of a country's level of development: freedom of association and collective bargaining, freedom from forced labour, elimination of child labour and freedom from discrimination in employment.

These standards are what the International Labour Organisation (ILO) calls "fundamental human rights of workers". They are included in the Global Compact, launched on the initiative of UN secretary-general Kofi Annan to forge a partnership for development with international business. Statoil has endorsed the Global Compact.

Our policy on human resource management states that our reward systems should be fair. Issues of pay and remuneration are determined in accordance with local conditions. There are no globally agreed standards. How could it be otherwise? The concept of a liveable, fair or competitive wage is a relative one. It only makes sense in the context of national or local labour markets, social legislation and costs of living.

PERFORMANCE

Freedom of association is not guaranteed in all the countries where Statoil is present. Neither is the right to collective bargaining. We have nevertheless seen to it that all our employees have a voice in the workplace, whether through councils, committees or general assemblies. We believe this helps instil a sense of trust and belonging.

In Norway, 75 per cent of our employees are unionised. Five different trade unions are involved in annual pay negotiations. Three directors are union officials elected by and among our workforce. The voice of employees is also heard through a system of works

WE HAVE SEEN TO IT THAT ALL OUR EMPLOYEES HAVE A VOICE IN THE WORKPLACE

Chief executive Olav Fjell meets the workforce on the Statfjord B platform in the North Sea.

THE STATOIL WAY – IN CHINA

To strengthen the voice of our employees and contracted personnel in the operation of the Lufeng field off China, we adopted best practice from Norway:

A working environment council has been estab-lished, and performance evaluation and planning (PEP) discussions are held with all staff.

We also participate in a dialogue on employment issues with other international oil companies operating in China's Pearl River Delta.

SUSTAINABLE DEVELOPMENT IS
ABOUT BEHAVING PROPERLY
TOWARDS YOUR FELLOW
HUMAN BEINGS AS WELL AS
THE ENVIRONMENT.

Rúni M Hansen (Faroe Islands)

councils *(bedriftsutvalg)* and working environment councils *(arbeidsmiljøutvalg)*. The unions and these councils are consulted on issues which affect the working conditions of employees. Grievances and complaints can be brought up in these staff forums.

We have a similar European works council, with members not only from the European Union countries in which we have operations but also from the EU candidate countries Poland, Lithuania, Latvia and Estonia. We established our first transnational staff forum in the petrochemicals sector in the early 1980s.

In addition, a performance evaluation and planning (PEP) discussion is held annually between each employee and their immediate superior. These discussions take place throughout Statoil, primarily for personal development and career planning.

The capital-intensive oil industry generally pays well all over the world. That also applies to Statoil. Our levels of pay are about average for the industry, and never below the national statutory minimum of a country.

Results from the working environment and organisation survey show that Statoil is considered a good company to work for. We also believe that low personnel turnover in the parent company – 3.84 per cent in 2001 – is an expression of job satisfaction among our employees.

JOB SATISFACTION				
1997	1998	1999	2000	2001
5.2	5.2	4.9	4.8	5.1

"I cite Statoil to my friends as a good company to work for"

Source: WEOS

THE AGREEMENT WITH ICEM

Statoil also encourages feedback from external stakeholders on issues of labour relations and standards. We accordingly have an information-sharing agreement with the International Federation of Chemical, Energy, Mines and General Workers Unions (ICEM), an international trade union secretariat with 20 million members in 110 countries.

The agreement with ICEM was first signed in 1998 and renewed in 2001, when it was adapted to the principles of the Global Compact. It aims to create an open channel of communication between ICEM and Statoil management on industrial relations issues, so that we can continuously develop good working practices in our worldwide operations.

ICEM head Fred Higgs says preventing human rights violations is a primary concern.

TARGETS
- We will continue to use the annual working environment and organisation survey to assess our performance in complying with corporate human resources policy in this area.
- A commitment to core labour standards, and the challenges we face in that respect, will be covered in assurance letters.

Knowledge and skills

Our ambition is to recruit, retain and motivate the most talented and dedicated workforce possible. The extent to which we succeed will in large measure also determine the success of the company.

CHALLENGES

Today, we produce seven per cent of our oil and gas outside Norway. Plans call for this proportion to reach 40 per cent by 2012. We are set for a major and rapid expansion of our international upstream operations.

This means that we will have to replenish our human capital base. We need to develop the expertise and skills of the people we already have, and we need to recruit new talent. We need more personnel who combine a global outlook with a deep knowledge of local conditions.

POLICIES

We are committed to giving all employees the opportunity to develop their expertise and skills in accordance with our business needs and their potential.

We offer a whole range of internal and external training courses and programmes covering important aspects of our business. However, the focus in our day-to-day operations is not so much on formal training as on work tasks. We develop most of our expertise through challenging assignments.

PERFORMANCE

Through extensive research and development in close cooperation with partners and contractors over 30 years, Statoil has provided competitive solutions to some of the greatest technological challenges on the NCS. Crossing the deepwater Norwegian Trench with the Statpipe gas trunkline is only one case in point.

Cooperation agreements with universities on research and training have been an important element in our skills development strategy for many years. As we see it, well-defined projects in which joint teams work on specific challenges are the key to mutually beneficial learning. These agreements have also given Statoil an edge in attracting talented students to the company.

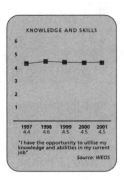

KNOWLEDGE AND SKILLS

6				
5				
4				
3				
2				
1				

1997	1998	1999	2000	2001
4.4	4.6	4.5	4.5	4.5

"I have the opportunity to utilise my knowledge and abilities in my current job"

Source: WEOS

SUPPORTING UNIVERSITIES IN NORWAY

Statoil provides seven Norwegian higher education institutions with a total of NOK 35 million annually for research and development projects which benefit both recipients and company. A substantial share of these funds is earmarked for modernising teaching methods and tools.

The seven institutions are the Norwegian University of Science and Technology (NTNU) in Trondheim, the Universities of Bergen, Oslo and Tromsø, the Norwegian School of Economics and Business Administration (NHH) in Bergen, the Norwegian School of Management (BI) in Oslo and Stavanger University College.

Statoil devotes NOK 800 million per year to measures for enhancing expertise. That figure has remained about the same for several years. However, we believe we are getting more value for money – or more training per krone – these days, partly because of the efficiency gains associated with web-based or e-learning.

TARGETS

- Review which expertise we need to retain and develop in-house and which can be sourced externally.
- Encourage our employees to take responsibility for their own life-long learning in order to ensure employment as well as employability.

IT STEPS 1 AND 2.

The first IT step was taken in 1997. We were the first company in Norway to offer all employees a home PC and an internet connection provided they undertook to complete an IT training programme in their spare time. Roughly 14 500 employees in 28 countries accepted the offer. IT step 1 improved the computing skills of our employees.

IT step 2 is being taken in 2002. This programme represents an upgrade, and will include new PCs with sufficient capacity to facilitate e-learning and flexible modes of working. Employees must again undertake to complete a training programme. However, the focus this time is not exclusively on IT. One training module will aim to increase awareness among our employees about HSE, CSR and business ethics.

Staff engineer Helge Joa and his family chose to sign up for the IT step.

Diversity

"A diverse organisation will out-think and out-perform a homogeneous organisation every single time,"says Alan Lafley, chief executive of Procter & Gamble. Statoil concurs.

CHALLENGES

The typical Statoil employee is a 43-year old male engineer from Norway. Promoting diversity means increasing the spread of our workforce in terms of age, gender, education, nationality, ethnicity, religion and culture.

Globalisation has helped us to gain access to new opportunities. To capitalise on these opportunities, we need to draw from a more diverse pool of talent when recruiting to the company.

The typical Statoil employee?
Steinar Strøm, a 43-year-old male
engineer from Norway.

POLICIES

We want diversity in age, gender and cultural background. We recognise the opportunities for innovation, creativity and insight which lie in bringing together people with different backgrounds in our company. We believe greater diversity will help us thrive in a business environment which is increasingly complex and global.

PERFORMANCE

We have strengthened our position as a preferred employer among students of business and engineering at Norwegian universities. A positive interest in Statoil was also evident when our trainee programme was launched last year.

We have adopted measures to recruit, retain and promote women. We offer solutions which balance work and life, such as opportunities for flexible and part-time working, liberal maternity and paternity leave, and day-care facilities.

Where gender equality is concerned, we set a target of 20 per cent women in managerial positions at all levels of the company by 2000. We are content that systematic efforts have given concrete results – especially among our younger employees. As illustrated by the table opposite, however, our target has not yet been reached. We currently stand at 15 per cent overall.

WOMEN IN STATOIL IN 2001

Women in the total workforce	27%
Women in managerial positions	15%
Women in managerial positions (below the age of 45)	27%
Women in managerial positions (above the age of 45)	7.5%
Women among recruited apprentices in 2001	35%

Why have we not reached 20 per cent? Figures from the working environment and organisation survey appear to indicate a lack of commitment to this target. For that reason, the different business units have been challenged to strengthen their efforts to promote women.

TARGETS

• Increase the proportion of women in managerial and senior specialist positions to 20 per cent.
• Increase the proportion of local staff in managerial positions in our international operations.
• Ensure that our workforce reflects the increased ethnic and cultural diversity of Norwegian society.

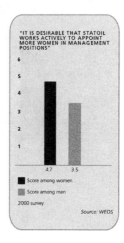

"IT IS DESIRABLE THAT STATOIL WORKS ACTIVELY TO APPOINT MORE WOMEN IN MANAGEMENT POSITIONS"

4.7   3.5

■ Score among women
  Score among men

2000 survey

Source: WEOS

CREATING AN ETHICALLY ORIENTED ORGANIZATIONAL VALUE BASE AND CULTURE

The second element that will be treated in this chapter is closely related to the issue of human resource management policies. As has already been mentioned, one big problem with policies, regardless of which area they pertain to, is the propensity for policies to remain just policies and never make it into practice. This problem will be attacked in the operational chapters later on, in the discussion of how policies must be followed through by designing and implementing processes and practices that bring the policies to life. However, even with the existence of processes and practices, an organization is fully capable of ignoring these and doing as it likes. As any change management expert will tell you, one key to achieving and sustaining change is ensuring that the new policies and practices become deeply rooted in the organizational culture and match the values of the organization and its culture.

While this might sound like a highly operational issue, a suitable organizational value base and organizational culture are parts of a strategic platform paramount in the implementation of and widespread adherence to any new policy. Thus, at an early stage in the transformation of the organization to an ethical business approach, building such a platform is important for two purposes:

• First, it serves as a basis on which the organization and its members at all levels can truly develop into practicing the spirit of the ethically oriented human resource management policy. In line with previous argumentation, keeping this hand clean, in terms of treating all employees with respect and fairness, is vital in the attempt to get employees to do the same when facing the external stakeholders of the organization. Employees who exist inside an organizational culture not centered on ethical values for internal conduct will never be able to credibly represent the organization externally in an ethical approach.

• Secondly, as will become evident throughout the next chapters, achieving a consistent ethical profile in the marketplace involves the formulation and implementation of numerous policies and practices, not only those related to employee treatment standards. Continuous and long-term adherence to all of these is not the result of coercion and using the whip on people, but must come from a shared sense of values that make such behavior an intrinsic part of the organization and its members.

Reaching this state depends on deliberate efforts to "design" the type of organizational values and culture that are desired, "implement" them through training and communication, and "maintain" them through constant reminders, rewarding suitable behavior, and altering behavior not in line with this culture. Some "tools" that have proven useful in this rather difficult and less tangible task are:

• The development of specific ethical guidelines for the organization and its processes. Being a truly operational element, ethical guidelines are treated in the next chapter.

• Training in business ethics, ethical guidelines, and ethical decision making. To the extent that traditional training will be dealt with in this book, you will find this material in the implementation chapter, chapter 2.

• "Experience-based" training, which sets itself apart from traditional training in that traditional training mainly aims at transferring explicit knowledge and practices while this type of "training" centers on having employees indirectly assimilate tacit understanding and skills.

• Value system and culture building through storytelling, which has emerged as a powerful approach to strategy implementation and the development of a shared culture within an organization.

This chapter will conclude by presenting some thoughts on the latter two, as they are particularly suited contributors in the aspirations toward an ethically founded organizational culture.

INSTILLING ETHICALLY SOUND TACIT KNOWLEDGE IN THE ORGANIZATION

By introducing the concept of tacit knowledge, the very foundation of human learning is brought onto the scene. There are a multitude of definitions and explanations of what human learning is, but most of them seem to share a view that learning represents some kind of a change process in the person that is based on experience and/or practical exercises. For example, this one by Reilly and Lewis (1983): "A retainable change in behavior resulting from practice or experience."

With these definitions in mind, it is surprising to what extent education and training, whether in schools or in organizations, take the form of theoretical passing of knowledge from the teacher to the recipients. However, effective learning of skills requires both theoretical training, which forms the underlying knowledge, and practical training, which builds and hones the applied skills. This is illustrated in Figure 3.2, where the two axes represent the polar situations of training in school or in real life situations, and whether the skills being trained are mainly theoretical or practical.

Together, these four training or learning modes develop both theoretical insight and practical skills, which are both required to become skillful practitioners within a field, including ethical business. In more scholarly terms, there are also denoted explicit and tacit knowledge, as originally coined by Nonaka and Takeuchi (1995), as depicted in Figure 3.3. The crucial difference between the two is that actions based on explicit knowledge come from rational thinking and deliberation while actions based on tacit knowledge stem from instinctive reactions. Granted, working in an organization, no matter which position a person holds, requires both types of actions, but the small tasks and deeds done every day, which ultimately aggregate into the nature of the organization's image and behavior, are very often based on tacit knowledge. These are the way you greet your coworkers, smile to your customers, deal honestly with suppliers, and so on, actions you do not think through before executing them, but rather do out of old habit and who you are and what values you hold. To ensure that an organization consistently performs all of these small tasks in a sustainable manner, ethical values must be rooted so deeply in people that they not only

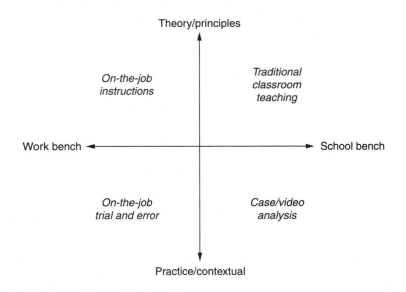

Figure 3.2   Four training modes.

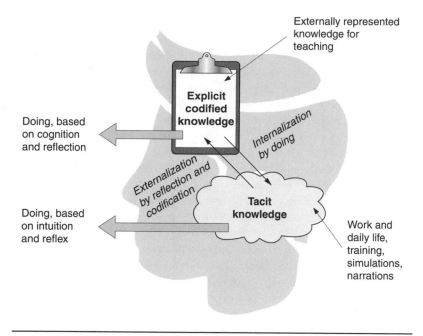

Externally represented
knowledge for
teaching

Explicit
codified
knowledge

Doing, based
on cognition
and reflection

Internalization
by doing

Externalization
by reflection and
codification

Tacit
knowledge

Doing, based
on intuition
and reflex

Work and
daily life,
training,
simulations,
narrations

Figure 3.3   Skillful execution of complex tasks requires both explicit and tacit knowledge.

represent ethical guidelines to be remembered in specific situations, but also tacit values that form the basis for all conduct. To achieve this, an alternative or additional approach to training is required, which moves to the left-hand side of Figure 3.2.

The problem is, the type of learning approach this requires is not readily available for training in an ethical value set and organizational culture. For a few types of skills, it does exist and has proven its merit. Aircraft pilot training is one good example, where the set of skills required is complex and not easily documented in a textbook, especially the kind of maneuvering that is required of a pilot in an emergency situation where things happen extremely rapidly and the consequences of error are fatal. As such situations obviously are impossible to train in real-life situations, flight simulators have been developed that expose future pilots to a large number of critical situations and allow them to train on handling them. The purpose is partly to ensure that the pilots know how to handle a number of the most likely emergencies they might experience and partly to hone their reflexes and instincts. In the latter case, the objective is to provide the pilots with a repertoire for improvisation, an experience base of situations, possible responses, their outcomes, and so on, developed through hours of training in the flight simulator. The result is an accelerated learning that allows a freshly graduated pilot to already have experienced many times over the number of critical situations she or he would during an entire career in real life.

Aircraft pilot is only one occupation, albeit perhaps an extreme example, with skills that are extremely difficult, if not impossible, to train through traditional classroom teaching. Other examples include other advanced occupations like surgeons and musicians, but also workers that we tend not to think of as highly advanced, for example, farmers or car mechanics, all of whom exploit their tacit knowledge to perform their jobs. Another example are project managers; some say that you can never become a truly excellent project manager until you've reached 50, because the job involves so many facets and so many different situations that you will not have time to develop the required experience base in shorter time. The skills required for functioning socially in an organization and performing explicit and implicit tasks are also sufficiently complex that some kind of accelerated learning of an extensive experience base is necessary to ensure that people act in accordance with organizational policies and values. The major question is, how can this be done?

Unfortunately, there is no clear answer to this question yet, and you cannot buy a solution off the shelf. However, scholars in the field of learning and knowledge management are beginning to see how this can be done, drawing on inspiration partly from the flight simulators for pilot training, partly from computer games, and partly by utilizing what is today common digital video technology. Regarding inspiration from video games, this is perhaps not so surprising. Speaking for myself, I remember some ten years ago when somebody gave me the game Civilization, a strategy game where the objective is to start from the stone age and develop science, inventions, arms, and skills to refine your civilization throughout the centuries. Even by today's standards, Civilization was a very complex game involving hundreds of different types of characters, entities, and rules, rules that were incorporated into the game's logic but not explicitly written anywhere. And the point is really that the game is quite similar to the real world in the way rules and the behavior of others are unpredictable, yet typically follow patterns that can be hard to put into words yet somehow understood. After having spent days, even weeks, one summer playing the game, I gradually understood, not explicitly, but by instinct, how the game worked and what actions on my part gave good results. Even though the game logic obviously represented a vast simplification of how the human civilization has evolved, it certainly captured many of the main points that history has taught us. Thus, by playing this game, I would say I learned quite a lot about evolutionary history and its success factors and pitfalls.

The parallel to modern organizations and business is that they are also governed by similar tacit rules and logic. If one is able to capture these in some way and incorporate them into a computer game/business simulator, this could contribute to accelerated learning of these tacit principles, which in turn form the basis for our behavior in business life. The only problem is that developing such advanced computer games as Civilization represents is an extremely difficult and expensive task. Unfortunately, there never seems to be sufficient funding available for developing such strategy games, which could have a tremendous impact on business life, whereas the market for arcade-type computer games is always large enough that the industry can pour out an endless stream of them. Thus, awaiting simulation training games surpassing the currently available very simple solutions, an alternative approach based on the use of simple digital video equipment might be what you need.

Basically, the idea is as follows: People experience a large number of different situations, both positive and negative, during the course of performing their jobs. Most of these are trivial, but now and then some are deemed sufficiently interesting and general that others could benefit from knowing how these experiences were handled. These few important experiences can be recorded, in some cases live as they happen, in others after the fact, indexed by use of keywords, stored electronically, and thus made available to the rest of the organization to learn from. Albeit with clear limitations compared to the flight simulators discussed earlier, the principle is still to foster accelerated learning and the creation of a repertoire for improvisation by exposing people to a large number of various situations.

But why make it so complicated that you have to use a video camera to record these experiences and situations? Well, if you are familiar with the field of project management, you might know that it is common practice in projects to write so-called experience transfer reports at the end of a project, documenting positive and negative learnings gleaned during the project. It is an equally common view that these experience transfer reports have very little impact; they generally become shelf warmers and dust collectors as very few take the time to read them. Research into this problem has revealed several reasons why:

• Re-creating situations, situations that those who experienced them found extremely useful in teaching them some kind of lesson, is very hard and difficult to depict in writing in such a way that others gain the same learning effect.

• Written reports tend to become lengthy as the writers want to include sufficient number of details to convey what truly happened, thus requiring much time to produce and in the end not being reader-friendly.

• The written word, although very powerful in the hands of skilled authors, is a difficult medium for a layman in which to convey emotions, moods, and less tangible aspects of the learning experience, thus often rendering such reports rather dull reading.

Ultimately, such reports have little or no learning value. In sharp contrast to such written reports, simple recorded video clips documenting the experiences have proven quite powerful in capturing and transferring the learning value from experiences. The reasons are probably the same as why written reports are not effective, only inverted; moving images capture the objects recorded with all their details, gesticulations, body language, and emotions; they are much more entertaining to watch; and much more information can be conveyed in much less time. Thus, many organizations have come quite far in building up libraries of such pivotal situations that everybody should be able to learn from.

In making such recordings, there are basically two distinct approaches:

• Recording the actual situation live as it unfolds, which is the most powerful way of doing this. However, only a small number of organizations and tasks within them are suitable for such an approach. For example, a group of laparoscopic surgeons at our local hospital represent an ideal example. Laparoscopic surgery, which belongs to the broader group of so-called minimal invasive surgery, is performed by using a tiny camera and very small instruments that are inserted into the body through tiny incisions. The camera's original function is of course to relate the internal operation site to the surgeon via a video screen. However, the camera is thus already present and the work space is very limited, thus recording the entire scene is extremely simple. In this particular case, after an operation, the surgeon quickly scans the video recording, selects short clips that contain situations worth storing (typically difficult or unexpected situations that occurred), adds narrative about how the situation was handled, indexes the clips by using a predefined set of keywords, and stores them in a database.

• Recounting the situations after the fact, which obviously is second to recording them live, but still has proven quite effective. In this case, simple video recording booths are placed around the organization. Each time an employee experiences a situation that gives her or him important new insight of some sort, she or he goes to the video booth and describes the situation to the camera. In some cases, this can be done immediately after, in others the person will not find time to do it until some time after the incident occurred. This does not seem to matter too much, as instant recordings tend to be more energetic and enthusiastic than those made some time after, but they also tend to lack the clearer organization of an incident recounted later. Luckily, both qualities enhance the benefits for those watching the recordings later. The clips are also indexed with keywords and stored in a database under this approach.

As with written experience reports, these video clips obviously have no effect if not used. Organizations that have started using this approach have, however, come up with a number of ways in which they can be put to very powerful use:

• Organizational training where the "curriculum" consists partly of a fixed set of material and partly of what is available of relevant video clips. If there is software allowing it, some of this training can be converted into e-learning where the participants themselves add to the course curriculum by recording their own experiences throughout the course. Training based on such a combination of standard material and real-life learnings from various parts of the organization has turned out to be very effective in both transferring specific knowledge and skills and helping build a shared sense of values.

• Preparation for demanding tasks, especially critical tasks that are not performed very often. In such cases, those who must do the job can review the video clips pertaining to the task and refresh their understanding of what have been critical points in the past and how they have been handled successfully. This application is used actively by the laparoscopic surgeons.

• Learning on demand, which is similar to preparation for demanding tasks, except in this case, the system is designed to enable people to access requested video clips as a situation or task unfolds. This is practiced in many complex assembly operations, where operators can call up a one-minute video of the next step in the assembly, displaying traditional problems and solutions to them. With the continued development of video capabilities on mobile phones, this application is becoming even more attractive, allowing personnel located outside the organization's facilities to call up such clips. One planned application of this latter type is for maintenance crews of signal masts located on mountaintops. If they need instructions on how to replace a certain component, they can access a recorded replacement operation via mobile phone.

All of these applications require that the video clips are short in duration, succinct, and contain only one element per clip. They must also be indexed so that simple searches will locate those that are relevant in a given situation. However, an inexpensive digital video camera, some software for video editing, and a simple searchable database are sufficient to implement such a solution, without too much bureaucracy or extra work to maintain and use it. The result is an alternative training approach that has proven much more powerful than traditional classroom training in transferring knowledge throughout the organization. As an ethical business approach represents a significant change in values, culture, and practices for most organizations, a change that can sometimes be hard to accomplish fully, this approach to training seems particularly attractive in such cases.

Recording experiences this way and "passing them around" for learning is also closely related to the next approach, namely storytelling for organizational culture building.

USING STORYTELLING TO BUILD ORGANIZATIONAL VALUES AND CULTURE

Experiences of the sort that are suitable for creating a repertoire for improvisation must by nature be described in sufficient detail and specificity to be able to learn from and emulate at a later date. For building deeper organizational values, such a level of detail is not required—rather it is the myths of the organization that need to be kept alive for this purpose. Just like a country has its set of myths, part true highlights from past history, part generalizations and idealizations of former times, that shape the country and its people, organizations do as well. However, where the myths of a country are passed on a little more systematically, through history books, teaching in schools, depictions in movies or TV shows, and so on, it is often left to accident to keep organizational myths alive. Instead, the management of many organizations spend their time and dollars on extensive training courses, launches of new strategic campaigns to glue the organization together, or the development of fancy logos. This is a shame, since myths can be a truly powerful way of building a shared sense of history, character, and direction, especially in cases where a change of strategy requires a revised or whole new set of basic values to direct the organization's behavior.

So how do you apply myths and storytelling in creating an organizational culture that embodies an ethical approach to business? Myths become truly powerful when they are simplified into a key observation, preferably containing some type of paradox, and formulated so as to stimulate the recipient to draw conclusions on her or his own. Metaphors are a classic way of "designing" myths to make people hearing them think for themselves and apply them to the specific situation. For example, whenever the discussion comes up whether to maintain a single-sourcing agreement for a set of key components used in the manufacturing of a product or start buying on the spot market, the purchasing manager of the organization uses the punch line: "If I'm having heart surgery, I'm not shopping around for the cheapest offer!"

A major advantage of myths or statements like this is that they can condense a myriad of often conflicting and confusing experiences into short stories, experiences that in their original form can be hard to glean anything from but which in this mode still communicate an important message. The concept of such learning stories was originally developed at MIT by Kleiner and Roth (1999). While storytelling has been extended in its use, the original application was for creating change by showing where the organization had gone wrong previously and illustrating what approach could work better.

Some prerequisites for using myths and storytelling this way are (Hatling, 2001):

• A paramount requirement for myths to generate the desired effect is a sufficient level of trust in the organization to allow the publication and spreading of embarrassing or deviating incidents.

• If the myths and stories are to capture people and create valuable thought processes on their part, they should normally contain contrasts and deviations from what is normal, in order to induce reflection and interpretation.

• The language of the myths and stories, either created or emerging ones, cannot be kept in the same tone that is normally used in strategic plans, that is, neutral, rational, and analytical. Such language covers up deeper meaning and is rarely suitable for motivating people. How many of the stories you were read as a child were written in such a way?

• Stories and myths are usually much more emotional and very often quite personal, thus the arsenal of myths that should constitute the value basis of the organization must be formulated accordingly to impact behavior.

• There is a lot to learn from classic storytelling, for example, fairy tales, sagas, or movies. The good myths of an organization have titillating titles and an inspiring introduction. They use metaphors: instead of explaining their message in detail, they rather hint at it. They try to appeal to many senses at the same time, are usually quite subjective, and focus on specific details.

Some trademarks of such organizational stories that do attain their goals of motivation, value-creation, and behavior stimulation are (Hatling, 2001):

• *A captivating basic idea*, such as the core idea of The Body Shop, which is to use sales of cosmetics and related products as a means for aiding the environment, developing countries, and animals. This is certainly a basic idea that can get many people on board who would normally not even consider working in a cosmetics firm.

A medium-sized Australian enterprise used to manufacture explosives for professional use at construction sites, typically road construction, tunnels, or large structures. During recent years, they had experienced some trying times when their customers had accidents in which explosives personnel, other construction workers, and even civilians, were injured or killed. In all such incidents, official investigations declared the explosives themselves safe and in working order, the cause of the accidents being human error in the use of them. The enterprise still saw these accidents as traumatic for the organization, both in terms of the suffering it knew its products had caused and the public mention of its name in conjunction with such incidents. Thus, it decided to radically change its operational logic, from selling explosives to selling explosive services, where highly skilled explosives consultants from the company would provide the desired end result.

This move would of course depend on the company's ability to maintain superior safety levels compared to those of their customers. Though already a safety-conscious enterprise, an even more solid platform would have to be developed. In pondering how to go about this, senior management saw similarities between the current strategic change and one that occurred more than forty years previous. Back then, the company stopped selling a line of minor explosives to farmers and other private customers for exactly the same reason, namely numerous accidents. The new line had targeted professional explosives personnel and reduced the accident count significantly, except for this latest surge. With help from the PR department, a set of short stories from the time of the previous big change, focusing on the safety concern, was developed and actively distributed throughout the organization. People who had worked there for a long time recognized these stories, and junior employees appreciated learning about the company's long tradition of concern for safety.

Using these "myths" in the development of the new business processes for explosive services and the organizational safety culture required for them, the company was ready to launch its new services after a six-month preparation period. During the approximately three years that have since passed, the company has seen no accidents whatsoever and has added 30 percent to its revenues.

• *An exciting cast,* where people in the stories come to life through their portrayal and are able to inspire the way movie heroes or heroines do. The Finnish design company Marimekko is an example of a company with colorful leaders taking on different roles and making good stories.

• *Based on events that in the end result in stories,* that is, recounting events or incidents that in some way represent crucial moments in the organization's history. Good examples of such stories use seemingly insignificant events that later on prove to be vital turning points to make people think and realize how important even the smaller tasks can be.

• *Presence at important stages,* that is, the stories must appear consistently inside the organization, in meetings with external stakeholders, perhaps even in media or advertising, to keep driving the points home.

• *Activating of knowledge,* from existing areas or business drivers into new areas. Many of the most successful companies have managed to leave behind declining or dying business segments and convert their knowledge to move into new ones, and such dynamics and change make fascinating stories.

Well, this is just the start of our journey through the business ethics framework, starting with a technique that may seem rather far-fetched and not closely related to the core of an ethical approach to business. If you think this is the case, do try to keep in mind the rationale behind this first step: you cannot keep one hand clean if the other is constantly poking around in the mud. Building a credible external image as an ethically oriented organization just won't fly if the effort is based on a dodgy organizational culture not holding ethical values. And although strategy and policy can be worth less than the paper they are written on and no guarantee for sound operational practices, the latter are more likely to emerge if there is a solid basis of direction, values, and organizational culture.

IMPLEMENTATION SUMMARY

In summary, the main elements to bring forward from the strategic, internal, and remedial part of the business ethics framework and into an implementation phase are:

• Developing ethically founded human resource policies for the different subareas listed in Table 3.1. This is typically a task undertaken by parts of or all of the executive team of the organization, very often headed by the human resource manager or person holding a similar responsibility.

• Developing an ethically oriented organizational value base and culture. This is by no means an easy task to take on, but can be made easier by ensuring that the tacit knowledge of the organization reflects ethical values. One way of achieving this is by using storytelling to shape the collective value base and understanding of the organization's history.

It is difficult to provide any specific advice on how to perform these tasks successfully. Policy development is typically a semi-structured, creative process that should take into account the organization's traditions, future needs, competing organizations' policies, and so on. Equally, developing, or rather changing, an organization's culture and value system is a complex undertaking for which there are no straightforward recipes. Storytelling is one somewhat more tangible approach to accomplishing this, but there are many others that can facilitate such a change.

Thus, hoping our efforts in developing sound ethically based policies and a set of organizational values have succeeded, the next area of the framework is operationalizing these into practice.

4

Turning Policy into Ethically Founded Remedial, Internal, and Operational Practices

Turning policy into practice is an age-old challenge most organizations struggle with in one way or another. This not being a book about strategic planning and subsequent strategy implementation, the concepts of experience-based learning and storytelling are included simply as two possible ways to aid this process. For any further treatment of this particular topic, you should consult other, more specialized sources on the subject. The focus of this chapter is rather a more specific outline of concrete practices the high-level policies presented in the previous chapter could encompass.

This outline, as indeed much of this book, should be viewed as kind of a menu. Start by selecting the items you find most attractive in terms of their match with your taste and "price." As you sample items, you can gradually expand your selection. As is the case in even the best restaurants, a seven-course meal is probably as much as you can manage; going for the entire menu on the first visit will surely be too much. Even if the outline of operational practices seems full of good ideas, trying to accommodate them all at once, especially if they represent quite a change from earlier practices, is probably infeasible and you will risk ending up getting nothing truly implemented.

THE MENU OF REMEDIAL, INTERNAL, AND OPERATIONAL PRACTICES

Like any decent menu, the menu of elements you can implement to develop a credible internal set of practices spans various sections. The main headlines are:

- Ethical guidelines for the organization and a sound ethical decision-making system

- Human resource management practices, building on the policies outlined in the previous chapter

- Cost consciousness and striking a balance between stinginess and extravagance

Developing a set of ethical guidelines can be seen as a start toward forming a platform for the practices you want to achieve. In terms of internal practices, human resource management is by far the dominant one and constitutes the main course. Cost consciousness, just like a sweet after the main course, can be something of a double-edged sword, but deserves attention. Let's look at these one by one.

THE BORING PART: ETHICAL GUIDELINES

This heading reflects the quandary as to whether a set of guidelines for ethical behavior and decision making is a useful tool, a necessary evil, or even an unnecessary evil. The decision probably depends on how such ethical guidelines, or codes of ethics as they are often termed, are designed. If they take the shape of obvious pleasantries encouraging "being nice, treating people the way you want them to treat you, and being ethical in all your conduct," they are a waste of time and might even be counterproductive by demonstrating to the organization and its external stakeholders that the organization is unable to convert an ethical approach into something tangible.

According to Solomon (1999), the practice of formulating organizational values in the form of a code or guidelines started only after the Watergate scandals of the early 1970s. Sometimes these represent nothing but an attempt to persuade employees to comply with a set of values that are far removed from their everyday work, sometimes even nothing more than a hypocritical attempt at public relations. However, if an ethical code of conduct is more specific in outlining which types of behavior the organization encourages within different areas, it is potentially useful. An organization consists of people from many different walks of life, perhaps various nationalities and religious origins, thus creating a multitude of different views of what is right or wrong in any given situation. It can also provide legitimacy for decisions and viewpoints taken by employees, for example someone working with procurement who declines a sponsored trip to a supplier's manufacturing site with reference to §4.2 in the code of conduct. To the extent that the code of conduct manages to clarify in broader terms what is acceptable and indeed desirable behavior and instill a more uniform understanding in the organization of these issues, it represents a necessary "evil." "Evil" in the sense that developing such a code of conduct takes time, can be difficult, and certainly requires some effort to make it known to the organization and eventually have an impact on people's behavior.

The truly useful approach to ethical guidelines is to make them even more specific. No doubt this can also require a considerable effort, but guidelines work best when they describe specific situations displaying an ethical dilemma and how these should be handled. To avoid having the entire organization spending massive amounts of time on identifying and describing such situations, it seems most suitable to start with typical high-risk situations. These will usually be readily identifiable and can form the basis of the guidelines. Expansion of the set can be done as new situations arise that seem to warrant inclusion in the code, either through being potentially serious enough to inflict damage or through occurring sufficiently often that large parts of the organization risk finding themselves in the situation. Such an approach ties in nicely with the approach of experience-based learning described in the previous chapter.

Combining these two, that is, an ethical code of conduct with a video-based experience database, the code of conduct need not even be a piece of text. Keeping in mind the argumentation as to why written experience-based reports rarely work as intended, the same applies directly to virtually any type of guidelines. Guidelines are nothing more than a structured manifestation of experiences made over time, and in the same way project experience reports or quality system manuals tend not to be read or actively used, the same probably applies to ethical guidelines sitting on the bookshelf in a binder. If instead the guidelines take the form of searchable video recordings of people in the organization telling about their experiences in ethically murky waters, how they handled the situation, and the results, they should prove more useful. For those missing the tangible binder, a transcript can even be made in this format as well. The key benefits from such an approach are:

- The "richer" presentation format makes the guidelines "livelier" and more likely to be understood, and with an improved ability to motivate.

- A dynamic selection of video clips of recorded ethical experiences is much easier to change, expand, and update. Experience tells that formal documents distributed in binders have a much higher threshold for updating and often remain static due to the time and cost involved in changing them.

To avoid having this type of guidelines become solely an indexed selection of video clips, a two-section approach can be taken. One section can contain generalized guidelines based on general issues of the organization and extracts from the library of experiences. This corresponds more or less to what would typically be included in a binder-type code of conduct, only these guidelines are also captured in the richness of video, graphics, cartoons. The other section will then be the dynamic library, which grows continuously as more and more experiences are added.

As for the design of the ethical guidelines and their focus and contents, there are many different approaches. Some major issues to consider are, for example:

• To what extent should the guidelines be derived merely from the senior management or board level of the organization versus through a process of broader participation from the entire organization? This is a question of both acceptance and organizational grounding and a question of time and resources. While a broader organizational effort in developing the code of conduct will generally ensure its wider acceptance, such a process can be both time-consuming and costly. A compromise solution consists of senior management being behind the development of a general set of guidelines while contributions from the organization are included in a specific experiences section as described above.

• What degree of specificity is needed, that is, very general value statements, hands-on guidelines for specific situations, or a combination of both? While it is generally agreed that "biblical" guidelines amounting to "be nice and do no harm" are of less use than specific directions for behavior in concrete situations, this also has implications for the extent of the guidelines. The longer and more extensive, the less likely that they will be thoroughly gone through and understood. However, by structuring the guidelines well and dividing them into subareas, even an extensive set can be easily navigable and thus be allowed a larger volume.

• Structure of the guidelines, keeping in mind their usage, as a lookup manual requires a different structure than a "read from start to finish" set of instructions. Connected to the previous point, the two main, extreme approaches in terms of structure are the type of code of conduct that requires a start-to-finish read-through to make sense and the handbook/dictionary type where people look up any specific item they may need help with. Again, compromise can be a reasonable approach, having a short introduction for complete familiarization, while the bulk of the code takes the shape of a lookup handbook.

• The type of language and "profile" used in the code of conduct, ranging from highly normative and strict to encouraging and supportive. This question depends heavily on having the tradition, culture, and tone of communication within the organization where some accept, even welcome, clear directions in the form of "do this, don't do this." However, in general, the time of the "commandment" style of organizational policies and guidelines is past. A tone of language and style where consequences of different types of behavior are explained, leading to recommendations, is probably more likely to elicit positive responses and compliance.

• Should the guidelines include sanctions for violating the code, or should such be included in individual job descriptions, or perhaps not mentioned at all? A predefinition of sanctions to be implemented in cases of noncompliance with the code of conduct is generally discouraged. To design a coherent set of sanctions that appear to be fair is a tricky task, the very existence of such suggests violations are expected, and the "police" mentality of such predefined sanctions tends to belittle people or instill negative responses. If sanctions are to be outlined in the ethical guidelines, at least limit them to a very small number of highly serious breaches that could jeopardize the entire organization and its reputation.

• The format of the code of conduct, that is, whether to publish it on paper, hang it on the wall, or keep in on the intranet, and whether to base it on written text, graphics, flowcharts, or possibly video. With the possibilities Web and video technology offer today for flexibility, richer presentation formats, and ease of distribution, the era of binder guidelines is past. This is of course also a matter of having the knowledge to do something beyond text-based guidelines and perhaps to some extent a matter of costs, at least initial investments, but thinking about a more innovative approach than the dreaded binder is recommended.

To illustrate better how such a set of guidelines can be designed, an example from the international restaurant operator Brinker appears in the example on the next page. It is a quite typical code of conduct, covering both general issues and some more specific aspects. It also informs the reader about the administration of the code.

BRINKER CODE OF CONDUCT AND ETHICAL BUSINESS POLICY

INTRODUCTION

The Brinker International Code of Conduct and Ethical Business Policy ("Ethics Policy") is established to ensure that all directors and employees at Brinker conduct the business of Brinker fairly, impartially, and in an ethical and proper manner. You may have additional requirements because you are responsible for significant decisions affecting the conduct of Brinker's business. This Code of Conduct represents the detailed standards and policies that must always be observed by you at Brinker. It is important that you know and understand these policies and standards, and acknowledge that you will comply with them.

It is the policy of Brinker International to conduct its business affairs fairly, impartially, and in an ethical and proper manner. Conduct that may raise questions as to the company's honesty, integrity, impartiality, or reputation, or activities that could cause embarrassment to the company or damage to its reputation, are prohibited. Any activity, conduct or transaction that could create an appearance of unethical, illegal, or improper business conduct must be avoided.

The highest possible standards of ethical and business conduct are required of Brinker employees and directors in the performance of their company responsibilities. It is the responsibility of every employee and director, and the policy of Brinker to encourage its employees and directors to ask questions, seek guidance, report suspected violations, or express their concerns regarding compliance with this standard of conduct.

To this end, when necessary, procedures and policies will be established to assist each person in resolving questions, providing guidance, and for reporting suspected violations of, or expressing concerns regarding compliance with, this Policy. Also, as necessary, a means of communication, other than through immediate supervisors, will be established for employees to express concerns regarding compliance with this Policy.

Any individual having information or knowledge of any prohibited act shall promptly report such matters to the general manager, department head, any officer in the human resources department, or the general counsel.

Source: http://www.brinker.com/corp_gov/ethical_business_policy.asp. Material that Brinker holds copyright for. Reproduced here with permission.

continued

A. CONFLICT OF INTEREST

You are obligated to act in the best interest of Brinker when you are in a position to be influenced by personal gain or benefit for yourself, a third party or both. It is very important to avoid any actual or apparent conflicts of interest. Any time a conflict occurs or you are concerned one will occur; you should immediately discuss the matter with your supervisor or the general counsel for guidance. The following paragraphs describe certain common conflicts and Brinker's policies.

Financial Interest. You should avoid financial conflicts of interest. The following two situations are common financial conflicts of interest, and must be avoided:

- Any ownership or interest (other than nominal amounts [1 percent or less] in publicly traded companies) by you or an immediate relative (that is, your spouse or close relative, member of your household, and those with whom you have a close personal relationship) in a vendor, supplier, competitor, or contractor. This information must be disclosed on a Brinker Ethical Business Policy and Code of Conduct Acknowledgment and Disclosure Statement ("Disclosure Statement"), which you may be periodically asked to complete.

- Borrowing or being financially indebted to a competitor or supplier of goods and services to Brinker, other than banks or other financial institutions for typical consumer debt generally available to non-Brinker employees. This relationship should also be disclosed on the Disclosure Statement.

Note: Brinker will not extend or maintain credit, arrange for the extension of credit, or renew an extension of credit, in the form of a personal loan to or for any director or executive officer.

Commercial Bribery. Giving or accepting gifts that equal more than the amount that would be considered customary courtesies may be deemed a bribe. Bribes are strictly prohibited by law and against Brinker policy. A bribe can expose a person to criminal penalties. Company payments (regardless of amount), or gifts or entertainment of any value to governmental officials and other governmental personnel of any local, state, or federal governmental agency or department are not permitted.

continued

If confronted with a demand for a payment, gift, entertainment, or the like, you must inform the general counsel.

Relationships with Vendors and Suppliers. Transactions with vendors and suppliers must be carried out on an arms-length basis. This means conditions should exist for competitive, willing buyer and willing seller transactions. Competitive bidding should be used whenever possible. Decisions should be made on the basis of quality, price, availability and service. All vendors and suppliers should be dealt with fairly, honestly and openly. This policy extends to all services provided to Brinker as well as goods used by Brinker. In addition, if the representative for the vendor or supplier is a former Brinker employee, family member, or close personal friend, you should disclose this information to your supervisor.

Gifts/Gratuities. It is generally prohibited to solicit or accept loans, gifts, gratuities, trips, or any other special treatment from a person or organization that does or desires to do business with Brinker.

You must not give or accept any "gift of value" which might indicate in any manner an intent to influence normal business relationships with vendors, suppliers, customers, or competitors. As a guideline, a "gift of value" is defined as a non-cash gift exceeding $100.00 in value. A gift in excess of $100.00 may not violate this policy only if pre-approved by the general counsel as being appropriate given the overall circumstances. A gift of value may be in the form of services, valuable privileges, vacations or pleasure trips, loans (other than conventional loans from lending institutions or typical consumer debt generally available to non-Brinker employees), and excessive entertainment.

Under no circumstances is a gift of cash or other form of money allowed.

You may accept:

- Meals and entertainment where business is conducted, such as recreational, sporting, or theatrical events that are of reasonable value considering the nature of the event and/or frequency of occasion; and

- Advertising or promotional materials, such as pens, note pads, calendars, paperweights, and other items of nominal value.

continued

Any gift or gratuity must have a clear business purpose. If you are concerned about the nature of a gift or gratuity offered or requested, you should discuss the situation with the general counsel.

There may be occasions where Brinker, as a company, solicits certain items from other persons or organizations in support of special company-sponsored events. In these circumstances, solicitations may only be made in furtherance of the event and for no other reason. All solicitations must be coordinated with the person or persons designated by senior management to be responsible for coordinating the special events.

Outside Activities. A conflict of interest may exist if outside activities (work, community service, and so on) prevent you from giving the necessary time and effort to your job. A conflict of interest may also exist if an immediate relative is employed by a vendor, supplier, competitor, or contractor. Special care must be taken to respect the loyalty and confidentiality you both owe to your respective employers. To avoid appearance of conflict, any such relationship should be disclosed on the Disclosure Statement. Individuals should not be considered for positions, which would place them in a conflict of interest. In addition "moonlighting" with a vendor, supplier, competitor, or contractor must be disclosed on the Disclosure Statement. Examples of "moonlighting" would be a cook at one of our restaurants who owns a janitorial service company providing cleaning services to the restaurant or a restaurant manager who provides consultant services to the restaurant industry.

Diversion of Corporate Opportunity. You should not take for yourself, or divert to another person or company, a business or financial opportunity, which you know, or could reasonably anticipate, Brinker would have an interest in pursuing.

B. COMPANY CONFIDENTIALITY

Confidential and Proprietary Information.

Brinker Information. You must not disclose any Brinker confidential or proprietary information or trade secrets to persons outside of Brinker, except as specifically authorized by management pursuant to established policies and procedures. This confidential or proprietary information includes nonpublic business, financial, personnel or technological information, plans, data, pricing and sales information, food and

continued

beverage processes, recipes and the like, and other processes or systems related to any portion of the Brinker's business operations that you have learned, generated, or acquired during your employment with Brinker. This prohibition extends indefinitely beyond your employment with Brinker. The use of any Brinker confidential or proprietary information or trade secrets for personal benefit is prohibited.

Other Companies' Information. You must not solicit, receive or use any confidential or proprietary information or trade secrets belonging or relating to any supplier, vendor, competitor, contractor, consultant, former employer, or other person or entity, except as may be lawfully received from the owner or an authorized third party.

Insider Information. You must not disclose any information that upon its release would be likely to affect an investor's decision to purchase, sell, or otherwise transfer any stock of Brinker and/or would be likely to affect the market price of Brinker's stock. Examples include periodic earnings prior to press release, projections of future earnings or losses, pending or proposed mergers, acquisitions, tender offers, sale of assets, changes in operations, changes in Brinker's dividend policy, or the declaration of a stock split. For more detailed information, please refer to the policy in the Employee Handbook entitled, "*Brinker International's Policy Governing the Improper Use of Material Nonpublic Information and Trading in the Company's Securities.*"

C. COMPANY PROPERTY

Books and Records. Federal and state laws require, and it is Brinker's policy, that Brinker's business records (including time sheets, expense reports, invoices, supporting documentation, and benefit plan information) be prepared accurately, reliably, and in a timely manner. It is very important that no employee create or participate in the creation of (or falsification or alteration of) any Brinker records which are intended to mislead anyone or conceal anything improper.

Company books and records should be maintained in confidence, safeguarded from loss and destruction, and subjected to internal control and audit procedures. You should always be honest and straightforward when dealing with internal or outside auditors with respect to the company's transactions, records, accounts, and financial statements.

continued

Improper Use of Company Assets. Company property may not be used for personal benefit or other improper uses. No company property (tangible or intangible) may be sold, loaned, used, given away, or disposed of without written authorization from the department head with budgetary responsibility for the property. Unauthorized copying of software, tapes, books, and other documents, which are legally protected, is prohibited. In cases where the department head initiates the transaction, authorization should come from his or her immediate supervisor.

Company property must be safeguarded from loss, damage, or theft. Abusing, destroying, damaging, or defacing company property, tools, equipment, or property of others is prohibited.

Information Technology Assets. As a Brinker director or employee you must:

- Protect computer hardware from loss, theft or damage.

- Protect computer software and company data against unauthorized access.

- Reduce risk of computer viruses.

- Comply with federal and state copyright laws, which provide copyright owners with exclusive rights against misuse of their proprietary programs, files, and databases, including making copies of software for non-backup purposes. Violations can result in civil and criminal penalties for Brinker and the employee.

- Limit personal use of company computer hardware and software.

- Responsibly use the companywide electronic mail system.

Abuse of these guidelines is prohibited and an employee may be subjected to disciplinary action.

Company Funds. You are responsible for company funds under your control. Funds should be spent for valid business purposes only at prices representing the best value to Brinker. Approval of payment should occur only if these two criteria are met. Specific authority limits are established within each department. Please discuss these limits with your department head to ensure compliance.

continued

D. COMPLIANCE WITH LAWS

You must obey all federal, state, and local laws and regulations while conducting business on behalf of Brinker. Many examples of laws are referenced in this Code of Conduct, but there are many other laws which apply to Brinker and each of us, including, for example, antitrust and trade regulation laws, environmental laws, franchise laws, liquor laws, employment laws, product safety laws, advertising laws, and so on.

With regard to antitrust and trade regulation laws, it is the duty of every employee having responsibility in areas affected by these laws to be sufficiently knowledgeable of the United States laws (federal, state, and local) and, if applicable, foreign country laws, to avoid unlawful conduct. No employee is authorized to violate these laws. Violations include price fixing, division of markets, exclusive dealings, and reciprocity.

You should not knowingly enter into transactions that would violate any laws or regulations. If you have a question as to the legal validity of an action, you should discuss the matter with the general counsel.

E. GOVERNMENT RELATIONS

Political Activity. Brinker encourages all directors and employees to vote and be active in the political process. Brinker does not in any way restrict your right to participate personally in political activities or to use personal funds for political purposes. If you choose to hold public office, either by election or appointment, you must take into account any potential for actual or apparent conflict of interest, and should also be disclosed in advance to your supervisor. Additionally, federal and many state laws restrict the use of corporate funds, assets, and time in connection with federal and state elections. Brinker is prohibited from contributing money, property, or services to a political candidate, party, organization, or committee. This restriction means that corporate facilities or other assets may not be used for the benefit of political candidates or parties. Any personal political contributions will not be reimbursed. Brinker only participates in the political process in the following manner:

Lobbying Activities. Brinker participates in lobbying activities only through the General Counsel. You must not lobby on behalf of Brinker without express written authorization from the General Counsel. Employees should not lobby on your personal behalf while on company time.

continued

Political Action Committee ("PAC"). Brinker is permitted to sponsor and pay the administrative costs of a PAC or effective citizenship programs. PACs are subject to strict regulation. Brinker sponsors the Brinker Good Government Fund.

Foreign Corrupt Practices Act ("FCPA"). Brinker, and the law, prohibit giving and/or offering money or anything of value to a foreign governmental official, agency, political party, party official or candidate under any circumstances which appears that such items were offered or given to induce the recipient to give Brinker business, purchase Brinker's products, or otherwise benefit Brinker's business in their country. The FCPA, as well as Brinker policy, prohibits bribing a governmental official or any other form of commercial bribery.

ADMINISTRATION OF THE CODE OF CONDUCT

This Code of Conduct is administered by the general counsel of the company. All disclosures required by this Code, requests for interpretation of any provision of this Code, and questions concerning this Code should be submitted in writing to the general counsel, unless stated otherwise in this Code. Responses, if necessary, will also be made in writing. All disclosures will remain confidential, and should be made on the form of Disclosure Statement attached to this Code.

From time to time you will be required to review this Code and acknowledge in writing your understanding and compliance with this Code. Where disclosure is required, you should consistently update the general counsel on a regular basis. Managers, directors, and officers will be required to complete and sign the Disclosure Statement annually.

At any time the general counsel may supplement or amend this Code for a particular department by issuing in writing more specific and/or stringent guidelines on any of the standards or policies in this Code, and if you are a member of that department, you shall be obligated to comply with those more specific and/or stringent guidelines.

OUR RESPONSIBILITIES

Each of us at Brinker is responsible for conducting ourselves in a manner that upholds Brinker's standards and values. We are all accountable for our business conduct, must obey the laws which apply to our business,

continued

continued

and must live up to the standards and values expressed in this Code. Your actions will be reviewed under this Code and applicable laws. If you do not act according to this Code and applicable laws, you may be subject to disciplinary action including suspension, reduction in salary, demotion, or termination. We at Brinker can not and will not compromise compliance with this Code or applicable laws to meet financial plans or maximize profits.

In addition to company disciplinary actions, violations of many provisions of this Code are against the law and may subject a violator and/or Brinker to severe penalties, fines or other consequences.

You have a responsibility to promptly notify immediate supervisors, department heads, or the general counsel of any violations of this Code of Conduct. You will not be subject to reprisals for reporting, in good faith, actions you feel violate this Code. Brinker further expects you to fully cooperate in any investigation of an alleged violation or other business conduct.

Any waiver of the Code of Conduct for executive officers or directors may be made only by the board of directors or a board committee and must be promptly disclosed to the shareholders.

OPERATIONAL HUMAN RESOURCE MANAGEMENT PRACTICES

These operational practices, needless to say, must be derived from the policies previously defined. Where the policies outline the organization's attitudes and values regarding its human resources, consistent practices constitute the proof of the pudding and are the tools to ensure a secure, self-confident workforce that will act as good ambassadors on behalf of the organization toward external stakeholders. Table 3.1 provided a breakdown of the area of human resource management and indicated issues covered by each subarea at a policy level. The aim of this section is to provide further specific inspiration toward various practices that could be part of an ethically founded approach to human resource management.

Physical Work Conditions

This is probably the area where a book like this is least able to add any additional ideas beyond what is already well known. The design of work places, be they industrial or offices, is an old and huge field of academic and applied research and practice. There exists extensive knowledge about the effects of various factors such as noise, light, air quality, ergonomic issues, and so on, and how these impact the well-being and productivity of those working under these conditions and thus how a place of work should be designed to accommodate a good quality of work life. An extension of this goes beyond simply providing working conditions that foster productivity, but also ensure the safety of the employees, both in general and of course in intrinsically hazardous jobs. This is also an area where much work has been done over the years and where much advice can be found in the literature. This book will therefore not go into the matter of such traditional design of workplaces, beyond stating the obvious that an organization with an ambition of being perceived as an ethically oriented actor must make a credible effort of providing good physical work conditions for its employees. This of course also applies to facilities in other parts of the world than their home base, but without reopening the question of global standards versus local adaptation touched upon in chapter 3.

A less-explored area of physical work conditions relates to what is frequently termed the "knowledge worker" and the characteristics of such work. Knowledge worker is perhaps not a very good term; every person is a knowledge worker in that she or he applies her or his skills and competence to perform a job. However, in this respect, the term is used to refer to people whose work tool is primarily their brain, not their body, in jobs like service developers, managers, researchers, journalists, and so on. There is a whole range of jobs falling under this category, and the number of them is growing rapidly. The main tools of this kind of employee are a PC, more often than not a portable one; a telephone, again usually the mobile, cellular type; and perhaps a so-called PDA (personal digital assistant)—all equipped with the latest means of fast network connection.

Common denominators for all of these tools are communication, availability, and mobility. These people often hold stressful jobs, juggling numerous activities at the same time, and are often on the move. Furnishing them with laptop computers, mobile phones, and so on, has been the typical approach to allowing them to be efficient and in touch with clients and the organization, and has normally been viewed as a positive gesture (especially considering the fact that many of these are relatively young people with an interest in the latest electronic gadgets). Is this really so? The number of burned-out professionals in this type of work has proliferated in recent years, and research suggests part of the reason is the "connectivity" that comes from such equipment. While it allows the parent to put in a couple of extra hours on that report after the kids have been put to bed, it eats away at what precious little leisure time that parent has. Sure you can bring your significant other for an extended weekend somewhere and still handle any requests from customers over the phone, but the result is that what is supposed to be a time for recharging batteries only becomes another drain on them.

This is not claiming that one should get rid of these technologies, not at all—I am an avid user of them myself, and would not lose them for the world. The point is to beware when dealing with these things. It is not a given that more is more. Providing the physical equipment necessary for this style of work seems very clever from an employer's point of view as you most likely will get more hours and efficiency out of each employee. But, if that same employee goes on sick leave for eight months and must be temporarily replaced by someone who needs to be found, trained, and gotten up to speed, it is not equally obvious that this is beneficial. Perhaps you either need to think carefully through what equipment each person really needs or lay down some guidelines on its use.

Organizational Work Conditions

If not equally well known and thoroughly researched as physical work conditions, quite a lot of work also has been done on organizational work conditions, or psychosocial aspects of work, to use another term. The position taken here is that practices that lead to a good working environment are also being ethically sound. However, the intention is not to rehash the body of literature on this aspect of work life, but rather to bring forward some ideas for practices that might be novel or are more specifically related to corporate social responsibility. Being a broad and diverse area, these practices also span widely, but will hopefully be of some use.

First of all, good working conditions and climate are virtually impossible to achieve in an organization characterized by fear, pessimism, and negative thinking. The mechanisms in play are probably much the same that cause economic recessions to reinforce themselves and create spirals that are hard to break out of. This is the opposite of the virtuous circles people, organizations, or indeed entire economies can create for themselves, where success builds on success and the sky is the limit. Organizations dominated by fear of authority figures, fear of failure, fear of loss of jobs—fear of anything—become self-fulfilling in their journey toward the very failure they fear. The answer is of course not to be naïvely optimistic, parochial, or myopic—one needs only to review the growth of Japanese electronics and automobile manufacturers during the 1970s and onward at the expense of American competitors to realize how equally wrong that can be.

There is, however, a marked difference between closing your eyes to the realities and just pushing forward, and encouraging an organizational culture based on positive values, exertion of leadership, and a reasonable tone to internal communication. The former will no doubt lead to trouble; the latter is an important part of a solid platform from which an organization can build success. The latter is a fusion of a whole range of "modern" (that is, post–Second World War) management and leadership theories, including flat organizations; human motivational theories; leading by example, not by fear; and so on. The use of the "and so on" in the previous sentence comes from the fact that such a "positive" atmosphere in an organization stems from a whole range of personality traits, leadership and management style, and organizational design that there seems to be no good common term for. However, in the recent book *Geeks & Geezers,* Bennis and Thomas (2002), looked at the concept of *neoteny*, a concept that sums up much of what this is about.

Having looked the term up in a dictionary, Bennis and Thomas quoted the following explanation of the zoological term neoteny: "The retention of youthful qualities by adults." These qualities include traits such as curiosity, playfulness, eagerness, fearlessness, energy, and so on, and often even physical appearance. *Geeks and Geezers* reports of a study of two groups of highly successful managers, one group of very senior people who are still active and successful, the geezers, and one group of surprisingly young highflyers, the geeks. Bennis and Thomas compared the samples within and across these groups, and brought the concept of neoteny into their book as a result of finding that the geezers shared many of the same qualities with the geeks—openness, willingness to take risks, hunger for knowledge and experience, eagerness to see what the new day brings. This "youthful" set of qualities, they claim, is one of the reasons why these people have managed to constantly renew themselves and look forward instead of slowing down while reviewing their past success.

After having learned this term and investigating it a little more closely, I sat down and reviewed some of the leaders I have been fortunate to meet during my work with different organizations. It was actually quite easy to pigeonhole most of them into two categories; the youthful, positive, polite, often humble, and successful ones; and the brusque, negative, often arrogant, and much less successful ones. This is, of course, no black-and-white picture; people of all types make good leaders and succeed, and "youthful qualities" is definitely not a precise term. (What about the youthful qualities displayed by some, perhaps even many, specimens of teenagers: sulky, rebellious, impolite; one minute invincible, the next depressed?)

But in embodying a somewhat intangible set of qualities that most of all centers around being an optimistic, positive, caring, curious, and simply good-humored person, the concept of neoteny sums up what is required of leaders and managers to stimulate an organizational culture of trust, fairness, and ambition. Leadership is essentially an emotional relationship, and leadership based on fear or heavy control can never succeed in instilling trust and loyalty the way leadership through positive involvement can. Some even go so far as characterizing people in general and leaders in particular as energy creators or energy drainers. The energy creators are optimistic, positive, see opportunities instead of problems, and frequently use humor as a deliberate "combat strategy"; energy drainers are pessimistic, negative, and prone to seeing all kinds of problems. The effect these two extreme archetypes of people have on others can easily be seen after 30 minutes in a meeting where they are present. The energy creators stimulate the meeting and keep it moving forward, the energy drainer slows it down and frustrates the other participants, much the same way they affect the organizations surrounding them.

Humor is a unique capacity of human beings, and humor has become a topic of management study in certain research environments. The U.S. Military Academy has characterized good leaders as possessing qualities such as caring for others, intelligence, physical ability, efficiency, and a sense of humor. Research on stress and professional burnout has shown that humor and laughter relieve many of the most severe symptoms of stress at work. A sense of humor is thus certainly a characteristic of leaders that stimulate their organizations in a positive way. There are, however, different types of humor, and not all of them are equally suited to creating a positive atmosphere. According to the "direction" of the humor and its quality, four types can be defined as shown in Figure 4.1 (this work has been led by Rod Martin at the University of Western Ontario, but has yet to be published in a referable form). To have a positive function in a work setting, humor must be good-natured.

		Direction	
		Toward Others	*Toward Oneself*
Quality	*Friendly*	Maintaining good relationships with others	Taking care of yourself
	Aggressive	Creating conflicts	Self destructing

Figure 4.1 Different qualities of humor.

Sethia and Glinow (1985) extended the concept of leadership styles into a characterization of organizational culture derived from management's concern for people and performance respectively. As shown in Figure 4.2, they arrived at four distinct types:

- The apathetic culture shows minimal concern for either people or performance. In this culture, individuals focus on their own self-interest.

- The caring culture exhibits high concern for people but minimal concern for performance issues.

- In contrast, the exacting culture shows little concern for people but a major concern for performance, focusing on the interests of the organization.

- The integrative culture combines concern for people and for performance, recognizing that employees are more than interchangeable parts—they are the basis for the organization's performance.

These four types are portrayed without much nuance to make it easier to understand their basic traits, and will rarely appear in their purest form in any organization. Still, for an organization trying to build a platform of ethics, there can be no doubt that the caring or integrative culture fits better. However, exhibiting traits like "minimal concern for performance," the caring culture is a sitting duck for criticism that an ethical approach is just like setting the organization up for bankruptcy. A business built around ethical principles need not be a naïve, self-excusing, turn-the-other-cheek type

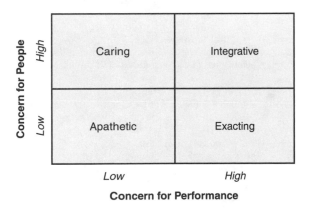

Figure 4.2 Characteristics of different types of organizational culture.

of organization that does not mind if it fails at meeting performance requirements. Thus, of these four types, the integrative culture is probably the one to pursue when transforming an organization to an ethical platform. Remember that people need something to live of and something to live for—ensuring attainment of performance standards aids long-term profitability and survival and provides food on the table; pursuing objectives that are generally accepted by society and mean something to different stakeholders gives work meaning.

Another source of support for the type of leadership that seems to create organizations capable of achieving greatness can be found in the book *Good to Great* by Jim Collins (2001). The focus of this book was to report the findings of a study of a sample of companies deemed to have moved from good to great, meaning a pattern of fifteen-year cumulative stock returns at or below the general stock market, followed by a transition point, then cumulative returns at least three times the market average over the next fifteen years. Among the common traits of these companies identified by the research team behind the book was a quality of leadership they termed *Level 5*, being at the top of a hierarchy of leadership capabilities (see Figure 4.3).

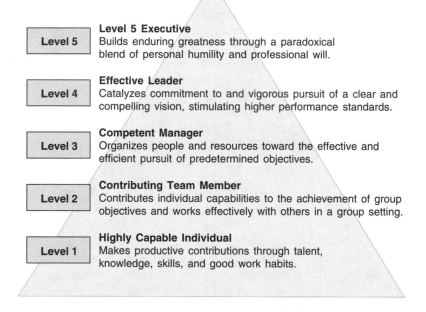

Figure 4.3   The hierarchy of Level 5 leadership (Collins, 2001).

Level 5 leaders were found to share some characteristics, especially a capacity for building enduring, great companies through what Collins described as a paradoxical blend of personal humility and professional will. These are not the charismatic leaders we have grown accustomed to reading about more often in celebrity magazines than business journals. In contrast, these leaders channel their ego away from themselves and invest it in the company. Some of those studied by the *Good to Great* research team were Darwin Smith of Kimberley-Clark, Colman Mockler of Gillette, David Maxwell of Fannie Mae, Ken Iverson of Nucor, and a few others. You might certainly have heard or read about these extraordinary people, but you have probably heard and read a lot more about other industrial leaders, for example Lee Iacocca, Bill Gates, or some of the others personalities well-covered by the media. Still, the numbers clearly show that the modest leaders, who dedicate their time to building great organizations and attribute the success of their companies to their organizations, are the ones who make great companies. Although not directly related to an ethical leadership profile, many of the traits described as being held by these leaders are exactly the qualities a fair and decent organization promotes: a belief in people, attributing success to the people, and humility. If you manage to grasp the qualities associated with the terms neoteny and Level 5 leadership and reach for these in your organization, you are very much on the road to an organizational culture that will not let you down when attempting to portray yourself as an ethically founded company to the outside world.

Other more specific practices that should be considered in order to develop the kind of organizational culture that will not "get one hand dirty" are covered below. First and foremost: a relentless fight against any type of bullying in the workplace. In typing the word bullying, images of kids being teased or harassed in the schoolyard quickly come to mind, but bullying is definitely also a grown-up pastime. Statistics indicate that as much as 10 percent of the workforce is regularly subjected to some kind of bullying or harassment at work. In my home country of Norway, this constitutes about 200,000 people, costing the society somewhere between 3.5 and 4 billion dollars annually in absenteeism. The ways of bullying might differ between a school and work environment, but the results are the same— ruined self-esteem, poor cognitive performance, absenteeism, low productivity, and so on, certainly detrimental to those that fall victim to such behavior, but equally damaging to the organization that allows it to take place. The damaging effects can be seen in the lackluster performance of the victims and those aware of the bullying (but who are unable to do anything about it), and in the organization's image if what is going on becomes public knowledge.

A large department store in a European capitol learned about on-the-job harrassment the hard way when an employee committed suicide after having been bullied at work for months. The story made the headlines in all the newspapers, and in a series of revelations it was made abundantly clear to the public that management at all levels had known about the situation, but simply closed their eyes and hoped the problem would go away on its own. Tragically, it did not and the clear lack of concern and empathy displayed by the store's management caused customers to shy away from the place in large numbers. A subsequent campaign attempting to restore the company's image has improved revenues somewhat but has not come close to restoring them to the levels of before the incident.

The department store described in the sidebar (after the tragedy had occurred), as well as many other organizations who have really taken the issue of bullying or harassment in the workplace seriously, have combined extensive training of all employees on the subject with appointment of "bullying police" to fight such behavior. The training normally focuses on the reasons why people turn into bullies, what forms bullying can take on, its consequences, and ways of fighting it. As for the "police force," it is not as serious as it sounds—normally it consists of a number of individuals selected from different areas and levels of the organization to have a role as "sentries." These people receive more training than the general employee and are alert to any bullying within their "jurisdiction," perhaps even trying to solve smaller problems. Serious issues are reported to the human resource manager and dealt with in a dedicated forum, which fortunately normally has to convene very infrequently after the introduction of the bullying police.

As for equal opportunity, affirmative action, nondiscrimination, or whatever term you choose to use, this should not be, but can still be, a difficult area. Whether the criterion is gender, race, creed, sexual orientation, or age, questions regarding recruiting or promoting tend to become highly political and very often go beyond logic. There will always be groups of people who feel, rightly or not, that they are being discriminated against and subsequently make a cause out of it. In addition, there are in most countries strict laws regulating these matters, with various watchdogs and institutions appointed to oversee their enforcement. The result is that almost any decision on recruitment or promotion can be interpreted by some group as overstepping some boundary, even in cases where the decision maker truly had no such intentions or seriously tried to do what was right.

Discrimination in the workplace can be expensive if brought before a court of law. Pennzoil paid $6.75 million to settle a discrimination lawsuit in which it was alleged that it paid black employees less and gave them fewer promotions than it gave their white counterparts.

Abercrombie & Fitch Co., a clothing retailer with 600 stores and 22,000 employees, is, as of June 2003, being sued on a charge of racial discrimination, accused of favoring whites for its sales floor jobs. The lawsuit was filed in U.S. District Court in San Francisco and charged that the retailer discriminates against Hispanics, Asians, and blacks in its hiring as it seeks to project what the company calls the "classic American" look. Several Hispanic and Asian plaintiffs said in interviews that when they applied for jobs, store managers steered them to stockroom jobs and away from the sales floor because they did not project what the company called the "A&F look." In a guidebook distributed to employees, the "Abercrombie Look Book," the company states: "America is diverse, and we want diversity in our stores. We do not discriminate, and will not tolerate discrimination in hiring based on race, national origin, religion, color, sex, age, or disability." Which just goes to show that there is often a large discrepancy between a policy statement and a working practice. Several plaintiffs said that top managers often visited stores and examined pictures of employees to determine whether they conformed to the Abercrombie & Fitch look. Jennifer Lu said she and four other salesclerks had been fired from a store in Costa Mesa, California, after a top corporate executive visited in February and told the store's managers that there were too many Asian salesclerks. What the repercussions will be for Abercrombie & Fitch remains to be seen at the time of writing.

You should also keep in mind that studies of group, team, or organizational composition are quite clear in their findings; the more homogeneously such units are composed, the less likely that necessary debates take place, that new opportunities are identified and pursued, and that the groups avoid becoming parochial in the long run. Collins (2001) also reported some findings of this type in the *Good to Great* study, where one hallmark of the great companies was that they first assembled management groups of the right people, then decided where to go. Furthermore, the right people referred to are not weak subordinates to strong genius CEOs, but rather, extremely talented people with their own minds. According to Collins, this is a somewhat paradoxical element in these "good to great" companies: that they all had executives who both voiced their opinions vehemently in debates, but also stood united behind decisions once they were made.

Related to an ethical organizational profile and behavior, a hypothesis has been put forward that organizations with a diverse set of people are more likely to be tolerant, open, and fair in both internal and external dealings. There are very few studies that have found evidence to support this, but the belief in the positive effects of diverse organizations, executive teams, even boards, is sufficiently strong that some countries have implemented or are planning to implement legislation requiring a certain percentage of female or minority representation.

Simplifying the issue of equal opportunity to its core, it is really nothing more than a matter of hiring and giving opportunities to the person best qualified for the job, completely irrespective of that person's gender, race, or creed. However, in the minefield you often invariably find yourself trying to navigate in situations where these traits are part of the decision, things are often a lot more complicated. So what can you do? Given that the organization is truly committed to the values of equal opportunity, perhaps even having formulated a strong policy on the matter, consistently practicing accordingly seems to be the only feasible approach. However, there are some measures that can be taken to ensure such consistency. Most often these involve appointing one or more special groups within the organization to oversee relevant decisions and also act as a support resource for managers facing decisions on hiring or promotions that involve potentially difficult cases.

One last issue under the heading of equal rights concerns female employees who give birth and subsequently take maternity leave. The duration of maternity (and indeed paternity) leave varies widely from country to country, from a law-imposed one year for both parents combined down to a couple of weeks. Where the rules allow mothers a leave of some duration, typically several months or more, there is normally an accompanying rule

In Norway, recent statistics show that a mere 7% of the board members in the largest companies in the country are female. In a country with a long tradition of womens' rights, female prime ministers and other cabinet members, this is certainly not impressive. The minister of trade and industry has set a milestone at the summer of 2005, by which the share of female representatives should be at least 40%. If not, the plan is to come down even harder and formalize the requirement through legislation. Since progress toward the goal has been slow, the public director for equal rights has demanded that such legislative changes be introduced even earlier.

protecting their right to return to the job they had before giving birth. This is of course done to make it easier for women to both pursue careers and establish a family at the same time. However, many organizations try to evade this rule by arguing that they needed to hire a replacement during the absence, the old job was reorganized, or demand changes made the job superfluous. These are unacceptable attempts at dodging an obligation that makes it more difficult for women to combine career and family. For an organization that truly wants to stimulate an equal opportunity climate, taking proper care of women returning from maternity leave is a sound practice.

After leaving a large IT company in 1998 following the clearly unfair promotion of a colleague to a department manager position, Kumar Mohanty,* a native of India, founded his own company, Dynamic Systems. Experiencing rapid growth in customer base and revenues, like most IT companies at the time, Dynamic Systems faced the paradox of finding it hard to recruit enough qualified people to sustain the growth, yet receiving plenty of unqualified applicants attracted by the boom in the industry. Kumar did not forget being passed over for promotion due to what he perceived as the wrongful promotion of a white, native Englishman, and from the very beginning vowed to review every applicant or candidate for promotion carefully, irrespective of personal characteristics not relevant to their ability to perform the job. Consistently hiring people from all parts of the world and of any religious beliefs, the company grew steadily and always maintained an image as an open and caring organization. As the sheer size of the organization grew too large for Kumar to handle recruitments and promotions himself, he appointed a diversely composed small team of personnel assistants. The team had two main functions: to act as general awareness-raisers throughout the organization for their equal opportunity policy and supporting anyone asking for their help in specific hiring or promoting matters. Until the global slump in the IT markets, Dynamic Systems saw the number of more-than-qualified applicants rise continuously, leaving their competitors far behind. Kumar estimated that the arrangement with the assistants cost the company around $10,000 per year in lost production from the team members, but paid off handsomely through the talent attracted to the company, who in turn helped shape it into a leader within its market segment.

* At the person's and the company's request, the names of both have been changed in line with standing company policy.

Professional burnout was mentioned briefly in relation to physical work conditions and the use of mobile/networked IT equipment. The problem is even more relevant under the heading of organizational work conditions, and has in some industries or sectors of employment created a truly serious situation. The causes of burnout are complex and compounded, but certainly a product of the times: an extremely fast pace in every aspect of life, ever-increasing demands from all types of customers, a plethora of things to get and activities to participate in, just to mention a few. Nevertheless, the trend is clear, at least in the industrialized countries; physical injuries and absenteeism caused by these factors are decreasing while there is a sharp increase in absenteeism due to stress, burnout, and related physical symptoms.

Having a compounded set of causes, preventing these problems is by no means only the responsibility of employers, but they must carry a significant share of it. As has been discussed already (see the section titled "Why Should You Change Your Ways?" in chapter 1), the incentives to the employer encompass productivity gains from keeping employees happy, avoiding negative productivity effects from people in the process of burning out, and portraying a consistent image externally as caring for both employees and customers. Luckily, research within this field has come far in proving that stress and burnout can be prevented or reduced, so let us look briefly into how.

First of all, however, a quick introduction to the concept of burnout, which is closely related to the more general problem of work-life stress. The term emerged during the 1970s following observations, especially in the healthcare sector, that people gradually fell victim to an emotional deprivation causing loss of motivation and commitment (in work pioneered by Freudenberger and Maslach, as described in for example in Maslach and Schaufeli [1993]). The term itself is still controversial (If you burn out, is there any hope at all for resurrection? Is it more relevant to talk about discharging, the way batteries discharge, and subsequently recharging?) and there has not been reached a generally accepted definition of it. An early and much cited definition was as follows:

> Burnout is a syndrome of emotional exhaustion, depersonalization, and reduced personal accomplishment that can occur among individuals who do "people work" of some kind. (Maslach and Jackson, 1986)

However, the phenomenon has spread, from originally being found mostly in "people work" type of jobs, often characterized by some kind of a "calling," for example, healthcare, education, the ministry, and so on, to appearing as often in other types of jobs marked by high motivation, high skills, and complexity. Today, more often than not, victims of burnout are young, skillful, enthusiastic people. In line with this, more general definitions have been formulated, for example:

> A state of physical and mental exhaustion following sustained emotional pressure in the workplace. (Roness, 1995)

Although being a relatively new concept, there is a fair body of literature to be found dealing with burnout, especially from a clinical view, explaining symptoms and treatment. It is not my intention to cover the topic in depth, though, so this book will focus primarily on the causes of burnout and its prevention and leave it up to you to consult other sources for more general information. To prevent stress, which is as much of a problem in its own right if allowed to reach high levels over long periods of time, and the resulting state of burnout, it is important to understand the causes of both. According to Maslach and Leitner (1997), the six basic factors that seem to provide the foundation for burnout are:

- Too much work (amount, type, and complexity)

- Lack of control over the work situation (objectives, tools, and results)

- Lack of feedback and recognition (material, symbolic, and social)

- Dissolution of the work community (belonging, loyalty, and caring)

- Unjust distribution of benefits and burdens (survival of the fittest, power alliances)

- Value conflicts between those of the organization and those of the individual

More specific factors of modern work life that also are believed to contribute to the negative trend are:

- To many people, work has changed its significance in life. Going back to the time of Taylor, scientific management, and the assembly conveyor, people felt little personal and mental involvement in their work and mostly saw work as a means to earn the money required to finance their real life, outside of work, where they looked for personal gratification. In stark contrast, many modern jobs are deeply engaging, to the point that many people experience their peak moments of achievement and gratification at work (in which cases work is often termed the "honey trap," being sweet and tempting, but also sticky enough to make escape difficult). At the same time, as work demands more and more time and attention, people find it hard to juggle their private lives and all the activities taking place there. An insightful observation in this respect is the so-called "time bind" (for a closer description of the time bind, see Hochschild [1997]): that professionals today live their lives at work and apply scientific management to their spare time simply to manage their relationships with friends, driving kids back and forth, being a spouse, and so on. And when work becomes this gratifying and this important, it is no wonder people channel much of their energy into it, seriously risking depleting their energy source (another proverb in the circles researching burnout is that "in order to burn out, you have to burn for something").

• It has become increasingly common to have more than one superior to relate to, both in matrix organizations, arising out of a marked increase in the project activity of many industries, and in general as organizations are tweaked and turned to find better solutions, for example, business process orientation, team structures, and so on. Although displaying some advantages, this is certainly a cause of stress for many people. Very often, these multiple superiors have some "right of disposal" of the individual employee, but there is only one of them who takes on the responsibility of line manager. The result is often that several people are pulling at the employee and her or his time and energy.

• Most organizations have become increasingly leaner as a result of general improvements, elimination of waste and streamlining of processes, cost reductions, downsizing, and so on. In some cases, there are too few people to do the job properly, in many cases the demand and supply of resources is just in balance. This of course means more work for fewer people and puts a general strain on organizations that is tiresome on people.

• More and more jobs are designed in such a way that an employee cannot simply check out of work and be 100 percent off work. One aspect of this is the aforementioned availability of electronic tools that allow connection to the workplace from anywhere. Beyond this, it is also a fact that more and more people become "knowledge workers" (which again is an imprecise term, suggesting that there are "non-knowledge workers" not utilizing their skills in their work) who hold some type of managerial responsibility, are in charge of paperwork, are involved in improvement projects, conduct different types of analyses, and so on. As opposed to purely manual labor or work that merely requires presence at a certain place of work, any such activity that involves thinking, writing, reading, and so on, can be done from anywhere, at any time. Combined with the erosion of unions as the traditional watchdogs over working conditions, people have generally become much more flexible regarding working times and hours. Again, the result is that people work more, at odd hours, have less leisure time, and spend less time recharging their batteries.

• Although perhaps about to change due to new conferencing technology and a general fear of travel, the number of people who travel in their work has risen dramatically over the last 20 to 30 years. There has also been a proliferation of meetings, training courses, seminars, and so on, which are no longer reserved only for management levels, but for everyone in an organization. Combined, these things keep people away from their regular "workstations" and their day-to-day tasks (not to mention the explosion of e-mail, which statistics show many people spend more than three hours every day simply processing). Combined with the increasing leanness of organizations, this means there is usually no one else who can take over the tasks of the employee traveling or attending a day-long meeting. The result is the same amount of work, only less time to do it in, which is bound to wear people down. This is also the start of a damaging spiral in which the increased stress often tempts people to call in sick once in a while simply to cool down, only to find that there is even less time left to clear away the pile of tasks waiting.

In all fairness, it should also be pointed out that most studies of burnout have found that burnout victims often have suffered from a combination of factors from both life at work and their personal lives. There are indications that stressful work conditions are tolerated over a much longer time and at much higher levels if they are balanced by positive and supportive personal conditions. On the other hand, in a very large number of cases, it seems as if events or conditions outside work, for example, marital problems, sudden illness or death in the family, financial problems, and so on, have been the triggers that finally induce burnout. This mutual reinforcement is illustrated in Figure 4.4 (Onsøyen, Andersen, Veiseth, Andersen, Røstad, and

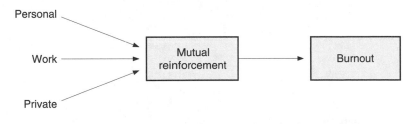

Figure 4.4 Burnout is often a result of mutual reinforcement between factors at work and personal aspects of one's private life.

In a recent study we undertook in a small sample of large Norwegian companies, the results were rather depressing:

- As many as 64 percent of the people surveyed, who were employees mainly involved in project work, perceived their work situation as potentially leading to burnout.

- Regarding their views of their colleagues, the respondents said 52 percent of them were in danger of burning out.

- A staggering 84 percent of respondents said they would go to work even on a day when they thought it perfectly acceptable to stay at home due to illness! The main reasons quoted for doing so are listed in Figure 4.5.

In terms of reasons why the respondents perceived themselves in danger of burning out, the main causes were given as (including the percentage of respondents citing each):

- Too much work compared with the available time—88 percent

- Too great demands for results—65 percent

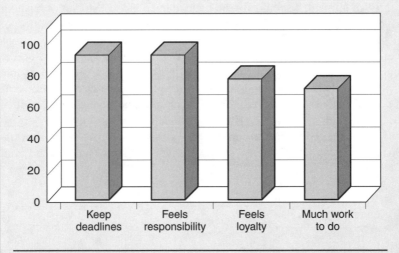

Figure 4.5   Listed in order of the number of respondents quoting them, these are the reasons why 84 percent of the surveyed people would go to work on a "bad day."

continued

continued

> • Too demanding requirements for revenues—59 percent
>
> • Difficulties in their personal life—49 percent
>
> • Little possibility for affecting one's own work situation—47 percent
>
> • Unclear expectations of one's own role at work—43 percent
>
> • Lack of feedback—41 percent
>
> • Lack of contentment at work—41 percent
>
> • Problems coping with the assigned tasks—37 percent
>
> • Unclear lines of reporting—31 percent
>
> Out of the total respondents, we also conducted interviews with a limited number of people including some that had experienced burnout. In all instances, this had occurred as far back as ten to fifteen years, but all of them still struggled with problems related to the burnout, some to the extent that they had never recovered and gotten back to work again. Common to all of them was that factors outside work had played an important part in creating the problems, but had also helped in supporting them and getting them back on their feet again.
>
> All of them agreed that even when it was obvious to everyone around them that something was wrong and developing in a disastrous direction, no one from the company put the brakes on. The effect was a feeling of being worn out and working just as hard, but still seeing tasks piling up and feeling that performance was deteriorating continuously. When the state of burnout was finally reached, one interviewee claimed, "Getting cornflakes and milk [was] like preparing a three-course dinner. . . ."

Ranes, 2002). This suggests that a superior cannot help prevent burnout in an employee only by providing sound working conditions, but must also know the employee well enough to have insight into the personal sphere of their life.

In terms of prevention, it is also useful to understand that burnout is not an instantaneous effect, rather it follows a gradual process of burning out, as depicted in Figure 4.6 (Onsøyen, Andersen, Veiseth, Andersen, Røstad, and Ranes, 2002).

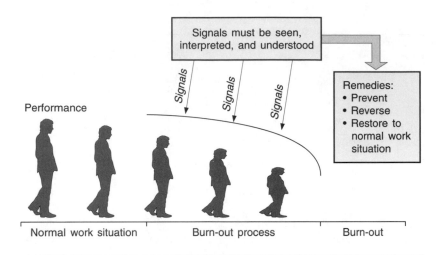

Figure 4.6   Burnout appears after a longer process of burning out.

The consequence of this realization is that treatment of burnout once it has occurred is too late, at least in terms of the organization doing its job. Rather, efforts must be directed at providing working conditions that do not start people on the process of burning out in the first place. Secondly, to understand the signals that indicate people have started the progression toward burnout and watch out for them. Finally, to develop a set of responses available when an employee is on the way toward burnout. Unfortunately, from our own studies and findings reported by others, we know there is not a "right" set of ways to prevent burnout. The specific causes appearing in an organization and the ways to combat these can be highly specialized from case to case. However, some generalized approaches that seem to have positive effects are:

- In general, provide some basic information or training on the topic of burnout, its symptoms, and the process of burning out to everyone in the organization.

- Emphasize "people skills" when selecting future leaders and their training.

- Focus on the role of leadership by not only having a system for performance appraisal of employees, but of leaders, based on the appraisals of their subordinates.

- Careful workload planning that leads to both an acceptable average level and allows temporary peaks where required.

- In line with the last bullet point, introduce "protected periods" in the wake of periods of peak work activity, where people are allowed to cool down and get themselves together again.

- Undertake a thorough assessment of all business processes and tasks in the organization to eliminate or transfer to others those that represent or are perceived as unnecessary bureaucracy or administration, and in general shield employees from disruption of their tasks.

- Carefully monitor levels of overtime, but over a period of time, for example, three to six months. When certain limits are exceeded, the organization must be the responsible party and make sure the employee slows down for a while.

- Organize work to allow introducing some kind of "backup system" where single employees do not carry the responsibility for extensive sets of tasks and where anyone can step in and take over some duties in cases of absence or reprioritizing of other tasks.

The last issue to be covered under the heading of organizational work conditions is the much-dreaded concept of "downsizing" and the related concept of "outsourcing." Starting with downsizing, this is a perhaps decade-old restructuring trend that at least in the beginning appeared to consist primarily of overhead reductions that targeted staff and white-collar jobs (see Skarlicki [1996] for a closer treatment of the subject). By definition, downsizing does not refer to termination of poor performers or departures due to retirement or voluntary resignations. Firm-related factors and not employee-related ones account for the terminations. As companies have cut as much as possible into staff and support functions, the next step has often been proportional overall cuts in the number of employees and subsequently their activity levels and revenues.

In one European country, the brewery industry has seen the "downsizing" form of restructuring lately. Brewing beer has for hundreds of years been a distributed business with a multitude of local brands. Some years ago, one of the larger breweries in the country's capitol started buying smaller units around the country. Most, if not all, of these were profitable and enjoyed high local market penetration, and all were promised that the acquisition would not lead to any of the

---

continued

continued

breweries being closed; on the contrary—backing by a larger company would only secure the future of these smaller ones. For a few years, this actually seemed to be true, until the large brewery started planning for a huge facility just outside the capitol. As the planning progressed and numbers were crunched, it soon became clear that the company could build a new brewery with the capacity to replace all of the smaller local units. Even if distribution costs increased, the cost reductions achieved through consolidation and economies of scale would outweigh these, so further plans were slowly set in motion. As the planning went into its final stages, preparations were started to transfer production and close down the small breweries. Eventually, the very smallest ones were shut down, only maintaining distribution and warehouse functions, and transferring production to the mid-range units in the larger cities in the country. Soon, only three relatively large units were left besides the main facility in the capitol. As construction went ahead and the new major facility was ready to start production, two of the remaining three local facilities were closed and their volume transferred mostly to the new unit, some to the last remaining old one.

The twist of this little story is that the entire time, all the way up until their closing, each and every one of these local breweries had been profitable, some of them with quite impressive results. Headquarters' calculations indicated even more profits could be made through consolidation into fewer, ultimately one, production site(s), but these figures were contested by local management and unions, and have yet to be proven. One reason why proof is still awaited is that as local units were closed, customers in the local markets revolted. Few consumers care strongly about where their ballpoint pen or their shirt was manufactured, but for some reason, beer is different. Like sports teams, beers have fan clubs and societies and are very much a local thing, carrying tradition and strong brand loyalty. Even though the large brewery believed this would be covered by maintaining the local brands but producing them elsewhere, customers got truly angry. Local newspapers covered the closings extensively, people signed petitions to keep their brewery, and local unions and soon-to-be ex-employees fueled the controversy through public appeals and wide media coverage. After each closing of a local brewery, the local brands now being produced elsewhere suffered up to 50 percent loss of market share. Obviously, this has impacted profit levels and so far it is impossible to prove that the consolidation has had positive financial effects.

In market segments where demand is slowing or competition is so fierce that many players experience reduced revenues, downsizing is of course a natural response. The same obviously is true in cases of general recession and reduced economic activity in an area or country. However, the reasons behind the use of downsizing appear to be changing. Initially, the most likely candidates for restructuring were firms struggling with high debt. Although the recent recession has been blamed for the bulk of this activity, a poll conducted by the American Management Association (continuously updated) of over 1,100 firms that downsized found that almost 50 percent of the downsizing had nothing to do with the recession. Instead, workforce reductions have become an ongoing activity that continues without regard to current financial performance. Firms who adopt downsizing appear to do so in part to imitate their competitors and peers. Firms have also begun to downsize "in anticipation" of continuing competition. Conventional wisdom includes downsizing as an effective management tactic, and changing societal standards support its use. Wayne Cascio (1993), in a study published in the Academy of Management's *The Executive,* concluded that firms are managing workers in the same way that they manage inventories of unsold goods—using just-in-time delivery with no stockpiling or inventorying of resources. A further observation was that layoffs are seldom one-time events; organizations now use them repeatedly as a competitive managerial strategy.

Outsourcing can perhaps be termed a sibling of downsizing. The effects on the organization are about the same, a reduction in activity and the number of employees, but through other mechanisms. One type of outsourcing involves transferring functions of the organization to external suppliers, for example custodial tasks, IT system management, human resource management, accounting, and so on. In such cases, there are massive changes in the work situation of those affected, where some retain their jobs but in a different organization while others do not. Another type of outsourcing is the kind where companies move their labor-intensive operations to low-cost countries, typically less-developed countries. In these cases, entire manufacturing plants are closed down and relocated to a different place, the result being that all original employees usually are laid off.

All of these types of downsizing and outsourcing, no matter how necessary they seem, have severe negative effects on the individual employees who are affected, on local communities, and also on the organizations that implement them. Restructuring and downsizing are considered to be activities to reduce redundancies, increase productivity, and, at least to some degree, redress a firm's financial woes. Evidence suggests, however, that these objectives are frequently not realized. Cascio found that fewer than half of downsized companies reported significant reductions in costs. Less than a third of the companies reported that profits or shareholder returns increased as expected.

The most recent trend is, however, not going to these lengths out of necessity or for survival, but as a strategy to increase already acceptable profits. As will be discussed in more detail in chapter 11, an ethical business approach does not imply that an organization should not make sound business decisions to secure profits and its future. Things become difficult when a sound pursuit of business objectives is replaced by greed for ever-higher returns without any concern for the consequences this has on others affected. Of the major downsizing or outsourcing moves to low-cost countries reported lately, most of them occurred in companies that are making profits but where these can be further increased by such moves. This is hardly a motivation that can be expected to be understood and accepted by the employees, a fact supported by research. It has been found that those employees who survive the cuts (the survivors) typically are less loyal, less willing to take risks, and provide lower levels of service to customers and support to fellow employees.

Not surprising, perhaps. Layoffs and reductions of this type induce pessimism in an organization. If downsizing is motivated solely out of the owners' and shareholders' greed for ever-higher profits, pessimism can turn into downright hostility. Dramatic cuts can eradicate entire local communities. The cumulative effects are still not known, but it is obvious that closing down or moving all manufacturing jobs out of the traditional industrialized countries does something to their ability to develop new products, commercializing them, and ultimately retaining their position as an industrial nation.

In terms of the individual employees, they are traumatized, disillusioned, and cynical. Organizations also tend to underestimate the potential for resentment and retaliation by employees for perceived unfair treatment. Layoff victims' responses can range from spreading ill will about the organization to workplace violence. Layoff survivors are in a good position to judge the fairness of the treatment received by those let go. Rousseau, in a book entitled *Psychological Contracts in Organizations* (1995), predicted that in the future, employees are likely to lower expectations and commitments to an employer, keep their emotions in check, and in this manner shield themselves from disappointment and avoid getting "burned" again. Loyalty will be restricted to one's work, not to the organization.

Furthermore, a paper in *The Lancet* (Vahtera et al., 1997) reported downsizing is a risk to the health of employees. Dr. Jussi Vahtera and colleagues from the Finnish Institute of Occupational Health in Turku, Finland, looked at the effects of downsizing on the health of 981 people who worked for local government in Raiso, southwestern Finland. The study was done between 1991 and 1995, a period when Finland faced its most severe economic decline since the First World War. The researchers used employers' records to investigate the relationship between downsizing and subsequent absenteeism because of ill health. They also looked at whether the effects of downsizing were dependent on other known predictors of sick leave.

"Individuals who remain in work during a period of economic recession may suffer from an increase in ill health," the researchers write. The extent to which employees' health was affected depended on the degree of downsizing. The rate of long-term sick leave (more than three days off work) was 1.9 to 6.9 times greater after major downsizing than after minor downsizing. Overall, long-term sick leave increased by 16 to 31 percent during this period of downsizing.

So how should you approach the situation if the need for downsizing or outsourcing seems to be imminent? Research has identified a number of strategies for firms to consider during restructuring that minimize negative effects for both the organization and the employees:

• First and foremost, consider alternatives to downsizing or outsourcing. Treating restructuring as a headcount reduction tends to adversely affect a firm's goodwill, productivity, and long-term adaptability. Pursuing such restructuring only out of a desire for increased profits will not be understood or tolerated and is bound to damage the external image of the organization.

• If action is required, involve employees in identifying what needs to change to achieve necessary improvements. Very often, voluntary (permanent or temporary) reductions in pay levels, extended working hours, and so on, will go a long way to get the organization through the rough waters.

• Overcommunicate as the restructuring process unfolds. Involve unions and the employees in fairly deciding who will have to go if staff reductions are inevitable and provide employees adequate advance notification of layoffs.

• Include severance pay and extended benefits to give displaced workers an economic safety net.

• Provide education, retraining, and outplacement programs to help employees develop new skills that will help them secure other jobs.

• Train managers to communicate the layoff in a sensitive manner. Layoff decisions must be clear, direct, and empathetic so that employees are clearly informed about the reasons for dismissal, can retain their sense of dignity, and can receive social support from supervisors and coworkers.

• Above all, approach restructuring and downsizing as a long-term strategy rather than as a single fix-it event. Research shows that by giving employees advance notice, providing employees with clear and accurate explanations, expressing remorse, and protecting the employees' dignity and respect, managers can lessen the negative effects of restructuring on both victims and survivors.

Compensation Structures

The question of pay and compensation can be a minefield, involving so many underlying issues that attempts at discussing it in a structured and fair manner are often stifled by the different sides jumping into their trenches, in part due to the fact that salaries and pay levels are by the very nature of modern society extremely important to people. Another factor making the issue difficult is that pay levels are often a private matter, but one that is discussed frequently. Most of all, perhaps, the discussion is made difficult from the age-old conflict between management and employees, where the intrinsic position is for employees to demand as much as possible and management to want to give away as little as possible. Add to this the constant revelations of how much money the executive level in some organizations actually get away with, and the fire is well kindled.

The intention of this book is not to nurture the arguments lobbed from the trenches, but rather to outline how an organization striving to develop or maintain an ethical profile should handle these issues. There are basically only two core questions to consider:

• Pay and compensation levels of the employees, employees in this case meaning everyone in an organization except for the executive level.

• Pay and compensation levels of senior management at the executive level.

For both questions, some core principles should apply. First of all, to be accepted and not cause any conflict, pay levels must be perceived as fair by all stakeholders in the matter. Fair meaning they must be in line with averages or norms for the industry; there must be a match between performance, results, and compensations; and internal variations within an organization must either be minor or justified in terms of workload, responsibility, or performance. Ultimately, this is a matter of achieving a tender balance between too little and too much, between management and employees, and between the organization and its external stakeholders. Any imbalance in this equilibrium will constitute the makings of a conflict and will sooner or later cause some type of problem:

• On the part of employees, being paid too little compared with either other comparable organizations or what they perceive to be a fair share of the profits generated by the organization will cause dissatisfaction, frustration, and lower motivation. Ultimately, this can also lead people to seek other opportunities, and external stakeholders, especially customers, can react negatively to what may be perceived as stinginess.

• On the other hand, if employees are paid significantly more than workers in comparable organizations, or at levels not in line with performance, perhaps to the extent that it seriously hampers profitability, this will obviously be a problem for management (it is much harder lowering than increasing pay levels) and will upset shareholders/owners. As for external stakeholders, customers in particular, the likelihood that these will react strongly to a deviation from averages is small. In the case of the greater number of employees, such a deviation is usually a matter of a few percentages. There is, however, also the risk that too generous pay levels will cause similar motivational problems as too stingy; the problem is that in both cases the logical link between performance and pay is severed.

• Turning to executive management, if they are paid less than the norm or what could be expected based on performance and profits, all experience shows that the gut reaction is to look elsewhere for better compensation. In organizations traded publicly, that is, not family-owned companies, management is normally much more volatile than the employees and will change more often, a fact that can be negative and partly avoided through decent compensation levels.

• Compensating senior executives more than what is seen as fair by the employees, owners, or external customers (very often all of them at the same time) is equally bad. To the extent that the overpay represents big money, it can hurt the organization's profitability and long-term viability. More often, the problem is outrage on the part of employees and stakeholders like customers or suppliers, as they can clearly witness how much management is "raking in," usually at the expense of themselves through lower pay levels for employees, lower prices to suppliers, and higher prices to customers. Outrage is not a good feeling in these relations and can only cause dissatisfaction and future problems.

Part of the reason why these problems occur is that what is construed as fair by one group can be far off the mark to others, even if the levels are based on averages. To an employee making $23,000 a year, it does not matter if all CEOs in the industry make $1.2 million, it will still seem outrageous that one person should take home more than fifty times her own outcome. Equally, to a customer barely managing to keep up with the

installments on a used Toyota Corolla, it is extremely frustrating to see the
dealership manager turning up in his brand-new Mercedes one day and his
Cadillac the next. Again, it is the imbalance and the perception of a lack of
cause-and-effect between effort, results, and compensation that are at the
heart of the matter.

This imbalance and perception of unfairness is also causing wider-
ranging problems than disgruntled employees or frustrated customers. In
the rally to constantly achieve higher standards of living, pay levels in general escalate. Management negotiates deals adding stock options, pension
schemes, and so on, to their pay levels. Employees use the increased pay
levels of management to claim healthy raises for themselves, fully backed
by unions. The economy of an industry or even a country can only keep
afloat for so long as cost levels skyrocket, and growth periods are followed
by the dreaded downsizings and outsourcings that were discussed recently.
Whole industries or local communities close down, to some extent people
recover and move on, and soon the cycle starts again. There are, however,
clear signs that the industrialized companies will not be able to keep on
reinventing themselves forever. Growth figures are slowing down or even
recessing, and at some stage, standards of living, cost levels, and the availability of new industries or new areas of income will be too imbalanced to
support our way of living.

Management pay levels, and related corporate behavior especially,
have reached a critical level in many industries, certainly enough to see the
formation of the Commission on Public Trust and Private Enterprise in
the United States. This is a blue-ribbon commission formed by the Conference Board, a New York business-research organization, and mandated
to issue recommendations on an array of items intended to improve corporate governance, auditing and accounting practices, who published their
recommendations January 9, 2003. According to its chairman, Peter G.
Peterson, chairman of The Blackstone Group, former secretary of com-
merce and chairman of the Federal Reserve Bank of New York, the latest
scandals in the corporate world are a breach of the contract on which the
entire Capitalist system is founded. He is supported by the commission
member John W. Snow, chairman and CEO of the CSX Corporation and
former chairman of the Business Roundtable, explaining that this contract
is based on the model where investors entrust their assets to the management of a corporation while a board is appointed to make sure there are no
conflicts of interest between management and the owners of the company.
The challenge has been and still is how to cut the cake, that is, the value
created by the company. Previously, the problem was that the owners were
left with too large a share. Now, the system is about to collapse because

management takes away too much of it. Some statistics to support this position were also provided by the Commission:

- More than 3 billion dollars were paid out in bonuses and stock option profits to managers of companies that later went bankrupt.

- More than 60 billion dollars were paid to managers of companies where the stock value later fell by 75 percent or more.

The Commission was formed to address circumstances surrounding the recent spate of corporate scandals and to offer suggestions for "best practices" to respond to the decline of confidence in American capital markets in the wake of the scandals. While the suggestions of the Commission do not have any formal impact on rules or regulations governing corporations, they may influence the best practices of some corporations and could impact regulators and legislators as they prepare corporate governance rules. Their recommendations will also be presented in other parts of this book; these are some interesting suggestions on compensation principles:

- Appoint a compensation committee within the board responsible for setting compensation levels for management. Any consultants or other external experts on compensation issues should only be hired by and report to the compensation committee.

- Incentives for management must be based on strategic, long-term objectives, not only share prices. In the event that management acts in a way that damages the company, the board must demand that bonuses and profits be repaid to the company.

- Stock options and incentives based on share price must be balanced between the value of the compensation and the costs for the company. The costs must be made clear to the owners.

- Compensation should have a long-term perspective, including a lock-in period for stock given as compensation to management. This lock-in period should not be shorter than the minimum lock-in period of pension programs for other employees.

- The cost of stock options should be included in the company's accounts as an expense, according to uniform standards for publicly traded companies.

- Stock option programs should be channeled through programs approved by the shareholders. Changes to these programs, including repricing of options, must be approved by the shareholders.

• Annual company reports should contain information about
results per share after a dilution of share value through stock
option programs.

Collins, in the *Good to Great* study (2001), found support for these
tenets. The researchers expected to find that changes in incentive systems,
especially for executives, would show a clear correlation with the good to
great transition. However, no such systematic patterns were found, even
after having conducted 112 different analyses. The only significant difference found was that the executives of the great companies received slightly
less total cash compensation ten years after the transition to greatness than
their counterparts in the comparison companies who had not made the transition. The theory put forward by Collins to explain the lack of correlation
between executive compensation and great results is that compensation and
incentives are important: not in order to elicit the right behavior from the
wrong people, but to get the right people on the team in the first place.

So, how do you turn these wise words from the Commission on Public
Trust and Private Enterprise and the example from Nucor (see sidebar) into
good practices in your own organization? As in most cases regarding ethics,
an important part of the answer is to use sound judgment and try to do the
right thing. However, some additional principles that could help in achieving a good compensation structure are:

• To the extent that industry or area averages are well documented and
act somewhat as normative pay levels, try to adhere to these. If deviating
significantly from them, this should be clearly explained and based on real
reasons, for example, deviating cost structures, better-than-average profit
levels, and so on.

• Try to strike a balance between base-level pay and performance-
related bonuses. If one or the other is too dominant, the result can either
be low motivation from the lack of additional incentives or people "killing
themselves" trying to achieve oversized bonuses. In any case, bonus
schemes that are linked to individual efforts and performance should be
avoided, as they tend to foster so much internal competition that they stifle
cooperation.

• In terms of executive compensation, try to follow the advice from the
Commission on Public Trust and Private Enterprise. Especially link executive incentives to long-term viability of the organization and avoid compensation levels that are clearly way out of bounds. This also includes stock
options, other compensation means like homes, cars, and so on, as well as
pension schemes and severance pay deals. Media coverage of cases of
CEOs working ten weeks at the helm before being let go and receiving

A good example of successfully applied, deliberate compensation structures cited in the *Good to Great* study is Nucor, the steel manufacturer. The basic idea was that you can teach a farmer to make steel, but you cannot teach the work ethics of a farmer to people who do not have them in the first place. Thus, Nucor's mills were deliberately located in farm areas instead of steel towns, to attract farmers and their strong work ethic. To motivate them, Nucor paid their steelworkers better than any other steel company, but based on a high-pressure team bonus mechanism. More than 50 percent of a worker's compensation was tied directly to the productivity of the team the worker belonged to, often consisting of 30 to 40 people. The result was that the ex-farmers retrained as steelworkers would show up for work thirty minutes early to prepare their tools and be ready to get going as soon as the shifts changed. The system's aim was not to convert lazy people into hard workers, but to create an environment in which hardworking people would thrive and lazy ones quit.

ridiculous sums of money in the process do no good to a company's image. In some extreme cases, the numbers have been in excess of 200,000 dollars per week's work. Crediting them with six-day weeks, that is more per day than the average annual salary of many of their employees!

• Staying within legal and ethical boundaries, it is often worthwhile to consider designing compensation structures that help employees (and executives) get the most out of their compensation. In many cases, the costs to the organization remain the same, but due to tax rules the recipient's net outcome can be higher if parts of the pay are given as free telephone, insurance, medical benefits, company car, and so on. If such approaches do not incur much administration or additional costs, they are one way of showing the employees that the organization is genuinely concerned about their proceedings from working there.

Perhaps not falling squarely under the heading of compensation structures, one last issue worth mentioning relates to the compensation of a company's owners. Regardless of whether a company is publicly traded and thus owned by shareholders or is not traded on stock exchanges and privately owned, the owners are obviously entitled to part of the profits the company makes. At least that is the ideal notion. The Commission on Public Trust and Private Enterprise claimed current executive compensation breaches the basic Capitalist logic, as opposed to earlier times when owner returns were the main problem. The Commission probably did not

One outrageous example of management getting away with too large a share of a company's profits was highly publicized in newspapers around the world after the pension deal of former ABB director Percy Barnevik became known. After the merger of the Swedish engineering company Asea with the Swiss Brown Boveri, ABB rose to become an engineering giant across the globe. After the rise of ABB, Barnevik had been viewed as one of the "kings" of Swedish industry, and a firm believer in ethical standards in business.

Following an incident in which one of the largest paper manufacturers in the world, a Swedish company, awarded a massive severance pay deal to their retiring CEO, Barnevik voiced strong criticism of such practices. He even went so far as to formulate the "ten commandments" for global executives, and of these emphasized two especially: "walk the talk," that is, stand out as a good example, especially in saving costs, and "communicate, communicate, communicate." Both principles seemed to have been forgotten when his own personal pension scheme was being negotiated, along with that of his colleague Göran Lindahl, who held a position as special advisor to UN Secretary General Kofi Annan in issues such as ethics, morals, and corporate social responsibility. Barnevik's pension deal secured him close to one billion Swedish kroner, about $100 million, paid in cash. At the time, ABB was, and still is, struggling with huge liabilities over the use of asbestos in the United States and a general downturn in revenues and profits.

The deal has sparked wide and massive criticism in Sweden and internationally. Old supporters condemn the deal and claim it damages the general reputation of business managers and ABB in particular. The Swiss lawyer Hans-Jacob Heitz has filed a claim against the two former ABB executives for fraud, the board of ABB filed a complaint to the Swiss tax authorities after Barnevik avoided Swiss taxes on the payment, and ABB employees around the world protest heavily against the deal. Suffice it to say, this level of personal greed has firmly dethroned Barnevik from his former position and left ABB a different company.

mean to say that the problem of too greedy owners is a thing of the past, though. There are still a large number of companies where the boards award the owners much higher returns than what is financially sound.

The shipyard example (see sidebar) is not a singular case. Owners taking out too high returns compared with the shares of profits other stakeholders get is a common problem. For an ethical organization, this is of

A relatively small, family-owned shipyard was for many years successful in winning prestigious contracts, culminating with a very large one for a major vessel. The project was huge, and the yard had to involve hundreds of local subcontractors to manage the job. For a couple of years, the local community enjoyed a bonanza of work and easy contracts. However, toward the end of the project, the yard ran into various types of trouble: excess overtime to complete the ship on schedule cost a lot and dug into the projected profits of the contract, the state withheld agreed subsidies due to various legal disagreements, and the owners of the vessel withheld payment in lieu of the yard properly completing the project.

As finding a solution to the various difficulties dragged on, the yard eventually ran into serious financial problems and was on the brink of bankruptcy. Negotiations with the bank and other creditors were initiated and the company was saved in the eleventh hour by the willingness of subcontractors to reduce or even forego their financial claims and the employees agreeing to reduced pay. Following the additional costs in legal and consulting fees and all the management attention the resolution of the crisis required, the yard is currently without any contracts and all employees have been temporarily laid off.

The head of the family that owns the yard and a couple of other enterprises had also been the CEO of the yard during the last few years. Having been very successful in turning the company around and winning a series of good contracts, she had originally been hailed as some kind of guru. The yard being located in a typical rural community, she had been quoted as being much more concerned about providing jobs for all the yard's employees than her own personal ambitions. Still, recent revelations have shown that even at the time toward the end of the huge contract when the financial outlook was direst, she awarded herself dividends and personal loans in the range of several million dollars. In the wake of the near-bankruptcy, several other companies in the area have either gone bankrupt from foregone payment from the yard or have ended up in serious trouble. Many of these are now outraged and feel they were victims of the CEO's personal greed.

course not acceptable. Rather, far more stringent criteria should be met when determining owner dividends:

• Never award owners dividends that eat into the company's equity capital, as this will weaken the company's position and come across as eating the cake before it is even made.

• Bankruptcy laws vary considerably from country to country, but in many cases (as in the shipyard example) owners are legally able to take out dividends of such a magnitude that creditors or employees cannot be fully compensated. Such behavior is extremely egotistical and completely unacceptable. Returns should only be awarded when the financial state of the company allows it.

• Even in cases where a company is financially sound and making profits, there is of course no automatic rule that all or most of the profits should be given to the owners as dividends. Profits made in good times are the lifeline that might be needed simply to stay afloat in bad times. Thus, dividends should be calculated from a perspective of building a solid equity before sharing the profits.

• As the Commission on Public Trust and Private Enterprise pointed out, there are several stakeholders that share a company's profits, including owners, management, employees, tax authorities, and so on. At least in the case of the former three, they all have a legitimate claim to part of the profits they have helped generate. Achieving a fair distribution of these profits, taking into account risk assumed, efforts invested, performance of tasks, and so on, should be a key concern.

Access to Information and Decision-Making Power

This is not necessarily the easiest area in which to convert policy into practice, in fact it is probably an area of organizational life where it is much easier to develop nice-sounding policies than living according to them. Still, that is no excuse for not trying. Basically, there are two aspects under this subheading to consider:

- Implementing ways to actively distribute and allow passive availability of any information that is seen safe to open up for the employees of the organization.

- Implementing ways to involve employees actively in decision making.

Arguably, these are two sides of the same coin. The more information is available to employees, the better equipped they are to participate in discussions and decisions, and vice versa.

Starting with access to information, this is probably the easier of the two. In this age of IT systems capturing any transaction inside an organization, the problem is rarely a lack of information, but some means of knowing what is relevant or not. Thus, some sort of filtering is required, it is no good simply opening the floodgates and unleashing massive databases onto the organization. As there is no way to provide you with a recipe for a successful practice of internal communication and information sharing, a few issues that you should consider when developing or refining current practices are:

• Segregate information into three main groups; information people need to perform their jobs, information that people might want access to but is not vital in the execution of their tasks, and information that should be restricted (the latter based on a better motivation than simply convenience). As different people inside the organization need or should have access to different types of information, this classification cannot be general for all employees, but will probably have to be made for various groups.

• Follow up this classification by making a crucial distinction among the groups of information in terms of how it is made available. Necessary information should be "pushed" to the employee and be readily available at their fingertips. Information which the employee has a right to access, but is not considered a necessity or used frequently should be "pulled" by the employee, that is, available but only by actively collecting it. Information deemed restricted should be handled accordingly, but be prepared to give a rational explanation why it is being kept "secret." The "push" and "pull" principles are extremely important. Lack of important information cannot be allowed to slow down the execution of tasks, but equally important is the point that information overload cannot be allowed to hamper people's work. Trying to stay abreast of all the information in papers, reports, e-mails, and so on, being loaded onto people is one cause of stress and burnout. The organization has a responsibility to filter information and relieve the individual of the job.

• Remember that the information needs of the organization are dynamic; you cannot decide once and for all what information is necessary, nice to have, or restricted. Especially in cases where changes are under way, be they reorganizing, downsizing, new market opportunities, new technologies being developed, and so on, the information "thirst" grows. These situations can be compared with the meteorological situation of a low-pressure system. The pressure inside the system being lower than its surroundings, the system sucks air into it, creating winds and turmoil. In an organization poised for change, where management fails to feed it with sufficient amounts of pertinent information, the situation takes on the low-pressure system capability of sucking in information, replacing facts with gossip and speculation. Allowed to continue, such a situation can easily get out of hand. Up-front information is the only way to counter it.

• Depending on the size of the organization, the nature of information systems in place, and so on, the ways in which information sharing and distribution is implemented can vary immensely in practice. There is no point in delving into the different technologies available, but keep in mind that people can be kept informed in a lot of different ways. Many organizations tend to try and "standardize" the information flow and confine it either to an intranet system, e-mail, or even paper reports. While having to relate to only one or a few sources of information can be positive and reduce confusion, it can be naïve to think that such standardization is possible to achieve in reality. Some types of information must be communicated personally, some is dependent on speed and might best be conveyed through e-mails, some is of a formal nature and requires a letter format, and so on. The general advice is to be flexible about the information carriers.

• So far, information has been referred to as if it is something you can precisely "measure" and portion out as you like. Perhaps the most extensive information system of them all in an organization is the informal system, that is, people talking to people, across departmental and hierarchical boundaries; word-of-mouth and rumor-spreading; coffee break discussions, and so on. One of the most important assets of an organization is people taking an interest in the organization, eager to learn what is going on, and applying what they learn to serve customers and other stakeholders. The informal information system is vital in this respect and trying to curb or contain it is a huge mistake. A networked organization where information flows from node to node is much more flexible and competitive than a strictly hierarchical one where information follows lines of authority. Thus, encourage this system.

The positive side effect of people being well informed about their organization, its affairs, and its challenges is that they are in a position where they can make qualified decisions. An organization is in fact nothing but a multitude of decisions being made every single day. Some are minute and of less consequence, others are monumental, and most of them are important in that they make up the collective effort of the organization in satisfying all of its stakeholders. Claiming that management should make decisions and the regular employees execute them is senseless and impossible; every person makes decisions all the time. The quality of these decisions improves with the level of knowledge and information. And the more that decisions can be left to people at the level where the need for the decision arises and the insight into its consequences are the highest, people at every level of the organization are allowed to make decisions that they are qualified for and paid to do. Time is saved in not having to send issues requiring a decision up and down the formal lines of communication, and

Table 4.1 Comparison of centralized and decentralized organizations.

Characteristic	Emphasis	
	Decentralized Organization	Centralized Organization
Hierarchy of authority	Decentralized	Centralized
Flexibility	High	Low
Adaptability	High	Low
Problem recognition	High	Low
Implementation	Low	High
Dealing with changes in environmental complexity	Good	Poor
Rules and procedures	Few and informal	Many and formal
Division of labor	Ambiguous	Clear-cut
Span of control	Few employees	Many employees
Use of managerial techniques	Minimal	Extensive
Coordination and control	Informal and personal	Formal and impersonal

people usually grow with the responsibility for making their own decisions. Thus, the availability of information and knowledge is inexorably linked to empowerment and decentralized decision making.

The distinction between centralized and decentralized organizations is probably the main one in this context. There are of course many variants and degrees in between the two extremes of a completely centralized and completely decentralized organization, but some typical traits of the two are listed in Table 4.1 (Ferrell, Fraedrich, and Ferrell, 2000).

In terms of ethical aspects of organizational design and the degree of centralization, centralized organizations display some inherent potential problems. These include attempts at blame shifting, lack of understanding of how unethical behavior impacts the larger whole of the organization, and lack of information flow upward in the hierarchy. In the latter case, this was seen in the Exxon Valdez oil spill in Alaska, where it took more than four days before Exxon executives had full insight into the extent of the disaster.

As with approaches to and systems for information sharing and communication, decision-making principles of an organization are a complex and multi-faceted issue to which entire books have been devoted. As far as they relate to a book on business ethics, these principles should contain a number of important aspects, some of which are:

• Allow decisions to be made at the lowest level of the organization that possesses the necessary overview, knowledge, and authority to do so. All people run their own lives and make major decisions regarding acquisition of homes, cars, marital choices, upbringing of children, and so on, why should they not be trusted to make decisions at work?

• In important issues, where decisions will impact the entire organization and its future, involve the broad masses of the organization in discussions leading up to the decision. This will both ensure that all of the knowledge and insight of the organization is utilized to shed light on the situation, and create better odds that people will stand by the decision and be loyal to it once it has been made.

• Be sure to make the distinction between everyday decisions that can be made at lower levels of the organization, major decisions that should be broadly debated before being settled, and regular management decisions that must be made by management at various levels without involving a huge apparatus of democracy before deciding. There are examples of organizations where the principles of empowerment and democracy have been pushed so far that they have become virtually incapable of making decisions, which is of course not the purpose. In one improvement project I was involved in a few years ago, purchases exceeding $100.00 had to be signed at three organizational levels, a practice that made life very difficult for people trying to do their jobs and one that almost stifled the entire capacity for management within middle management.

• Put in place systems or practices that capture ideas and opinions from the employees. After Mintzberg (1987) pioneered studies into strategic planning showing how bottom-up emergent strategies very often prevail over top-down decided strategies, several studies have demonstrated that perhaps as much as 85 percent of strategic choices, new ideas, and innovations indeed "bubble up" from the organization. Chances are, however, that this is not the result of "suggestion mailboxes" scattered around the organization's facilities. Rather, a culture of taking seriously any idea, suggestion, even complaint, from any person in the organization must be developed over time and consistently practiced. Communication channels must be open, and preferably some kind of incentive system for capturing good ideas to promote creativity and a culture of innovation should be in place. In this area, there are even some distinct geographical differences in approach that can offer inspiration. Japanese companies, at the advent of the *total quality management* movement, became renowned for their ways of involving all employees in continuous improvement work and problem-solving through quality circles and other types of improvement teams. Many of these ideas have since also proven to work well in the United States and Europe. The worshiping in the U.S. of the "lone ranger" or hero making it big through hard work and genius has fostered a culture where achieving personal success is perfectly legitimate and looked up to. This induces people to work hard, follow their ambitions, and often end up building great new products or companies. While personal success is perhaps more envied and frowned upon in many European countries than in the United States, these countries often have century-long traditions of strong farming or fishing communities. Farmers and fishers are their own bosses, used to hard work and getting by under tough conditions. While both farmers and fishers are all but disappearing, some of their spirit still lives on and, although now members of large organizations, these people still display ingenuity, stamina, and personal initiative that benefits their employers.

Respect for Laws and Regulations

In a book about business ethics, laws and regulations are arguably an important topic, one that pertains to many more aspects of an organization than just human resource management practices. Thus, laws and regulations will surely be recurring topics throughout the book. Still, human resource management is a highly pertinent topic under which to raise the issue first. Laws and regulations apply both to how the organization deals with relevant rules in the human resource management area and how to motivate employees to develop a general respect for and adherence to laws and regulations.

The first issue, making sure that the organization adheres to relevant laws, regulations, rules, agreements, and so on, that apply to the area of human resource management is by far the easiest one of the two. Although many countries have extensive sets of rules governing work life, these are, generally speaking, "logical" in the sense that they are based on common sense and regulate obvious issues like working hours, employment contracts, working conditions, pensions, and so on. Many of these are overseen by a human resource manager or department; others fall naturally within the responsibilities of line managers throughout the organization. Ensuring that breaches are avoided is more or less a matter of sorting out responsibilities and implementing routines where required. There certainly are many breaches of these laws and regulations in industry, but not because avoiding them is particularly difficult—rather because many organizations take these issues lightly.

There are certainly other areas within work life law that are more complicated, for example, sexual or other types of harassment, equal rights, or unfair terminations, especially in countries where a tradition of "opportunistic lawsuits" has developed, such as the United States. These are areas where the text of the law is ambiguous, and precedent and judgments made by juries dictate what constitutes a breach and what is acceptable. This makes it difficult to advise how to avoid any trouble, but many of these issues have already been dealt with in other sections of this chapter.

The second law-related issue, general adherence of the organization and its employees to laws and regulations that are relevant, is a slightly different matter. Relevant in this case means any type of legislation that applies to the organization's operations and deliveries, be they product safety laws, accounting rules, maintenance standards, even speed limits if applicable. Every single employee of an organization has the "power" to commit breaches of a large number of different rules and regulations, every single day. In some cases, this is personally motivated, for example, making the job easier, getting things done quicker, getting a little extra out of a deal personally. More often, such conduct is motivated by a wish to make the organization come out ahead in one way or another, either through lower costs, higher sales, better productivity, and so on.

This being the case, it seems quite clear that the problem, to the extent that this can be defined as a singular problem, is not a general lack of morals on the part of the organization's members. Since most breaches are committed on behalf of the organization, the causes must be found in the incentives and messages provided by the organization. These can be of various types: continuing to cut corners the way it has always been done to save time or money, "leading by example" by showing that management personnel take laws lightly, looking the other way when rules are stretched, or setting such strict performance demands that they can in practice only be met by bending a rule or two. How do you handle such concealed messages?

First of all, no matter how hard legislators strive to make their laws and rules crystal clear, there will always be room for interpretation (why would there be lawyers otherwise?). Some behavior will invariably fall into a gray area, being either generally perceived as acceptable behavior, being tangential to existing laws but not crossing the line, or being over the line but having very small consequences. If an organization fanatically tried to eradicate any behavior from any member of the organization that either crosses the line or is in danger of doing so, that organization would be a strange and not very appealing place to work. Some sound judgment is required, which is exactly the case for ethical guidelines presented in chapter 4.

This is no coincidence: when push comes to shove, ethical guidelines of some sort are about the only way to tackle the question of adherence to laws and regulations on a broad scale. And as discussed, ethical guidelines of a specific nature are required, not the "biblical" ones that simply tell you to be good. Regarding laws and regulations and their mention in ethical guidelines, some steps are:

1. Deciding on a general level of "compliance expectation"; that is, agreeing whether a zero-tolerance approach is preferred or a somewhat more relaxed position. Relaxed in this sense certainly does not mean condoning illegal behavior, but not being fanatical in areas where rules and precedence are not crystal clear.

2. Reviewing assumed relevant legislation and sorting these into a few categories, for example irrelevant (no need to dig deeper into), marginally relevant (must have passive knowledge about), relevant (must have active knowledge about), and highly relevant (crucial to the organization, and specific procedures should be developed).

3. Develop appropriate routines for education and compliance in each category. For the marginally relevant, it is sufficient that one or a few persons gain passive insight into the rules and thus know how to relate to them. For the relevant category, the organization must ensure that those persons affected by it receive the information and training required to stay within bounds, and someone must be responsible for monitoring the area for any changes in rules or practices. For the highly relevant category, instructions should be developed detailing how affected employees should act in general and in specific situations.

Beyond this, the treatment of ethical codes of conduct and compliance with laws and regulations have very much in common, thus going back to "The Boring Part: Ethical Guidelines," page 90, can be a good idea.

One striking example of how employees break laws on behalf of the company they work for and not out of personal profit can be found in the grocery industry. Although this specific case is taken from a chain with national coverage in one country, it is a more general problem. In this case, the government health authorities first found some irregularities in one of the chain's stores. Within a few weeks in the fall of 2002, a number of instances were found in which the employees in several of the chain's stores had tampered with food in different ways:

• When the expiration date of various types of meat had expired, the meat was taken out of the sales displays. Instead of being destroyed, as is of course the proper procedure, the meat was instead used by the stores for producing various types of premade meals, for example, casseroles or stews, and sold afterward.

continued

continued

- After expiration dates had been exceeded on various types of goods, employees in the stores had deliberately repackaged the products, thus extending the expiration date, and continued selling the goods.

- In various storage facilities in the stores, products past their sell-by date were still stored. This in itself is an offense; worse is the fact that they were probably intended for the same treatment as described above.

These breaches were discovered one after another, in more and more stores, as the authorities intensified their inspections following the first offenses. As new findings were made, they were published in the media as part of the authorities' policy for exposing such behavior. To make matters worse for the company, this was the chain of stores that had most ardently profiled itself as premium food stores, having an extensive range of fresh foods of high quality. Needless to say, this seriously impacted customers' perceptions of the company's 140 stores.

As matters further unfolded, it became quite clear that the decisions taken to cheat this way were made at the individual employee and store level. To what extent they acted in accordance with some unspoken or even spoken rules originating from higher levels in the company is impossible to know. Some stores have been thrown out of the chain in the aftermath of the problems. Following the revelations, the company also hired external consultancy assistance to revise procedures and implement new ones to avoid similar incidents in the future. Among others, these include clear routines for dealing with health authority regulations.

Competence and Career Development

Under this heading, areas such as knowledge management, competence management, and the like come into play, and there is no intention of covering them in detail in this book. Their relevance in a business ethics text stem from the fact that a fair good citizen organization should facilitate competence and career development for its employees in a way that allows them to take full advantage of their potential and constantly evolve on a professional and personal basis. Another fact, that this also makes good business sense, is not an insignificant side effect.

Establishing clear and alternative career paths, allowing employees to educate themselves further, either through schools/courses or practical experience, and ensuring that people can pursue their interests and ambitions inside the organization have been proven many times to pay off. These methods avoid having people leave the organization from being denied opportunities to develop and grow, constantly add new knowledge and skills to the organization, and keep people motivated to do their best in return for promotions and new challenges. In a study conducted by Hayes and Wheelwright at the peak of the industrial thrashing of American manufacturing by its competitors (1984), different approaches in manufacturing industries were compared among the United States, Germany, and Japan.

One important finding pertained to dramatic differences in recruitment and development of managers. American companies had by then come to believe firmly in "professional management" exerted by generalists, often with a financial or legal background, moving from company to company, and industry to industry. German companies were found to have managers who had worked their way upward through various positions inside the company, most of them with an engineering background, but also with skills and education in management subjects. The result was that German managers knew the organization, its people, its products, and its processes, and could relate to these to a much greater extent. Running a business always involves some kind of risk (if not, there would probably not be an upside), risk that cannot be eliminated, only replaced by another type of risk. Human beings are predictable in that they choose to live with the kind of risk they are familiar with and can assess in some way. Thus, economists will generally prefer to run a company in a way that exposes it to risk stemming from currency fluctuations, rate changes, tax issues, and so on, instead of technological risk. Marketing people will prefer market- and product-related risk, whereas lawyers will probably feel most at home with risk stemming from mergers and acquisitions or other legal issues. German managers, having been "brought up" through the technical departments of their companies, preferred technological risk, and accordingly demonstrated a much higher willingness to take risk related to the development of new processes and products that would be the basis for future revenues.

Some of the same findings were discovered in Japanese companies, but Hayes and Wheelwright also focused on the "lifetime perspective" of many Japanese organizations. This practice is not as entrenched anymore as it was, but by viewing human resources as assets that are expensive to hire, train, and hone to perfection, they were perceived differently than in the typical American company at the time. Maintenance of people was just as important as maintenance of machines and other equipment, which is a concept that is still highly valid. Maslach, the best-known researcher in the field of professional burnout, claims that burnout is a consequence of organizations blatantly neglecting to apply the same principles of regular preventive maintenance to their people as they do to their "precious" machines. Developing the skills of the employees through career and competence development is at the heart of such human maintenance.

Given that the organization truly believes in this tenet, how do you go about putting this sound principle into practice? Reciting extensively from works on competence and knowledge management is barely fruitful, but some practical approaches include:

• Implementing a system for structured assessment of the skills and capabilities of each and every employee of the organization. There are many good assessment tools of this type available.

• Systematically making use of such data in deciding on job selection, promotions, training needs, and so on. This is probably the hard part—many organizations have invested heavily in huge database solutions through which competence searches can be made and people selected for teams, projects, new jobs, and so on. While there certainly are good examples where these work, there are probably equally many where little value is gained from such systems. With evolving data mining and database technology, this will improve, though.

• Acknowledge that training and competence development is a form of maintenance and an investment that, although often hard to measure the return on, is the only way to secure the organization's future. Business environments, technology, products, market preferences—everything changes continuously—and an organization that does not upgrade its skills accordingly will no doubt fall behind.

• Establish clear career paths inside the organization, but not only one path for each type of employee. The best organizations manage to create network organizations where different career paths result in a web of skills tied together by experience in many areas of the organization and personal relationships criss-crossing the organizational chart.

• Through employee conferences, performance assessments, and a well-developed system for internal recruitment to vacancies, ensure that training needs are systematically mapped and filled through internal or external courses or other types of training.

Concern for the 24-Hour Employee

This is, quite suitably, the last issue under human resource management practices. While not really being part of the traditional concerns and obligations of an organization toward its employees, the field of human resource management has gradually adopted a more holistic view of employees. To make employees productive, high-performing assets to an organization, they need to be complete and content persons. If work requires so much of them that there is no time for a family life, they will not be content. Vice versa, if employees frequently injure themselves during leisure pursuits, this also affects the employer. Thus, the prevailing modern view is that an organization has a right and an obligation to take an interest in people outside the time they spend at work, often termed the *24-hour employee* approach.

Some elements of this approach have already been explored. Providing work conditions and workloads that allow people to actually have a life outside work is certainly an important element in this. Other approaches that have been successful in many cases include:

• *Encouraging, enabling, or even providing means for physical exercise.* It is well documented that people in good health and form perform better at work, have higher quality of life outside work, and are less susceptible to sickness. When investigating why many people never exercise or exercise much less than they should, despite these known benefits, researchers have found lack of time and lack of easy access to suitable facilities to be important causes. In companies where the employer actively organizes fitness activities during work hours, estimates are that the time and money invested yield a high rate of return. This is completely in line with the ideals of a good citizen organization and is at the same time probably a profitable investment. Even if the organization does not actively organize various types of exercise sessions, negotiating good deals with health clubs and other sports groups can help a lot.

• *Promoting a focus on safety.* The reasons why employees are involuntary absent from work fall mainly into the two categories of sickness and injuries. Statistics clearly show that most personal accidents occur outside of work, either in the home or in traffic. This is not surprising, as workplaces are quite strongly regulated and subject to authority inspections, and their safety handled by professionals. At home, people do all sorts of activities according to their own safety standards, including working with power tools, chemicals, ladders, and so on. A few years ago, I helped a steel plant undertaking a benchmarking study in the area of safety. One of their benchmarking partners had achieved dramatic reductions in absenteeism levels over a couple of years and claimed that most of this was due to their efforts in educating their employees in safe work and developing a safety culture. This way, they had maintained their low injury statistics at work, but also removed close to 60 percent of absenteeism stemming from injuries outside of working hours. Their approach included both general training in how to make activities safer and keeping a very visible scorecard of injuries and dangerous incidents. A similar approach is certainly a worthwhile initiative for any organization trying to develop an ethical approach; it shows employees that the employer cares about them, it can help employees avoid accidents that cause pain and expenses, and it pays off in terms of reduced absenteeism.

 • *Identify potential burnout cases before they happen.* When we dealt with the topic of burnout, it was explained how the state of being burnt out comes after a long process of burning out, which can often take months or even years, see Figure 4.6, page 120. A typical symptom of this process is that the individual undergoing it displays some signs of the process being under way long before it culminates in the condition of burnout. Some are able to keep it together and keep these signs hidden at work but not at home, others the other way around. Further, stress often leads to true burnout when compounded by difficulties in the personal sphere. In any case, a key element in identifying that someone is on the road to burnout and thus reversing the process before it gets there is being able to read these signs. This of course requires that managers and colleagues know what the typical signs are, but it also requires them to know the person in question well enough to spot a change in behavior. For a manager to know their subordinates this well has some implications for organizational structure and control span, but equally for organizational culture and what it is concerned with. A "cold" (apathetic or uncaring) organizational culture (see Figure 4.2), where managers and colleagues in general care little about the organization's individual members is in a poor position regarding spotting such signs. Under the caring or integrative organizational culture, you as a manager should know "your" people well enough that you know how they behave when in good shape and know what is happening in their personal lives.

Through this rather extensive section, I have attempted to put some flesh on the bones of the human resource management policies outlined in chapter 3. Mind you, this is not a textbook on HR management, and thus what has been presented are practices that tie in with the ethics aspect of this area. For a more extensive treatment of the topic in general, you will have to consult other sources. Please also try to appreciate the need for positive, caring HR policies and practices not only in times with an oversupply of workers, but also when employment is scarce. There are many examples of organizations that added various benefits to attract and keep people in times of low unemployment, only to revoke them when unemployment figures increase. This is both an ethically questionable approach and a practice that is bound to backfire at some point as good workers will shy away from the organization, both in better and poorer times.

Let us move on to the last element of an internal, operational setting: cost consciousness.

Many organizations realize that their employees can get hungry outside of the open hours of the in-house canteen (if indeed there is one). To address this, it is very common to find vending machines selling chocolate bars, chips, crackers, and so on, in the hallways of companies. As a snack, such food is probably the worst you can find health-wise; it's fatty, provides empty calories, and does not help clear a weary head or body. Some employers are changing their practice and are taking advantage of a recent offer that has become quite popular: having baskets of fresh fruit delivered to the organization every Monday morning. Fruit is much healthier than prepackaged snacks, both in terms of calorie and fat intake, and boosting energy.

NOBODY LIKES A SNOB—BEING COST CONSCIOUS

Assuming you are not one of those who have made a fortune from being an executive manager (and if you are, all the more reason to keep on reading this): how do you feel when you read the story about the CEO of the manufacturer of the last item you bought with your hard-earned money that shows her or him boarding a private jet to set off somewhere exotic for the weekend? Or when you make a complaint about the problems with the product you bought and the store where you bought it puts up a fierce fight to avoid having to replace it or repair it, only to see the store manager cruising up to the classiest country club in the area in his new Mercedes the day after? What about struggling hard to scrape together enough money to pay the electricity bill during the winter, almost believing the utility company's explanation of why prices are so high this year, only to see them build a lavish new headquarters the following summer?

Several similar examples could be listed, but no matter the shape or form extravagance takes on the part of organizations you are dealing with, it leaves you with a bitter taste in your mouth. There is no way helping the feeling that you either paid too much, were given a poorer product than they could have produced, or simply were taken by the nose. As any skilled marketing person will tell you, a purchase can be seen as consisting of three phases, see Figure 4.7.

Any "purchase," be it of products, services, shares, even donations, is initiated by some kind of prepurchase assessment where alternatives are considered and compared, costs are evaluated against the means available, and so on. Ultimately, this assessment culminates in a decision not to buy

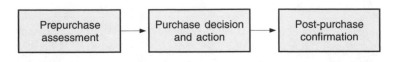

Figure 4.7   The phases of a purchase process.

or to buy, and the actual purchase is performed. However, the process does not end with that. Every "purchase" is an action that involves placing your trust in the seller, giving away money for something in return, and then gaining what effect was sought from the purchase, either momentarily or for a long time afterward, depending on the object being purchased. It is a psychological fact that for some time after having made the purchase, we perform a kind of post-decision assessment of the purchase: "Did the service provide what we wanted? Does the product work as it should? Did we pay too much? Is perhaps the other alternative we considered better looking after all? How do other people who made the same decision feel about their purchase?" What we are really looking for is a confirmation that we made the right choice, that the object procured is of good quality, the supplier a reliable one, that the price was right, hopefully even a bargain, and so on. In the cases where we get this confirmation, we feel good and at peace with the purchase. Such confirmation can come from hearing that other people are satisfied with the same choice, reading favorable reviews of the product or service, seeing the same object advertised at a higher price than we paid, or otherwise having our perception of the supplier confirmed as positive. Receiving such confirmation, we are prone to becoming repeat customers (customer being a buyer of products, services, or shares), a luxury every company hopes for.

Lack of such confirmation or, even worse, confirmation that we made the wrong choice, leads to the other extreme situation; that we become ex-customers—ex-customers that are likely to talk negatively about the supplier, one of the worst "enemies" a company can have. This type of negative confirmation comes from experiencing that the product we bought functions poorly, hearing our neighbor complaining about the service delivered, finding that the same product is later offered for sale at 50 percent off, or feeling that we paid too much—so much that the supplier and its managers and employees live the big life on our money. There are many things an organization can and should do to avoid producing this negative confirmation and maximize the likelihood of producing repeat customers, much more than being cost conscious, and many of these will be revisited in other chapters, especially those dealing with external dimensions of the business ethics framework. Nevertheless, avoiding giving the image that products or services are priced so dearly that enormous profits are made and all kinds of luxuries are afforded is one sound approach.

This is no purely black and white picture, though. There is a line, or perhaps more a vague zone, between the concepts of ascetic, "sound," and lavish:

• Being ascetic means an organization that is really stingy and tight with its expenditures, to the extent that it probably bothers and frustrates both its employees and external stakeholders. Going this far means taking a basically positive cost consciousness too far and turning it into something negative. Of course an organization can maintain an ethical and caring profile and still allow itself to have comfortable and performing facilities, benefits for its employees, and other aspects that cost money but probably also represent profitable investments.

• Going to the other extreme and being lavish crosses a different line/zone and moves into an area where money is wasted on luxuries no organization really needs, for example, pricey designer furniture, champagne-stocked limousines, or $100,000 country club memberships. While it most certainly is enjoyable for those who benefit from the luxury, it is both likely to upset external stakeholders and a waste of money that probably will be needed some day when economic cycles have turned and business is slow.

• "Sound," then, is a not-well-defined middle course where both an ascetic and lavish "lifestyle" is avoided. Being too stingy can be just as bad as too lavish. A nice and decent office or other facility can help give a solid impression of a quality organization, but there is a line that should not be crossed into a style that "ticks people off. " What falls within the sound category and what does not will typically vary, both from industry to industry and country to country, not to mention over time. Perhaps the most telling test is whether an expenditure in any way, directly or indirectly, contributes to creating value for the organization's external stakeholders—if not, it can most likely be defined as unnecessary and over the line into lavish. Instead of trying to outline what constitutes the sound category, it is probably easier to give examples of what falls within the other two, most importantly the lavish category. From experience, very few organizations are bordering on ascetic; the vast majority that risk straying from the sound middle course are on the verge of becoming lavish.

The question is, what represents spending that might upset stakeholders and risk turning them into ex-customers? Three examples that capture the essence of the lavish style are related in the following sidebar.

A mid-sized engineering firm called Professional Engineering developed gradually over the years into a successful, competent company designing and building complex industrial facilities and infrastructure. Its management being dominated by people who had climbed through the ranks of the organization, its operations were marked by a culture of earn-before-spend and a general risk aversion that made it a solid unit. Following the bold move of hiring an outside lawyer as the new CEO of the company, its profile changed significantly. The new CEO threw Professional Engineering into a series of acquisitions and high-profile risky projects. For a while, things looked quite good; money was made, a new headquarters erected, even a mansion was built to house the CEO. Nothing was spared in the design of the mansion, using a large number of in-house engineers to work on various innovative solutions and decorators to give it the highest sheen of class. It was rumored that the drapes of the master bedroom alone cost $200,000, drapes that were ruined after three months while being cleaned and immediately replaced by the exact same type. Needless to say, the story goes as you can expect: the formerly cautious and somewhat dull company presented a completely different image to the world, shareholders jumped ship, customers looking for a solid engineering firm to undertake huge projects avoided the company, and after a few years problems became dramatic. After reintroducing the former type of CEO, the company was saved and still exists, but it has never reclaimed its previous position.

When a small law firm was chosen to represent a small number of sufferers from cancer caused by exposure to asbestos when working on the manufacturing lines of a brake component manufacturer, the firm managed to settle the case against the manufacturer at a record compensation level. Taking 30 percent off the settlement value as attorney's fees, the firm and its partners made a gigantic profit. This money was used to acquire top-of-the-line yachts, cars, and so on, even a company jet airplane, some paid for with cash, some with borrowed money. As business slowed (partly due to the new "toys" taking more and more of the partners' time) and the operating and maintenance costs materialized on the budget, the financial situation became difficult. Associates who had enjoyed stable and secure jobs for many years had to be let go, and finally the firm ended its existence in a nasty bankruptcy.

continued

continued

A French consulting firm was tendering a bid for a large contract with a multinational company to reorganize a large Paris branch of the company, a prestigious contract with a nice profit to be made. Among the other contenders were all of the big global consultancy companies, but they were trailing the French company since the multinational had expressed skepticism about these players. Knowing this, the local consulting firm had made a selling point out of their low operational costs and level-headedness with projects. After having completed a successful first round of negotiations with the potential customer, a few of the account managers were so excited, they booked an extended weekend in New York via the Concorde. Having the worst of luck, one of their customer's counterparts saw them boarding the flight at the airport and developed serious doubts as to whether the local firm was any different from their infamous large competitors. In the end, the contract was awarded to a different, smaller French firm.

The examples in the sidebar may not be entirely representative; to some extent they are rather extreme and to some extent they are marked by one-off incidents as opposed to a general problem. They do, however, illustrate how extravagant inklings can lead to negative repercussions. Keeping in mind that what is acceptable or not varies highly from setting to setting, the following are some areas and practices that hold potential to be construed as over the top and irritating to different stakeholders:

• *Facilities and fixed infrastructure.* Practically every organization needs some kind of physical facilities and/or infrastructure, typically offices, manufacturing facilities, service provision sites, and so on. The invisible line is crossed when these are of a size or standard that is significantly larger or higher than averages in the industry or region. Erecting glass-and-marble towers when competitors make do with standard office buildings can be seen as a statement that "we make more money than we can possibly spend on useful things." By standard, I mean aspects like interior design, materials used, furniture, art, and so on. These things are nice to afford and have, but should be on a reasonable scale. In terms of size, any facilities that do not contribute to the organization's core activities are suspect, for example, company cabins on the coast or close to the skiing slopes, great ballrooms, mansions for managers, and so on.

• *Equipment.* Equipment in a broad sense, perhaps not so much actual production equipment for products or services, but more along the lines of computers, cellular phones, PDAs, and so on, typically electronic equipment that comes in a wide variety of price ranges. Most such equipment is characterized by ever-evolving technology, constant introduction of new versions or product types, high prices for the latest features, and the fact that much simpler types will do just fine for the vast majority of people. Equipping managers or employees with expensive gadgets of this sort makes the statement that the organization has been able to elicit more money from their customers than is strictly required to keep the wheels turning.

• *Transportation means and travel.* Many organizations own different types of transportation means, that is, cars, buses, even airplanes, and most organizations conduct business in a way that necessitates travel for many different groups of employees. Common to all of these aspects is that vehicles and travel can vary extensively in style and cost. The range is enormous, from beaten-up fifteen-year-old cars to brand new limousines, from second-class train journeys to executive-class transcontinental flights, the latter typically costing tens of times more than the former alternative. Sometimes the higher price means better performance, performance that can be important in the value creation processes of the organization, but often it is merely a matter of comfort and style. Granted, a person traveling business class to an important meeting can probably argue the morning after that her or his performance at the meeting improved from getting more sleep than in coach, but the client who eventually pays the travel costs would perhaps not see the issue as clearly. Thus, some level of curtailment regarding style and cost of such means can be wise.

• *Representation.* Representation in this respect encompasses elements such as business dinners, participation at fairs and trade shows, internal or external seminars or conferences, and other types of hosting undertaken by the organization. These types of events are of course very common in most businesses; many decisions are made over a good meal and a nice bottle of wine, and future customers are attracted to the organization through the hosting of seminars. Again, it is not the existence of such things that may be considered over the top, but the level of expression. There is a huge difference between a $50 meal per person and a $500 one. An internal seminar can be held on company turf almost for free, at a nearby hotel or conference center for a reasonable price, or on a different continent at a high-class resort—the expenses adding up accordingly. In some cases, the $1000 dollar per person meal with a potential client can be what finally wins the contract (which raises the question whether this is due to the client's satisfaction with your offer on behalf of her or his organization or her or his own), whereas in others, it can be what confirms to the potential client that your organization is a big spender that acts irresponsibly and cannot be trusted with the contract. Thus, care should be exerted when deciding on these matters and their style and cost level.

• *Bonuses, incentives, and management and employee benefits.* The matter of executive and employee compensation levels has already been dealt with, arguing the need for striking a balance and trying to keep some pace with norms and industrial or regional averages. This is of course also an aspect that falls under cost consciousness, where extremely generous pay levels, stock options, compensation in the form of a company car, housing arrangements, interest-free loans, free access to company phone for personal use, free or significantly reduced tickets to sporting or cultural events, shorter working hours or more vacation time for normal pay levels, and other types of better-than-usual benefits can send undesired signals to stakeholders. As with any other expenditures that seem uncalled-for, such spending can be irritating to customers, shareholders, and others with an interest in the organization. Again, establish procedures that take into account these effects and the image such spending produces.

• *Personal style and appearance.* This area might be stretching it a little in terms of what an organization can dictate regarding their employees. However, there is no doubt that the personal appearance of representatives of an organization is part of the image it portrays and takes part in influencing stakeholders' perception of it. This of course applies to both "directions," that is, ascetic and lavish. Poorly dressed frontline personnel can be as damaging as employees showing off Armani suits, Rolex watches, or Gucci shoes. Where suitable, the organization can dress their most visible representatives in uniforms, where not, easy-to-follow dress codes can be implemented.

The area of personal appearance is one where it is obvious that how much you spend is meant to state a message. Certainly the same can be said about facilities, cars, travel habits, and so on. This is a main point under the cost consciousness heading; there is a huge difference between indulging a desire for a little luxury, but doing it "quietly", that is, not showing it off, and deliberately doing it to demonstrate wealth (topping this list of particularly unappealing behaviors is the concept of "see our beautiful home" stories in magazines where CEO and wife invite reporters to document their wealth to the world). The former will probably be forgiven by an annoyed stakeholder, but the latter is almost guaranteed to create frustration.

As should be clear by now, the question of cost consciousness is something of a double-edged sword. Too little or too much can be just as bad; in some cases it probably does not make much of a difference; and in some cases, spending that little extra (or even that much extra) can be the deciding factor in making a good impression, getting a contract, or attracting a particularly suitable candidate for a job. Thus, deciding what is sound and what is lavish for itself must be at the discretion of each organization, in any situation. The points above merely represent some areas where a lavish style can elicit negative responses from stakeholders.

IMPLEMENTATION SUMMARY

In implementing internal, remedial, and operational practices based on ethical principles, some advice follows:

• Develop ethical guidelines or a code of conduct, a code that of course should correspond with the policies developed for the various strategic areas of the business ethics framework. This is, as the development of an ethically founded organizational culture, a fairly complex task. Such ethical guidelines can easily become trivial, so general that they bear little consequence, or so detailed that they stifle activity in the organization. The task of developing these should be a combination of top-directed setting of premises and the utilization of local knowledge within different organizational areas to design more specific parts of the code.

• Implementing operational human resource practices is an extensive job that must push forward along a number of frontiers. These could span as diverse areas as improved physical and organizational work conditions, inside and outside the workplace; compensation structures; employees' access to information and decision-making power; law and regulation compliance; and career development. From the range of these areas, it is evident that there is no simple implementation approach that will work for all of them. For physical work conditions, basic problem-solving tools that span the phases of problem identification, analysis, and improvement will probably be quite helpful. Within the total quality management area, there is a large toolbox of such tools that would be helpful described in a number of different books, for example, *Juran's Quality Handbook* (Juran, 1999), *The Quality Improvement Handbook* (Bauer, Duffy, and Westcott, 2002), *Fundamental Concepts of Quality Improvement* (Hartman, 2002), *Quality Problem Solving* (Smith, 1998) or even my own *Business Process Improvement Toolbox* (Andersen, 1998). Typical tools you could consider are Pareto charts, check sheets, flowcharts, cause-and-effect charts, root cause analysis, process streamlining, force-field analysis, and so on, while for the other human resource practices it is difficult to suggest specific aids.

• Turning cost conscious is the last element of this chapter, and again not a uniform path that can be aided by specific tools. This is really a matter of scanning the organization and its operations for extravagancy or unnecessary spending and finding ways to reduce or eliminate any uncovered. This is a matter of being systematic in the search and creative in ways of improving things.

As a final note, many of the tools mentioned above, tools that have been developed over some time by quality management professionals, are very useful in any change or improvement effort. They span many purposes and are often very intuitive and easy to adapt, and are often also graphical in nature thus making it easy to understand mechanisms at play or see patterns. Acquainting yourself with a basic set of such tools will no doubt be an advantage on the road to an ethical organization.

Well, that completes the review of the menu of elements that you can keep in mind as areas for credible internal practices, which were organized under the headings of ethical guidelines, human resource management practices, and cost consciousness. The next chapter takes the first look so far at external issues when dealing with remedial, external, and strategic questions.

5

Setting Things Right with the Outside World: Developing a Remedial, External, and Strategic Profile

As the title implies, still being in the remedial sphere of the business ethics framework, this chapter deals with evening out any "damage" the organization might inflict on its surroundings and staying on the "straight and narrow" with regard to its external profile. Covering the strategic aspect of this, as a prelude to the operational approaches discussed in the next chapter, the focus here will be on higher-level decisions regarding business segment, products, and strategic business policies.

BUSINESS = WAR?

First of all, let us take a minute to reflect on the relationship between an organization and the outside world, its surroundings, and external stakeholders. If you try to review in your mind different kinds of management thinking and literature you have been exposed to over the years, what kinds of metaphors have been used to describe it? There are quite certainly more than one, for example a systems analysis approach, a cybernetics view on the world, and probably others, but the war analogy has prevailed. This ranges from consulting old war strategy sources, for example, the ever-popular *The Art of War* by Sun Tzu (1963) and *The Prince* by Niccolo Machiavelli (1532), to using war metaphors and language when portraying various concepts, for example, attack, defense, guerrilla warfare, and so on. This is prevalent in literature on strategy, marketing, contracts and negotiations, economics, and many other subjects taught to future managers.

From history lessons about former wars, endless movies depicting the horrors of war, and live coverage of recent conflicts in former Yugoslavia, Iraq, and elsewhere, I know enough about war to understand it is no attractive setting and one it would not be desirable to transfer to business life. Besides the gory side of casualties, maiming, and destruction, no matter how high we hold the principles of the Geneva convention of warfare, war is a situation plagued by distrust, aggression, disinformation, sneak attacks, the use of illegal weapons, atrocious treatment of prisoners, and so on. Although the war metaphor probably makes for better stories to be passed around the campfire, business is much more reliant on mutual trust, predictability in adherence to generally accepted rules, integrity, and human compassion. Covey (1999) encourages companies to examine the impact of trust on the bottom line and documents that when trust is low, organizations decay and relationships deteriorate, resulting in politics, infighting, and general inefficiency. As ethical compliance decreases, employee commitment to the organization falters, product quality declines, customers leave, and employee turnover skyrockets. The public's trust is essential for maintaining a good long-term relationship between a business and consumers. All of the "virtues" mentioned above are cornerstones of a working capitalistic system and are not traits that appear too often in wars. (Some are keen to portray war as a gentleman's undertaking marked by exactly these virtues, but these are rather unconvincing attempts at glorification.)

If a metaphor is needed to provide a framework for explaining various concepts of strategy and management, perhaps the game analogy is better. While games of various types involve many of the same "competitive" aspects as war, no one is physically injured or killed (usually at least). Games are competitive and end up declaring winners and losers, but are dependent on a common understanding and respect for the rules of the game. Cheating and unfair play ruin the game. Well-designed games stimulate competition that spur self-improvement toward better performance and excellence. Poorly designed games, as war, motivate competition whose aim is to harm or destroy the opponent and which more often than not ends up as a zero-sum game.

The game metaphor holds true for any view of business, but coincides particularly well with an ethical approach to business. To come across as a credible ethically founded organization, you must deal with the outside world and external stakeholders in a manner that instills trust and generates benefits for all parties. This does of course in no way imply that you are responsible for generating profits for your competitors, but it means treating them with respect. Being seen as a fair contestant improves the chances that customers will regard you positively. As for other stakeholders, for example, customers, suppliers, authorities, media, and so on, the general principle is that you get what you give. If doing business with your organization means a customer or a supplier comes away feeling a good deal has been made and value for money has been received, chances are it will be positive toward future deals as well.

There is even some mathematical proof that head-on competition is not always the best strategy. The Academy Award–winning motion picture *A Beautiful Mind* portrays the life of the genius and Nobel laureate John Nash. In 1950, Nash published the dissertation for which he later received the Nobel Prize in economics, in which the Nash equilibrium is presented. Nash proved that in so-called noncooperative games (where participants make no beforehand negotiations or arrangements) there exists an equilibrium point where the participants' strategy is optimized related to the other participants' strategies. The consequence of this is that instead of pursuing completely individual competitive strategies, all participants will benefit from finding this equilibrium point. (In the film, the principle is explained by means of an example set in a bar where four men are all attracted to the same entering lady—if they fight head-on for her, nobody will win.) The Nash equilibrium also represents support for a concept termed *co-opetition*, which will be referred to in chapter 10 about philanthropic business practices toward competitors. For now, let us close this brief reflection on business metaphors by giving my answer to the question posed in its heading: No, business does not equal war. Business can in many cases be viewed as a war for the sake of having a lingo to describe it, but an ethical approach to business comes from an intention of dealing with external stakeholders in an atmosphere of trust and mutual respect.

WHAT DO YOU DO FOR A LIVING? BUSINESS SECTORS WITH INHERENT ETHICAL ISSUES

Ethics is one of those volatile concepts that do not translate into clear boundaries between right and wrong. Rather, there is a huge gray area where tradition, norms, and personal interpretation decide what is acceptable and what is not. This also applies to business sectors and to what extent these are by definition unethical may hold some inherent issues that could be questioned, or may be perfectly acceptable. As such, it is obvious that any "sector" where the core "business idea" contradicts laws is unethical, for example, illegal drug trade, prostitution, forgery, and so on, "sectors" that quite frankly fall outside the scope of this book. It is equally clear that hairdressers, lamp manufacturers, or book printers are legal businesses that have no apparent ethical issues connected with them. However, there are a number of sectors in which there are to a smaller or greater extent inherent factors that make them susceptible to criticism or questioning, for example, arms manufacturing, the tobacco industry, even healthcare and the legal profession.

What consequence does the existence of sectors that for some reason or another fall within a gray area ethically speaking imply? If you happened to belong to one of these, would you have to get out of it, find a new sector, and start from scratch to be ethical? Of course not! It simply means that, opposed to sectors where there are no such apparent potential ethical issues, you need to have an active attitude toward the inherent issues of the sector. In fact, in many cases, due to the fact that there are well-known ethical factors within a sector, these sectors have a much more clarified ethical position than industries without such factors.

Before looking more closely at some sectors with such apparent issues, let us briefly look at some possible "sources" of such issues:

• *Products or services delivered.* An obvious reason why some sectors score highly on the scale of questionable issues is their products or services. Selling products that are designed to injure or kill people, that create addiction, that can inflict psychological disturbances, and so on, will by definition put an organization in the eye of the public.

• *Raw materials used.* The delivery of products or services involving raw materials that are nonrenewable or endangered is a classic source of ethical turbulence.

• *Environmental concerns.* Negative effects on various aspects of the external environment, whether pollution during manufacturing of products, discharges from use of the products delivered, or other types of problems, are another source for such inherent issues.

• *Mixing of roles.* In many cases, an organization may act as trusted advisory, control body, and supplier of services simultaneously. Keeping watertight bulkheads between these roles has often proven difficult and been the basis for criticism.

• *Influencing attitudes.* Through their products, services, or marketing, many organizations have power to influence how people think and feel about different issues. This power is a potential source of problems if the organization acts irresponsibly.

• *Confidentiality and privileged information.* An organization or its members gaining access to information that is confidential or privileged through the conduct of their business can often be a potential source of ethical problems.

• *Regulating authority and funding power.* Especially in the public sector, there are a vast number of departments and units whose primary, or at least very important function, is to process applications for permits, grants, and so on, making decisions with potentially significant consequences for those affected. This is a setting that has traditionally been prone to bribery and similar unethical (and illegal) conduct. Another main function of the public sector is to provide funding for various societal functions, for example, welfare, police, schools, and so on, and failure to uphold an adequate level of these services can easily be seen as an ethical issue.

• *Fundamental decisions.* Some sectors have the authority to make "fundamental" decisions, that is, of life-and-death importance, and simply having this type of power makes a sector prone to questioning.

There are probably even more such generic sources, but these cover quite a bit of ground. Not a source of inherent issues itself, but rather a symptom that a sector has such issues, is the existence of industrywide ethical standards. In acknowledging that an industry has specific issues that could represent ethical quagmires, industry boards or councils often initiate the development of ethical guidelines as attempts to bridge such risky ground. So, which are the sectors that display such inherent issues? The list is not exhaustive, rather, the following are a number of examples of such industries and their issues, roughly in the same order as the ethical issues sources listed above:

• *Sectors with questionable products or services.* Typical examples are arms manufacturing and trade, ranging from knives that are designed to be used as weapons to battleships and bomber airplanes. The common denominator is of course that the purpose of the products is to injure or kill people. Within this large sector, there are again volatile boundaries; some weapons are primarily made for target shooting, others for hunting, and some solely for human targets. While many question the viability of hunting, it is mainly the segment that delivers weapons aimed at people that is in question, and even for this segment, the answer is not simply to stop producing or selling such arms. There is an "acceptable" need for arms (police and armies) and an "unacceptable" demand (criminal purposes). Being ethically responsible in this industry probably means both doing what is possible to avoid arms falling into the hands of criminals and also acting responsibly when dealing with the legal market. The latter means complying with international conventions regarding the design of weapons and

As the war on Iraq was developing early in 2003, the different coalition forces involved in the operations restocked their supplies of ammunition. The Norwegian ammunition maker Nammo sustained massive criticism for their role in the supply chain. The company produces bullets called MK-211s, which are sold extensively to the United States. They are part of the standard gear of the American forces, and the "problem" is that the projectiles have a hollow point that creates the same effect as so-called "dumdum" bullets when they hit a human target. Their main purpose is to penetrate armor, but they can of course also be used on people, and the 12.7 mm ammunition is particularly well suited for rifles. Under the Hague convention these projectiles are illegal. The International Committee of the Red Cross (ICRC) has appealed to every country in the world to stop the production, use, and exchange of this type of ammunition. The committee claims that Norway, as a country that opposed the Iraq war as long as it progressed without a UN resolution backing it, is operating in a gray area in terms of international law.

ammunition and exerting caution when selling the products, especially in terms of whom they are sold to.

Another obvious example of issues related to questionable or harmful products is found in the tobacco, alcohol, and to some extent the pharmaceutical industries. Common to certainly the two former ones, in many cases also the latter, is that they create addiction—addiction to smoking, drinking, or drugs. Tobacco and alcohol especially have damaging health effects. If being extremely conservative, one could even go so far as to say that the ethical issues of the tobacco and alcohol industries are so severe that it is impossible to develop an ethical platform when belonging to these. However, as pointed out earlier, the intention of this book is to offer advice on how an organization can pursue an ethical profile, not to harass it into changing sector.

Furthermore, as long as a product is legal in most parts of the world and there is a demand for it, it hardly seems fair to pass such judgment. Thus, given that producing and selling tobacco and alcohol is an acceptable line of business, the inherent issues revolve around honesty and openness about health hazards and addictive patterns, restriction of sales and distribution to those who are allowed to buy and use the products, and advertising and other promotion of their use. The large tobacco companies have been adamant in their denial that they have known how dangerous or addictive tobacco is, while evidence has surfaced that has clearly shown that they have known and made good use of that knowledge to create a solid demand through habitual smokers.

Equally, everybody knows that there is a market for these products among underage people, thus incentives for restricting these groups' access to the products are perhaps not very strong. Certainly, actively promoting use (or abuse) of tobacco and alcohol products among people under the legal age is a highly questionable ethical matter. The proliferating varieties of alcoholic beverages tasting very little of alcohol, for example, wine coolers, soda with vodka, chocolate milk with alcohol, and so on, are clearly targeting younger persons who have not yet acquired a taste for regular beer, wine, or liquor. Statistics show that as much as 75 percent of these beverages are consumed by underage people, a fact the manufacturers know very well and are highly criticized for.

A final example of products or services that can lead to addictions is gambling, from state lotteries to slot machines. It has become abundantly clear that gambling is an addiction just as powerful as that to tobacco or alcohol, but often much more expensive to fuel.

A third category of products with some questionable characteristics, especially a potential for having psychological effects on people, consists of computer games, movies, perhaps even music, with violent content. Although there is no truly irrefutable evidence available to demonstrate the link, a general assumption is that being exposed to such violence can lead some people to commit violence themselves. There have been age restrictions for motion pictures shown in theaters for decades, but in latter years there have been more and more incidents where music albums have been fitted with advisories due to language. Finally, after having been an industry virtually without any control bodies in place, age restrictions have now been implemented for computer games as well. There are more and more games being restricted after a few highly criticized games paved the way, for example, the series of Grand Theft Auto games and the BMX XXX game which many large store chains in the United States have refused to sell. For organizations producing and distributing movies, music, and games, the ethical issues revolve around the level of violence, the use of violence to draw audiences, its effect on people, especially younger persons, and access to this material for underage people. Related to violent content is of course pornographic content, but almost the same considerations apply to this particular genre.

• *Sectors with inherent issues related to the raw materials used.* This is another large group of industries, where problematic issues are related either to the materials being nonrenewable and/or "endangered" or to their provenance, especially if they originate in developing countries. The former is an issue in most industries making heavy use of natural resources, for example, foresting, especially in rain forest, products made from tropical wood (furniture, boat trimming, and other types of décor), fisheries, oil and gas, and so on. The latter typically appears in sectors where important raw materials are sourced from developing countries at low prices, for example coffee, cocoa, rubber, and so on, for further refinement into finished products.

• *Sectors with environmental concerns.* There are quite a few of these around, industries where the products, services, or the delivery of these by definition cause harmful effects to the environment. Environmental impact is a topic that will be explored later on, in chapter 6, so it will not be covered in detail here, but the harmful effects can be divided into discharges to sea or land, emissions to air, depletion of nonrenewable natural resources, and probably many other effects as well if making the categories more detailed. Some examples of industries having such negative effects are chemical industries generating pollution during the manufacturing of various products; every electronic industry sector that uses lead, PCB, or other materials that pollute when the products are discarded after use; industries that produce products that are fueled by gasoline or other energy sources that are both nonrenewable and emit exhaust fumes when used; and so on.

• *Sectors that could experience a mixing of roles.* This is a source of inherent ethical issues that may sound harmless compared with weapons of war, tobacco manufacturing, or pollution, but the last couple of years have proven this to be as potent a set of sectors as anything else. As the

There has been a growing awareness in recent years regarding the use of, and subsequent destruction of, tropical rain forest. As pressure groups have voiced their protests and consumers have made a statement through refusing to buy products made out of endangered tropical wood, manufacturers have been receptive to these messages. Contrary to what the situation was a few years back, almost all furniture for outdoor use sold in Europe today is made out of wood from plantations, very often carrying a certificate that it is not taken from old-growth forests. Completely out of touch with this development, the boat-making industry still uses teak and other types of tropical wood for décor in boats. These types of wood are found in significant amounts in all types of boats from small open craft to large luxury yachts. When questioned about this, the industry replied that the market wants this type of wood and there are no plans to change the practice.

Enron and WorldCom scandals have demonstrated very well, accountants have a number of such inherent issues to deal with. They are supposed to act as external, neutral bodies that approve the accounts of organizations, but have an interest in what the numbers show. Most accounting firms also have large consulting units who to some extent make use of information learned by their accountant colleagues through their accounting function for clients. Lawyers are in a position where defendants rely on their advice in terms of defense strategy and pleas. In many cases, defendants would receive lesser punishment by cooperating with the police or plaintiffs and either pleading guilty in criminal cases or settling civil cases before they go to trial. However, attorney fees are much lower in cases that are settled quickly than those that proceed to trials, especially lengthy ones, often involving several rounds of appeals. Thus, lawyers have an incentive to advise their clients to pursue strategies that often are less favorable for their clients and cost the judicial system huge amounts of money. There are many other sectors in which the role of trusted advisor does not go very well together with the incentive structure of the same advisor, one more example being stockbrokers, as shown in the following sidebar. Numerous news stories have documented how brokers juggle their sell or buy recommendations based more on their own views to profits than their customers' best interests.

The owner of the Stride-Rite shoe store in Brooklyn, New York, Steve De Villo, together with his wife, saved about $2000 dollars a year for twenty years. At the age of 65, they had $192,000 in their savings account and were looking forward to a comfortable retirement, perhaps in Florida. Two years later, after having invested based on "safe" advice from Merrill Lynch, they have only $50,000 left in their account. Much of their money was invested in companies like Cisco, Ericsson, Lucent, and EMC. How the safe investments could go so wrong is perhaps easier to understand after highly embarrassing, personal e-mails from Merrill Lynch analyst Henry Blodget became public. Stocks privately labeled "such a piece of crap" or "a piece of junk" were officially given strong buy or long-term buy recommendations. The district attorney of New York, Eliot Spitzer, became aware of these dealings and started an investigation into the entire Wall Street group of elite analysts and financial advisors. The investigation has uncovered numerous highly questionable and illegal practices, including issuing strong recommendations for stock in return for investment banking jobs from

continued

continued

the same company. What is equally shocking is that not only have all the major players in the American financial system been part of this, but also that the stock exchanges and their governing body, the Securities and Exchange Commission (SEC), have failed to do their work in a setting where "everyone" knew what was going on. Of course such conduct, when exposed, has a price: an initial settlement was made in the amount of $1.4 billion. When all the small-time investors who took the analysts' advice, like Steve De Villo, sue them for their losses, this settlement could seem like a minor detail compared to the final bill.

• *Sectors with the power to influence attitudes.* This is also a wide group of industries and sectors, interpreted to the letter perhaps every sector. However, in particular these are organizations that truly have the power to influence broad masses of people through their position, prestige, reputation, and so on, and which can use this power to instill "wrong" attitudes. The fashion industry is an example, where brand-name power, an image of glamour, and advertising force allow companies to "dictate" what people think of as beautiful. There can be no doubt that the massive increase in eating disorders during recent years is in part linked to the image of what is a suitable figure and weight as promoted by the fashion industry. To the extent that a company within the fashion industry contributes to such images and thus perhaps pushes more people into eating disorders, they are at the edge of an ethical dilemma. As the following sidebar shows, at least one fashion company has taken this seriously and changed their ways. Other types of organizations that reach large numbers of people and whose messages are regarded as credible include publishers of newspapers, magazines, and journals; artists within music, TV, or movies; perhaps even political organizations. All of these push their message out into the world and people explicitly or implicitly receive, interpret, and act on these messages. When this power is used to promote questionable attitudes, it is reason to be careful, especially when the incentive for doing so is either to sell more products or for payment, for example, actors and movie producers being paid to portray smoking in a favorable light.

• *Sectors with issues regarding confidentiality and access to privileged information.* This is a rather general issue that concerns many different types of industries, both in the private and public sector, and an issue quite often being the cause of dispute. Information that is confidential often can

Women's fashion is a world of glamour, gorgeous models, and beautiful clothes. Research has often reported that women base their views of normal bodily proportions and looks on ads, magazine articles, and other sources controlled by this same fashion industry. As most people tend to look different than professional models, the gap contributes to negative self-image and self-confidence. As a response to the general approach in the industry, that is, using very thin, often downright skinny or emaciated models, a chain of fashion stores decided to take a different approach. In an ad campaign, they selected quite ordinary people as models, people with regular jobs, kids, and normal looks, and built the campaign around the "ordinary lives" of these "ordinary people." The campaign immediately sparked yet another debate about fashion models and beauty ideals, but for once on a positive note. The chain received much acclaim for the campaign and grateful letters from thousands of women who praised the use of ordinary models.

This was arguably a positive approach to fashion advertising, but perhaps more manipulative than done just out of a concern for women around the world. At the time of the launch of the campaign, coincidence would have it that the largest newspaper in the home country of the chain published a story on how fashion advertising ruins women's self-confidence. The story was based on a survey of 500 women and found that three out of four suffered from poor self-image from seeing such ads. The only flaw was that the survey had been commissioned by the very same store chain.

be of interest to other parties who can use the information for their own benefit. Such information can therefore be seen as a commodity that can be sold for money, favors, products, and so on. Many might view such disclosure of information as harmless, but it is a breach that can sometimes have serious consequences. Organizations in which such access to confidential information is common include healthcare organizations, legal practices, and public welfare departments. Much of this information is personal and perhaps not of much use to anyone else. However, other groups of organizations gain insight into privileged information, for example business consultants, banks, financial analysts, stockbrokers, journalists, public sector planning authorities, and so on. Such information is potentially highly valuable to the right (or perhaps wrong is a better term) people, and these sectors need to have clear rules and solid procedures to ensure such information does not go astray.

• *Sectors with issues related to regulating authority and funding power.* As has already been mentioned, this is particularly a public sector issue. Planning authorities decide what type of use is allowed for different areas and which type of buildings might be erected there, decisions that could have immense financial impact depending on whether say, a shopping mall is allowed on a premise or not. Aviation authorities appoint flight slots to airlines, again decisions that impact business attractiveness. Tax authorities put the tax rules and regulations into practice through local decisions, decisions where some degree of interpretation is required to make rulings. Again, the potential economic impact can be enormous. Judges make the rulings in many lawsuits, and even if a jury has the final word, judges still have much influence over the court, certainly in decisions of great import. In the private sector, perhaps the most similar setting is found in the insurance and banking sector, where compensation or financing cases can be compared with these public sector ones. Anyway, the list goes on and on, and common to all of these is the fact that decisions made by individuals or groups of individuals representing their bodies have potentially grave ramifications for other individuals or organizations. Acting justly in this setting requires a high moral code and an ethical fiber of the organization that can stand against attempts to make it waver.

Another typical public sector ethical issue stems from the sector's function as financer of a large number of societal and welfare services to the community. Depending on the country in question, these range from police, firefighting services, and schools to churches, healthcare, transport infrastructure and services, roads, and so on. In a time when wealth seems to be accumulating in the private sector and public poverty is common, decision-makers at all levels face extremely tough settings where the choice is between cutting school seats or hospital beds. Still, such cuts that undermine the core functions of society, which are paid for through taxes, exist in an ethical gray area.

• *Sectors with issues related to the power of making fundamental decisions.* This is again perhaps a rather generic source of ethical issues that can apply to a few different sectors. However, the most common ones are probably healthcare related, for example doctors in a position to decide whether treatment is worthwhile and, if so, which course of treatment. Certainly the question of euthanasia, active or passive, is one such fundamental decision that is right in the middle of a huge ethical debate. Perhaps not as obvious in terms of making on-the-spot decisions, organizations working with genetics research, cloning research, or developing ways of testing whether fetuses are healthy or not early enough for abortion, are also very much in the public eye as part of an ongoing ethical discussion. And while dealing with the healthcare sector, the segment of this industry devoted to cosmetic surgery is certainly also one with inherent ethical issues. Many of these organizations perform plastic surgery that is clearly necessary after accidents, and so on, but an immense amount of resources and skills are channeled into cosmetic surgeries with the sole purpose of altering appearances, operations that many would deem completely uncalled-for.

As was mentioned at the start of this section, the point of exploring such inherent ethical issues is not to say that you should stay clear of any sector with such issues. Rather, it is raising a flag that different sectors and industries have strongly varying propensities to struggle with ethical issues. Some are perhaps so much on the fringes of what is generally acceptable in the population that staying clear of them could be the best approach. Others have some issues that need to be handled carefully to avoid problems and negative exposure. Especially in this latter case, making an assessment of the core business idea of your organization and how this stands the ethical test is a good exercise to raise awareness of any inherent issues. Having understood what these issues are, if there are any, policies and codes of conduct coupled with appropriate procedures are typically the way of keeping them under control. The list of possible sources for such inherent ethical issues serves as a reminder of things to consider when searching for potential "ethical hot spots" in your organization.

DEVELOPING POLICIES FOR
EXTERNAL CONDUCT

As was the case in the chapter dealing with remedial and strategic issues internal to the organization, strategic issues of a remedial nature directed at the external surroundings of the organization are largely about policies and general attitudes. Such policies define the point of view of the organization on various issues while operational practices ensure that this point of view translates into action. Under the heading of policies for external conduct, most policies will be specific to different external stakeholders. As a result, this section is structured around specific stakeholder policies. Please also keep in mind that it is still the remedial half of the business ethics framework that is being analyzed, meaning that these policies are designed to "make up for" any damages or liabilities an organization inflicts on the outside world. Any more radical policies and practices that are often associated with business ethics will appear in the chapters dealing with philanthropic issues.

Of course, coming up with a generalized list of stakeholders that is relevant for a broad range of industries can be something of a challenge.

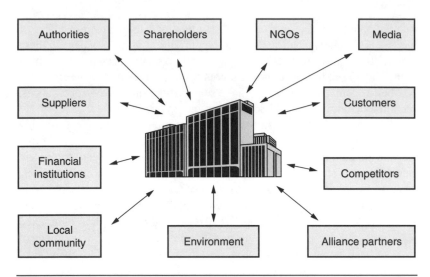

Figure 5.1   A generalized external stakeholder model.*

Depending on the peculiarities of the sector in question, there can be quite a few specific stakeholders that play important roles. The point of this exercise is thus not to cover such more specialized ones, but rather the general stakeholders that most organizations will relate to in one way or another. Removing the internal stakeholders from the model, Figure 5.1 portrays a general stakeholder model (Andersen and Fagerhaug, 2001).

Table 5.1 lists these most common stakeholders, in no particular order, together with possible ethically founded policies of a remedial nature. Chapter 6 will then deal with more of the operational details for each of these policies.

As in the case with the internal, remedial policies listed in Table 3.1, when reviewing this table one might get a feeling that some of these policies are obvious, perhaps trivial, and some might even come across as too "goody-goody." To counter this sense, one could argue that a) the list represents the most extensive set and the idea is that you should choose those elements from it that are relevant to your organization, and b) policies have a tendency to come out very soft around the edges, but translate into more useful practices when brought forward to the operational side of things (as they will be in the next chapter).

---

*   NGO is an acronym for nongovernmental organization, a common term for interest organizations and pressure groups which are neither commercial, for-profit, nor governmental.

Table 5.1 Remedial policies toward external stakeholders.

External Stakeholder	Policy Element
Authorities	Policy for meeting obligations regarding laws and regulations, truthful reporting, and payment of taxes and other dues.
Shareholders	Policy for being truthful in all communication with shareholders, both pertaining to financial issues and any other issues.
	Policy for trying to convey as correct an image of the organization and its status to the public as possible and not trying to manipulate share prices.
	Policy for having a long-term view on the organization's development and viability, both in terms of making decisions that do not produce short-term gains at the expense of long-term prosperity, and maintaining a positive image in the marketplace.
Suppliers	Policy for being honest about future prospects and giving suppliers a fair chance to bid for renewed contracts.
	Policy for paying on time and in general adhering to existing agreements.
	Policy for agreeing to fair prices for purchased products or services, especially when dealing with suppliers in developing countries, and not squeezing suppliers to a point where their viability is at risk.
	Policy for posing strict requirements on suppliers regarding ethical issues like environmental impact, labor rights, compliance with laws and regulations, and so on, and conducting supplier assessments to enforce these requirements.
Financial institutions	Policy for honoring obligations and payments due.
	Policy for being truthful about current status and future prospects in matters of relevance to the institutions.
	Policy for imposing requirements on financial institutions regarding their ethical conduct.
Local community	Policy for making up for any damages/strain inflicted on the community, through actions or monetary compensation.
	Policy for being honest about the organization's future, to allow the local community to take necessary action.
	Policy for contributing to maintaining a positive image of the local community through the organization's conduct and image.
The environment	Policy for minimizing any environmental impact resulting from the organization's operations.
	Policy for continuously striving to improve the organization's environmental performance and developing new solutions and technology that support this effort.

continued

continued

External Stakeholder	Policy Element
The environment *(continued)*	Policy for being willing to rectify any inflicted environmental damage where this is feasible.
Alliance partners	Policy for being honest about future plans and prospects to allow partners to make informed decisions.
	Policy for imposing strict requirements on partners regarding ethical issues like environmental impact, labor rights, compliance with laws and regulations, and so on.
Competitors	Policy for complying with laws, regulations, and unwritten rules when dealing with competitors or aspects that impact competitors.
	Policy for not undertaking marketing efforts that are derogatory toward competitors.
	Policy for not engaging in any unlawful or unethical pricing or market sharing cooperation.
Media	Policy for being honest in communicating and informing any part of the media and not using media as a means for manipulating public opinion or share prices.
	Policy for treating all parts of the media equally unless past experience dictates otherwise.
Nongovernmental organizations	Policy for supplying NGOs with accurate information when asked for it where this does not conflict with the organization's own interests.
Customers	Policy for ensuring the best possible product or service safety.
	Policy for being truthful about the organization's products and services in marketing and other communication with the market and customers.
	Policy for fair pricing of products and services that reflects their value, quality, and durability, and not exploiting monopoly or oligopoly positions.
	Policy for handling complaints, warranties, and recall issues in a forthcoming manner.
	Policy for handling product take-back after their end of life in a responsible manner.
Third-parties and other stakeholders	Policy for treating third-parties with respect and honesty.
	Policy for refraining from giving or taking bribery from any stakeholder.

THE PROOF OF THE PUDDING— SUBJECTING THE ORGANIZATION TO EXTERNAL VALIDATION

Going into the marketplace with an ethical image and offering is almost like putting on armor and going into battle—there are so many out to hurt you or bring you down that the armor needs to be strong; everyone will be looking for a chink in it. With all stakeholders out there looking to find flaws in companies, every type of organization is susceptible to this kind of scrutiny. However, when an organization publicly claims to follow standards that are even higher than those applied to everyone else, they are especially vulnerable to any discoveries of breaches.

One way of ensuring to the outside world that these higher standards are indeed complied with is for an organization to take the initiative to be validated by external parties. Whether related to quality, environment, labor conditions, or many other areas, there are many services established whereby a qualified assessor of some sort reviews the organization and its performance in the area and gives it a stamp of approval. A related practice is that of so-called triple bookkeeping, where the accounts are published in approved annual reports. Especially in relation to external stakeholders, such approaches are useful. However, they apply to other areas as well, and have therefore been compiled into one section in chapter 2 about implementation of the ethical profile.

IMPLEMENTATION SUMMARY

When developing elements of the strategic, external, and remedial part of the business ethics framework, the main task is developing ethically founded external policies for the different stakeholders listed in Table 5.1. This is, as is the case for internal policies, again a job that must be led by the executive team of the organization. Unlike human resource policies, for external policies there is an approach to make this task easier to conduct. Stakeholder analysis is a proven series of steps that provides the organization with an overview of important stakeholders, classifies them according to potential for cooperation with the organization and their impact on it, positive or negative, and helps develop strategies for dealing with the different stakeholders. There are many sources that provide a description of stakeholder analysis, for example Freeman (1984), Donaldson and Preston (1995), or Jones (1995).

When implementing these policies and making sure that the organization lives by them, the various validation approaches mentioned in chapter 2 are useful tools. External assessments, performance measurement, benchmarking, and so on, are all ways to keep the organization "on its toes," encourage and reward suitable behavior, and uncover unsuitable practices.

So let us leave the remedial, external, and strategic aspects on that note, and move on to more specific aspects of the remedial and external area in the next chapter on operational practices.

6

Walk the Talk in Dealings with External Stakeholders: Remedial, External, and Operational Practices

Just as chapter 4 presented operational practices to support the policies outlined in chapter 3, this chapter will review specific ways of fulfilling the spirit of the remedial and external policies from the previous chapter. Some of these will probably be perceived as obvious ways to implement an ethically based relationship with external stakeholders; others might come across as far-fetched. This is not a major concern; hopefully you as a reader will construe most of this book as a varied selection of alternative approaches that you can choose to make use of or not. Thus, elements you find less appealing can easily be skipped.

The policies in the previous chapter were structured according to which external stakeholders they apply to. If you read them carefully, you will have realized that many policies are similar for two or more stakeholders. This chapter has therefore been organized along areas of practice rather than stakeholders, starting with some general ones and moving on to more stakeholder-specific ones later on.

THE RECURRING ISSUE: LAWS, REGULATIONS, HUMAN RIGHTS, AND SO ON

The issue of laws and regulations as related to internal human resource management practices was dealt with already in chapter 4, under Respect for Laws and Regulations. You were then "warned" that this would be a recurring issue throughout the book, as it is so fundamental when discussing an ethical approach to business. As you remember, the first treatment of the issue also touched upon ways of ensuring compliance with relevant legislation throughout the organization, so those points will not be repeated here. Rather, I will focus briefly on the relationship with external stakeholders, as opposed to your own employees, in this respect.

The reason for the somewhat inaccurate heading of this section is that there are several levels of legislation or standards that apply to an organization. Some are part of criminal legislation and can result in prison sentences if breached, other are perhaps not formalized as legislation but rather represent international, national, or industry standards or norms that most organizations abide by. In between these extremes, there are various types of formal or informal laws, regulations, codes, and so on, with much variation from country to country or state to state. Not taking these differences into account, a coarse and helpful classification can be as follows:

• *Formal legislation.* Laws and rules imposed by various lawmaking bodies like the national assembly, government, directorates, agencies, counties, cities, and so on. These are "absolute" in that breaches are not accepted (perhaps except for gray areas of the law) and can result in fines, injunctions, even prison sentences.

• *Formalized standards or norms.* Agreed practices and codes of conduct administered by international or national bodies, industry associations, or other types of organizations where such topics are on the agenda. Examples of this type can be the International Labour Organisation, a United Nations agency that has defined minimum standards for labor rights, or the International Benchmarking Clearinghouse, an interest organization focused on the tool of benchmarking that has defined a code of conduct for benchmarking. Breaches of such standards or norms will rarely result in any formal prosecution, but can involve fines or other punishment. Still, the most severe punishment is probably publication of breaches and the ensuing disgrace.

• *Informal standards and norms.* Unwritten rules or mutual understandings of what is acceptable and what is not. Such standards are rarely administered by an organization or the like, but exist based on tradition and accepted practices. These can vary widely from industry to industry or between geographical areas, but some are also universal, for example the rather nebulous term "human rights" which embodies the basic rights to freedom, food, work, and so on. Failure to comply with them will seldom result in any consequences beyond perhaps loss of trust and esteem.

Many of these different levels of legislation and standards apply to internal labor conditions of an organization, but most of them deal with the organization's relations with various external stakeholders. There is also considerable variance in content and enforcement from country to country, and being aware of local singularities is important for any organization operating internationally. It goes without saying that for an organization with a high ethical profile, compliance with all relevant legislation and standards is mandatory. Breaches will undoubtedly represent the chink in the armor that such an organization cannot afford to allow developing. The consequences are several, of course depending on the nature and severity of the breach:

• *Any official response from the judicial system.* Fines, compensation for damages, prison sentences, and so on, all of which can be both costly and highly inconvenient.

• *Reactions from stakeholders if breaches are made publicly known.* Everything from loss of trust or faith in the organization to cancellations of contracts to severing of all relations. These can often be much more serious to the organization than the official responses.

• *Impact on the organization's moral code.* Breaches that are silently approved, perhaps even encouraged, will counteract all efforts made to raise the organization's ethical standards. In the longer term, this can be a very serious effect as a culture can develop where breaches are okay as long as you manage to hide them. Of course, in such cases, it is only a matter of time before they are discovered. The pyramid in Figure 6.1 illustrates quite well the principle of the tip of the iceberg. For every case where charges are brought against an organization for breaking laws or rules, there are probably four to five instances of media mention of possible infringements. Behind the four to five such news stories, there are probably 50 to 100 serious cases of breaches of laws or rules. Behind these, there will be a large number of cases of minor overstepping of boundaries. In order to prevent negative media coverage and lawsuits, the minor and serious breaches must be prevented.

As for more specific practices that an organization can implement to eliminate breaches, these are partly of a general nature (these were to some extent treated in chapter 4) and partly of a highly specific nature depending on the legislation in question. It is far too detailed for this book to venture into the specifics of the legislation and standards that apply to different industries, so it will be up to you to review these and determine how to relate to them.

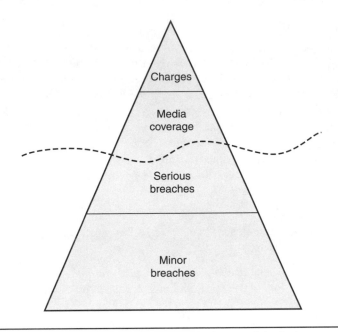

Charges

Media
coverage

Serious
breaches

Minor
breaches

Figure 6.1   Criminal or civil charges are only the tip of the iceberg.

One interesting question raised by the healthcare diagnosis re-coding scandal (see sidebar) is whether this is simply a matter of morals and the personal integrity of those coding the diagnoses. It seems quite clear this is not the case. Investigations undertaken by the Ministry of Health in the aftermath of the initial revelations have found this practice to be systematized; in some cases software applications have even been developed to identify the diagnostic code that will produce the most funding. This raises (at least) two important issues: For one, it is pertinent to ask whether this behavior has actually been induced or encouraged by the system and its rules. Money is a very strong motivator, and the newly formed regional health enterprises are eager to show that they can run their hospitals at budget or even with a profit. When everyone knows that diagnoses are often inaccurate and can be bent a little, especially when the difference between two largely similar diagnoses can be many thousands of dollars, this is of course tempting. The result is seen in the institutionalized procedures for squeezing as much as possible out of this system. The important observation is thus how incentives can drive behavior. In this case, the incentives are aligned so as to encourage an unethical behavior, but the principle works just as well the other way around. This is a mechanism that can be exploited to

In one of the European countries where most hospitals are owned and run by the public health system, recent reforms transferred ownership to regional healthcare enterprises wholly owned by the state. These enterprises are responsible for all aspects of running the hospitals, including income. Income is generated through the public healthcare system according to a unit price structure for all types of treatment performed. Underlying this structure is an extremely detailed system of diagnoses used to classify every consultation, operation, and treatment undertaken by the hospitals. Based on the reported diagnosis types and the number of each, the state then calculates the funding for an individual hospital by applying predefined charges for the different diagnoses.

Recently, many hospitals in the system have come under public scrutiny for so-called creative diagnosis coding. The case started when one of the major newspapers in the country discovered how simple operations to remove tonsils were re-coded as complicated palate operations. The newspaper did not let go of the story until it had uncovered that this re-coding was part of a systematic and deliberate scheme to maximize the income for the hospital. The chairman of the board of the regional health enterprise was given a tough lecture by the minister of health, and the story played out in the media all over the country. As of today, fourteen hospitals are under investigation for tampering with diagnosis codes and estimates are that they have reported in excess of $100 million in illegitimate funding.

make the organization and its members act as desired under an ethical profile, something that was discussed regarding performance measurement in chapter 2 about implementation of the business ethics approach.

The second issue that can be derived from the diagnosis coding case is how strong the discipline of such an internal "coalition" to cheat and deceive can be. In the cases of these hospitals—organizations with thousands of employees—large shares of these have been privy to the practice. Yet no one came forward and questioned it or "blew the whistle." It really takes only one person to sound the alarm, which is the concept of whistleblowing, a general approach that can form part of a platform for "melting" the bulk of the iceberg of minor and serious breaches. Formally, a whistleblower is defined as an individual that believes that his or her organization is engaged in or willfully permits unethical, unlawful, or otherwise reprehensible activities. Whistleblowers bring attention to the objectionable activity and attempt to effect change. They generally report these actions internally and may ultimately resort to reporting the activities to external authorities or interested parties.

Unfortunately, whistleblowers can be divided into two main groups when it comes to their motivation:

• *Those who are motivated by personal reasons and ambitions,* often greed or revenge, who often claim to blow the whistle because it is the right thing to do but later admit to hating the boss. They are often seen as scoundrels by their colleagues and have no true place in an ethical organization.

• *Those who are motivated by their morals and social concern,* typically when organizational practices or corruption threaten public safety. They are often seen as cultural heroes and are the type that can help build respect for laws and standards in an organization.

Surveys show that approximately two-thirds of employees who observe misconduct report it. However, contrary to the common belief that whistleblowers hold high moral standards, the studies have shown that there are no major differences between the ethical beliefs of whistleblowers and non-whistleblowers (Miethe, 1999). Nevertheless, by functioning as watchdogs that have both a preventive and corrective effect, whistleblowers are a useful asset to an organization trying to develop its ethical position. Sadly, many organizations treat whistleblowers as something completely opposite of assets. Martin (1992) outlined three general approaches to whistleblowing:

1. To condemn whistleblowers as disloyal troublemakers who betray their companies, undermining teamwork based on the "chain of command" within the corporation. Such a view is a form of organizational ethical egoism, which states "an action is morally right if the consequences of that action are more favorable than unfavorable only to the agent (that is, the organization) performing the action."

2. To consider whistleblowing as a tragedy to be avoided, being indicative of trouble within the organization and management failure, and threatening the careers of managers on whom the whistle is blown.

3. To unequivocally affirm the obligation of professionals to whistleblow in certain circumstances and confirm that this obligation is paramount, overriding all other considerations, whatever the sacrifice involved in meeting it.

Obviously, an organization pursuing an ethical approach to business must choose the latter of these. Responsible and justified whistleblowing can be very good news (both episodically and systemically) for both the public that is protected by it and the organization it helps to keep alert to its moral code.

The problem has often been that whistleblowers, irrespective of whether they were motivated by social or personal reasons, have been victims of firing or liability prosecution by their organizations. However, as society more and more has come to see whistleblowing as a positive asset, legislation is being developed to protect whistleblowers. The federal government in the United States, as well as several states, has determined that the public policy regarding reporting wrongdoing by employers is important enough to enact laws designed to protect whistleblowers from retaliatory dismissal or harmful action by their employers. So-called "whistleblower laws" make it illegal for employers to fire, discriminate, or otherwise harm whistleblowing employees as a result of having blown the whistle. The Federal Whistleblower Protection Act of 1989 protects federal employees from all discrimination or retaliation in the workplace when reporting illegal acts by federal agencies. Minnesota has also enacted a Whistleblower Protection Statute protecting public and private employees from retribution by an employer in a whistleblowing case.

To conclude this section on laws and regulations, the tables will be turned to introduce the question of how an ethical organization handles criminal acts committed not by it, but against it. This is really not a trivial question and organizations have developed many different ways of dealing with this all too common problem. Stores are victims of shoplifters, manufacturers see their products illegally copied, customers fail to pay their invoices, or competitors commit industrial espionage. No matter what the offense, the organization at the receiving end is a victim of acts that cause monetary losses or damage of some other nature. Such offenses can subsequently be handled in various ways, ways that should set an ethically founded organization apart from one that is not. Very simplified, an organization can take three approaches:

• Acting as severely as the situation allows, prosecuting where possible, adding penalty fines where contracts contain such clauses, and generally coming down hard on any offender.

• Choosing the middle road of taking measures against serious offenses and handling minor ones more leniently.

• Overlooking almost any breach made against the organization, except perhaps for the most serious ones, where the prosecuting authorities would make a case even without the organization initiating it. This might be termed turning a blind eye or turning the other cheek.

Not surprisingly, the general recommendation to an ethical organization would be the middle road. The severe approach can easily be perceived as unnecessarily harsh, even vindictive, and will rarely help build a positive reputation. Pressing charges against any 14-year-old committing petty shoplifting can come across as cruel and will clutter the judicial system with misdemeanors. However, acting naïvely lenient will only make the organization look like a sitting target to anyone who bothers to take advantage of it and can harm it seriously. In addition, employees who frequently witness unethical behavior against the organization being condoned can hardly be expected to act ethically toward the organization's stakeholders.

Under the middle road approach, the organization should make an effort to define in advance what offenses it will "overlook," treat mildly, or treat severely. This can obviously not be done in great detail, but a coarse classification along with guidelines for their treatment can be developed without too much effort. Most important of all, severe actions that an offender can expect should be announced in advance where relevant. This both works as a deterrent and creates a predictability that can avoid a negative perception by the public when offenders are pursued.

An example of how a store treats shoplifters was reported in International Herald Tribune earlier this year. Although consistent, this is perhaps on the severe side (see sidebar).

CARING FOR YOUR CUSTOMERS: PRODUCT AND SERVICE SAFETY AND QUALITY

My own basic scholarly platform is more or less the traditional total quality management movement, an area which developed gradually from a narrow quality control focus to the current wide-reaching philosophy of customer focus, employee empowerment, zero defects, business process streamlining, excellence, and performance management. With today's focus of quality as a field (or perhaps rather lack of focus), many of the strategic policies and operational practices reviewed so far in this book could probably be interpreted as quality management elements as well. If the definition of quality has changed from conformance with product specifications to achieving customer satisfaction and delight, it does not take a vivid imagination to see that honesty and fairness toward stakeholders, sound supplier conditions, safe and durable products, good complaint and warranty routines, and so on, can be included in a quality perspective. Furthermore, this is certainly in line with the message promoted by the

Macy's department store in Manhattan has furnished a holding room for shoplifters containing two chain-link cells in which shoplifters are body-searched, photographed, and handcuffed to a long steel bench. Personnel from Macy's conduct an interrogation, and a verdict is reached as to whether they tried to steal or not. Their social security numbers are punched into a national database before they are turned over to the police or freed. If they sign a confession, they are asked to pay a private penalty in the amount of five times the value of whatever was stolen.

In 2002, more than 12,000 people were transferred through detention rooms in 105 Macy's stores, including more than 1,900 at the Manhattan store. The company says more than 95 percent of those detained confess to shoplifting, many of them agreeing to pay the in-store penalty before leaving, with 56 percent sent to the police. This system, which is run entirely by private security officers with dogs and large amounts of equipment, is legal. Retailers say they find it necessary, as an overburdened public police force has no time for chasing shoplifters.

There is some concern, though, that this system deprives accused shoplifters of some of the basic assurances usually provided in public law enforcement proceedings: the right to legal representation before questioning, rigorous safeguards against coercion, and the confidence that the officers in charge are adequately trained and monitored. The New York state attorney general's office is not aware of any complaints against retail security operations, but has investigated other forms of private policing and said the practice can lead to serious problems. In May, Macy's was sued by a Bronx paralegal and other people with a range of claims, from racial profiling to false imprisonment, concerning how Macy's polices shoplifting.

In contrast, Wal-Mart's policy is to always contact the police when it detains a suspected shoplifter.

pioneering quality gurus such as Deming, Juran, and Crosby. One of their main teachings was that putting the customer first and delivering the best quality possible is the only strategy a quality organization can pursue.

Product and service safety and quality is an extensive issue, but one that is primarily of interest to the customers of the organization. Both product and service and both safety and quality have been included under the same heading, as they are closely related. However, there are also some distinct differences between them. The approaches used to ensure safety and quality in a product cannot always be transferred to a service or vice versa, and sometimes quality and safety must be handled in different ways as well.

Common to all, though, is the prerequisite that the organization is genuinely interested in providing products and services of high safety and quality. This is a basic tenet that must be in place before the organization even starts discussing an ethical approach to business (albeit that the motivation for such a commitment can be as much to avoid negative consequences from poor products or services as a true concern for the customers). Given that this commitment is indeed in place, the next few pages provide some practical insight into and examples of how to deliver such products and services. Keep in mind, though, that this is not a textbook in product development or design—there are no ambitions about teaching you how to go about designing your customer offerings.

Product Safety

Product safety is another of those rather nebulous concepts that could mean everything or nothing. Thus, some clarifications are in order:

• First of all, when talking about product safety in this book, it is in this context limited to safety for the user of the product and the surroundings of its use. This means that the manufacturing of the product falls outside the scope of product safety, as this issue is covered under safety for the organization's human resources.

• Safety implies an absence or reduction of risk levels, and risk in this case applies to human lives and health, any relevant animal lives and health, to some extent the external environment in general (more specific aspects of the environment are treated in chapter 6), and damage to property.

• Product safety has both a short-term and a long-term component. The short-term component refers to any risk of injuries or damage that appears immediately during the use of the product, for example an injury from a power tool. Just as relevant are gradual effects that materialize after some time, for example health problems from exposure to substances in a product.

When designing a product, or revising the design of an existing one, there are often literally thousands of factors to consider: functionality, appearance, durability, serviceability, costs of parts and manufacturing, spare parts, safety, and so on. It is really no wonder a good product is a key component of competitiveness. All of these are important, and which one is more important will invariably differ from product to product; some products hardly have any safety issues at all, in others safety is the key concern. Thus, to give any general guidelines on how you should arrange your product development and design process is virtually impossible within the scope of this book. Rather, some issues to consider during such a process are as follows:

• The obvious one: structural integrity of the product, that is, that it does not break during use and thus cause injury or damage.

• The other obvious one: risk of safety hazards during use of the product which are related to its functionality and design in general, for example, pinching a finger, tearing clothing with sharp edges, bicycle brakes failing during high speed, and so on.

• The last obvious one: safety hazards from poisonous or otherwise dangerous or harmful substances, materials, or chemicals, for example, exposure to a gas intended to be enclosed but which is released accidentally.

The problem for any manufacturer of products is that they are rarely used in only the intended way or for the intended purpose. There is therefore a whole range of other, less obvious issues to consider as well during product development:

• *Safety hazards during unpacking, assembly, or installation of the product.* There are many products that require some kind of assembly or installation before being put to use, for example, furniture, electrical products, building supplies, and so on. It is often easier to ensure that a product is safe to use once it has been properly assembled or installed than making this process sufficiently safe. I remember vividly my own experience with a spring-loaded door I was installing in my house. The door came equipped with a safety mechanism that prevents it from slamming shut over your fingers, but there was nothing to stop the spring bringing the hinges down hard on my hand when trying to install it.

• *Safety hazards during disassembly or servicing of the product.* A large range of products require some sort of maintenance or service during their life span, and even more difficult than predicting all the ways amateur customers might try to assemble a product is predicting all the ways they can try to disassemble it.

• *Safety hazards during or after product disposal.* For most products this is perhaps not an issue, but it is a fact that once a customer is done with a product and wants to get rid of it, it is often handled differently than when it was being used. There are for example quite a number of people every year who are injured by flying glass erupting from fluorescent tubes being thrown into a trash container. Before the tubes burned out, the same people treated them delicately and mounted them with care not to harm them.

• *Safety hazards from unintended use of the product.* How many times have you used whatever is at hand as a hammer, or stacked whatever you could find to reach that high spot? People will use a product in every conceivable and inconceivable way, and a manufacturer does wisely in at least trying to predict some of these ways so as to limit the risks involved in such usage. The classic tale in this respect is the old lady who used her microwave oven to dry her dog after a walk on a rainy day and sadly ended up killing it. A variant of unintended use is unintended users, typically regarding products that are normally quite safe for adults, but can be dangerous for kids who happen to use them.

• *Long-term harmful effects that might not be obvious initially.* At one time, asbestos was believed to be a miracle material with many useful properties, properties that led to its use in a large number of products. Today, scientists know that it is a dangerous material that causes cancer. The problem with this type of effect is that negative consequences often appear only after years, even decades, of exposure and it is almost impossible to conduct any reliable tests on long-term effects. There is currently an intense debate about whether cellular phones can inflict damage on the brain due to microwaves and the heat they generate. Let us hope this is not the case, but it is not possible to rule out a situation in the future where lawsuits against phone manufacturers are abundant and damages are being paid to customers in amounts far exceeding those currently being bestowed upon asbestos victims.

In 1989, the electrical engineering giant ABB acquired the United States power generation company Combustion Engineering. At the time, claims against the parent company were rather small. According to an analyst report, ballooning asbestos litigation and clean-up expenses in the U.S. could now cost ABB $3 billion. Asbestos claims could grow tenfold over the next decade to 660,000 cases, said BNP Paribas industry analyst Thomas Ringkvist in a report on the issue. "The final cost to ABB of pending and future asbestos claims could be substantial compared to the $595 million sum currently provisioned in its balance sheet," Mr. Ringkvist predicts.

The latest news in this case is that the court has approved the firm's proposed asbestos deal, capping potentially ruinous liability claims at $1.3 billion, pending additional information from ABB. ABB said it was confident the court would finalize the recommendation and a district judge would sign off on the deal soon.

• *Indirect safety hazards from use of a product.* It was mentioned earlier that industries that make and distribute violent movies, video games, TV shows, toys, and so on, are under fire for influencing attitudes and values of people, especially children and teenagers. Many researchers believe there is a link between exposure to such violent content and the exercising of violence. Although this is a far more tenuous connection to prove, it is not infeasible that companies can be sued or at least held morally responsible for resulting violence.

• *Risks of inducing addictions.* Products that are known to cause addiction, for example tobacco, alcohol, certain types of drugs, gambling, and so on, have been mentioned earlier. Such addictions can be a hazard in themselves, as the costs of feeding such habits can be immense. To make matters worse, the case is often that the objects of addiction are in themselves dangerous as well. Combining a product with long-term negative health effects with an addiction that make people continue to expose themselves to the product is a disaster (but a goldmine for those companies that sell these products, at least as long as they do not have to pay the victims of their vices).

A singular aspect of addictions and the long-term negative health effects of a product group has emerged as a news story recently, namely fatty, unhealthy food. It is a well-known fact that fatty food leads to overweight and obesity. Recent research at Princeton University, published in the *New Scientists* magazine, indicates that in addition fatty, salty food and food with much sugar may be highly addictive, even as addictive as nicotine or heroin. Estimates are that as much as two-thirds of the U.S. adult population can be defined as sufficiently overweight to be termed obese, costing employers across the United States more than tobacco-related health problems. Ford Motor Company has estimated that weight-related costs add $12 billion a year to the costs of employers nationwide, including medical bills, reduced productivity, increased absenteeism, and higher health and disability insurance premiums.

The World Health Organization, an agency under the United Nations that previously targeted the tobacco industry, has now set its focus on the food industry, especially fast food and beverages containing large amounts of sugar. Discussions are ongoing as to how people can be encouraged to change to healthier diets and eating habits and how the food industry can contribute to this. In the United States, the

continued

continued

fast food restaurant chains fear lawsuits over obesity issues, especially since George Washington University law professor John Banzhaf has started preparing for this. Mr. Banzhaf is a veteran of litigation against the tobacco industry and has now been masterminding the development of lawsuits against food companies over what the U.S. surgeon general has called America's "obesity epidemic." The first lawsuit of this kind was brought against McDonald's by a group of overweight Bronx teenagers, but was initially dismissed by a New York judge. Banzhaf has asked the six fast-food chains McDonald's, Burger King, Wendy's, KFC, Taco Bell, and Pizza Hut to display warning signs in all their restaurants about the allegedly addictive nature of fatty foods, and intends to file lawsuits against them in the case of their failure to comply.

So, is unhealthy food really a question of business ethics? Yes, although some might find the connection a bit tenuous, it can easily be claimed that it is both a matter of product safety in its broadest meaning and also a matter of ethics. Having had the pleasure of both living in and visiting the United States on a number of occasions, there is no doubt that the contrast to Europe is dramatic in terms of obesity problems. Certainly people are partly responsible for what they eat, but it is obvious that the culture and tradition that has developed among food manufacturers and restaurants has been instrumental in exacerbating these problems. To the extent that obesity has become such a huge problem for both the individual sufferer and the country and its industry as a whole, continuing to contribute to the problem by purveying fatty food is unethical. Making unhealthy food, promoting it, and selling it is one of those inherent ethical issues that were discussed earlier. Even the size of portions and meals falls under the heading of questionable practices. Again, being used to European portions, eating out in the United States is often a matter of being stunned and amazed by how much food is loaded onto the plate, certainly out of an intent to give value for money, but with the result that people get used to eating much more than they really need to sustain them. A last point is of course the fact that this planet seems unable to supply sustenance for all its inhabitants. Running a business in a manner that keeps some of these inhabitants constantly overweight is part of the global problem, not to mention the enormous amount of food that is thrown away each day in restaurants and private homes due to excessive serving sizes and an overabundance of food. When there is a huge strain on the world's food supply, this is clearly also an ethical matter.

Again, when developing new products or revising existing ones, all of these issues are factors to consider in striving to make products as safe as possible. There are even some specific techniques that can be used to facilitate high-performing development processes that are likely to uncover any safety hazards and remedy them:

• *FMEA/FMECA,* acronyms for, respectively, *failure mode and effects analysis* and *failure mode and effects/criticality analysis*, two analysis methodologies to be used in the design phase of a product or system. Their purpose is to uncover ways in which a product or system can break down or fail, the consequences of this, and then trace back to the causes to eliminate them. The methodology has been extended and refined over the years and comes in a few different variants, but a basic reference is Stamatis (1995).

• *Fault tree analyses,* a group of different analysis techniques that use a graphical tree structure to foresee future events and product failures. Again the purpose is to identify how a product can fail or be used in such a way as to create risks, for the sake of eliminating these.

• *Concurrent engineering,* not as much a specific technique as a principle of performing development processes in parallel instead of in sequence to ensure that every actor in the process can have her or his say throughout the entire development job. One advantage of this approach is that the collective insight and creativity of the entire development team is exploited at the same time instead of "throwing things over the wall" to the next department in sequence, thus making it easier to identify possible product risks and eliminating them. For more details, see Syan and Menon (1994).

• *Quality function deployment (QFD)* a technique originally developed to carry the "voice of the customer" all the way through the different phases of a product development process. This technique has also been developed further over the years and can now be used to carry the "voice of safety" along the process instead. QFD uses a so-called *house of quality* diagram to decide which design features should be included in the product. For further reading, you could look up Akao (1990).

Product safety has become a hot issue over the last decade or so, with a proliferation of lawsuits and tort claims. In the worst cases, where thousands of customers have been affected by, for example, drugs with damaging side effects or faulty vehicle components, the damages paid are in the range of billions of dollars. This has led to dramatically increased attention to product safety issues, and development of product warnings that sometimes border on the ridiculous, such as, "Do not use this ladder as a striking weapon as its weight and resulting momentum can cause serious damage or injury."

These warnings are one approach used by manufacturers to protect themselves from liability and lawsuits. Other avenues include:

• Along the same line as product warnings: enclosing good, easy-to-understand assembly/installation/use/service manuals for products. The more precise and "intuitive" such a manual is, the less the risk that a product will be used in a manner that does damage.

• Obtaining various approvals, certificates, or marks that confirm that a product has met certain tests. There are a number of such schemes, some aimed specifically at product safety, others at factors like environmental impact, human rights, and so on. In Europe, the CE mark is the dominant product safety certification (CE is an abbreviation of Conformité Européenne, French for European conformity). As opposed to many such schemes which are voluntary, the CE mark is a mandatory European marking for certain product groups to indicate conformity with the essential health and safety requirements set out in European Directives. Without the CE marking, and thus without complying with the provisions of the Directives, the product may not be placed in the market or put into service in the fifteen member states of the European Union and Norway, Iceland, and Liechtenstein. However, if a product meets the provisions of the applicable European Directives, and the CE mark is affixed to the product, these countries may not prohibit, restrict, or impede the placing in the market or putting into service of the product. Thus, CE marking can be regarded as the product's trade passport for Europe. Other countries have similar arrangements, and these are a way of pretesting a product's safety performance before launching it into the market.

• Foolproofing, an approach that the Japanese have systematized under the heading of *poka-yoke*, which means implementing means to eliminate possible ways to misuse a product. There are a number of ways to foolproof a product, from making it impossible to assemble it incorrectly to designing a machine that could be dangerous to fingers such that two hands are necessary to operate it to installing child-proof safety locks on guns.

Many of the issues raised under the heading of product safety also apply to service safety, but service safety involves other issues as well.

Service Safety

Service safety is very akin to product safety, and these two sections could just as easily have been merged into one. As there are, however, some distinct differences between product and service safety, they are separated, but keep in mind that most of what was said about product safety also applies here.

Some points worth mentioning are:

• When dealing with product safety, I limited the discussion to the safety of the user of the product and its surroundings. For services, the case is very often that delivery of a service involves both people from the supplier and the customer engaging in some activity at the same time. A taxi ride is a combined effort between the driver and the passenger, a medical examination between the doctor and patient, and so on (although there are many examples of services that can be supplied either without intervention from any type of service personnel or such personnel being present together with the customer, for example, an unmanned monorail or online processing of a loan application). However, the focus of service safety is still on the customer or user of the service, not the provider of it, as the provider is covered under internal human resource policies.

• Like product safety, service safety involves safety of lives and property, both from short-term and long-term influence.

• As opposed to a customer's use of a product that has been sold to her or him, provision of a service will often take place under the supervision of one or more representatives from the vendor of the service. To some extent, this aspect of many services makes safety easier to control (as opposed to a buyer of a product using it for a completely different purpose than it was intended for). On the other hand, the presence of some type of supervision during the supply of the service also implies a higher level of responsibility. When a customer uses a product on her or his own, much more care is usually exerted than when in the presence of a service provider. This means the service provider must be more alert and that the likely consequences in terms of accountability are higher in such cases.

• Finally, rendering a service for a customer or user very often involves the use of some means, for example a vehicle, hairdressing equipment, medical devices, and so on. As a result, service safety is a combination of the safety of the products being used to supply the service and the actual service.

Some issues to consider regarding product safety were listed in the previous section, and the corresponding list of issues for service safety follows here:

• The obvious one: safety in the execution of the actual service, that is, that no injury is done to living objects or damage inflicted on property. This encompasses, for example, collisions in transport services, health risks during personal treatment, and so on.

• The other obvious one: safety hazards related to the physical means used to produce the service, for example vehicles, equipment, and so on (which are then subject to most of the considerations mentioned under product safety, as the service provider can fall into the same trap of misusing a product as any other user).

• The last obvious one: safety hazards from poisonous or otherwise dangerous or harmful substances, materials, or chemicals used in the provision of the service.

• Safety hazards during preparations for the service or after service delivery. This is similar to the fact that many product manufacturers give much thought to the actual use of the product but often overlook installation or assembly risks. Many more people are injured or even killed waiting for buses, taxis, and trains than from accidents when on board these transportation means. Had these service providers put as much care into waiting and boarding facilities as the actual ride, these could have been prevented.

• Safety hazards from unintended behavior during service delivery. Again quite similar to product misuse. In many cases, the customer is free to do strange things during the time when the service is being delivered, for example stick an arm out of a train window, jerk an arm back when receiving an inoculation, and so on. Service safety is a matter of both making the service safe when the customer behaves as intended and fool-proofing it so it is safe even if the customer behaves in unexpected ways.

• Long-term harmful effects that might not be obvious initially. When silicone breast implant operations became common, they were believed to be completely safe. However, years later many patients have had serious problems related to these implants, effects that were not foreseen at the time. In many cases, services involve the use of materials, substances, or otherwise that can be harmful in the long run.

As for how to identify these risks and prevent or at least reduce them, the approaches are identical to those available for product safety work. Perhaps the only additional item, but one that is extremely important when it comes to service safety, is that of maintenance. As already explained, a large number of services rely on the use of one or more physical entities in their delivery. While safety of the service is of course related to the properties and design of the products used, the properties that are determined by their maintenance are often of higher importance. A roller coaster can be designed to be a reliable and safe structure, but that is of no help if the maintenance of it allows it to develop hazards that were not part of its original

Some years ago, a large chain of hairdressers saw their business declining as other salons were taking over much of the hair dyeing and other more complicated treatments and leaving them with the simpler haircuts. To counter this trend, they tried to take advantage of the practices developed by one of its salons that was still highly successful in attracting customers who wanted their hair colored. It turned out that this salon had developed their own blend of coloring by blending three commercial products. This one salon had tested the new formula on their own employees for some time before starting to use it on customers and the chain undertook further testing before distributing it to all their salons. Combined with a marketing campaign, this self-made blend was a success and boosted revenues. Several years down the road, an alarmingly high share of their customers had problems with hair loss and baldness in patches. A small law firm became aware of the situation through the wife of one of the partners (being a customer with problems herself), had the product tested by external laboratories, and sued the chain. The jury found the evidence linking the coloring to the hair loss compelling and awarded large punitive damages to the customers who took part in the suit.

properties. Thus, proper maintenance is a key component in a safe service environment, and failure to undertake the required maintenance (most often out of a cost-saving perspective) is truly an unethical act.

Product and Service Quality

This is where the connection between business ethics and quality is clearest. Under a total quality management heading, organizations strive to deliver the best quality possible of their products and services, out of a motivation of being more profitable by putting the customer first. Delivering quality to the customer is the main focus under this belief system. The exact same focus, delivering quality to the customer, is valid under a business ethics heading, however out of a slightly different motivation. Here, the assumption is that failure to provide true quality to the customer is a matter of breaching the agreement a purchase really is, and not holding up your end of a deal constitutes unethical behavior. Both, that is, being unethical through breaching an agreement and being of poor quality through delivering less value for money than expected, will result in customer dissatisfaction, loss of market share, and ultimately financial problems for the organization. As such, both quality and ethics have the same goals and same end results.

Under no circumstances, however, does this book intend to go into the core of quality management. It is an extremely extensive concept, and it has been covered very well in numerous volumes before. For this book, suffice it to say that a commitment to product and service quality is vital under any business ethics approach, and that textbooks on TQM will explain available techniques to ensure quality is indeed delivered. Instead, the word "decency" will be introduced into the equation. The question of value for money will be revisited when dealing with pricing practices later on in this chapter, and value is a concept that is hard to define with any accuracy. The same can certainly be said about decency, but somehow decency has a ring to it that helps explain value.

Many companies take the view that they should charge as much as they can for as little cost to them as possible, often without considering the value delivered to the customer. This is an egoistic, introverted, and certainly indecent view that almost certainly in the long run will prove detrimental to the company. In contrast, a "decent" company will focus on delivering true value to the customer and setting the price based on this value. This decency materializes in the way products and services are designed: care for functionality, a quest to make them durable, to treat customers with respect, and so on. Ultimately, it comes down to an intangible quality that can easily be sensed in the organizational culture, in employees' behavior toward customers, and in the feel of their products and services. Although intangible, customers have no problem in recognizing this decency and dedication to quality when exposed to it, and it is a sure winner of repeat customers. A few examples are probably the easiest way to ensure that you grasp the meaning:

• In recent years, there has been as explosion in the different varieties available of alcoholic beverages sweetened and spiced to taste like anything but alcohol. While there obviously are adult customers of these products, the prime target is people under the legal age for drinking alcohol, people who have not yet acquired the taste for beer, wine, or liquors. All over the world, organizations against alcohol and alcoholism are protesting over these new products, but to little effect. In fact, some companies have gone even further and developed popsicles containing alcohol. This is a product that traditionally clearly was meant for children, and there can be no doubt children are also the target group for the alcoholic version. Of the major players in the market, a few have said they will not enter this niche as they realize they have a responsibility toward limiting the use of alcohol to people old enough to consume it. Although suppliers of alcohol products are by definition a sector with inherent issues over their products' negative health effects and actions performed while under the influence, having the wit to stay out of such a lucrative, but highly questionable market segment is a sign of this decency.

• The insurance industry is an industry notoriously being made victim of fraud. People sell their cars and claim they were stolen, set fire to their homes and claim the insurance coverage, take out medical insurance after finding out they are ill, and so the list goes. Consequently, all insurance companies have developed procedures to discourage fraud and expose fraud when victimized by it, a perfectly normal response. However, this has gone so far and become so much a part of their way of life that the knee-jerk response to any claim is to try to dismiss it. Insurance companies use all kinds of tactics in this process, from hoping a simple no will deter the claimant (as it indeed does in a large number of valid cases) to stalling to trying to make them back down at the prospect of a lengthy trial to perhaps the worst practice of all: accusing fatalities of road accidents of being suicidal and willfully having caused the accident (to the utter despair of the next of kin who not only must deal with the loss of a loved one, but are also denied compensation and faced with devastating allegations that the deceased wanted to leave them for good). A few shining examples of decent insurance companies exist, which pride themselves in processing all claims fairly and not using these tactics originally intended for illegitimate claims on legitimate claimants. The excuse that everyone else in the business does it is really not good enough and it takes such a decent company to demonstrate it, both to customers and competitors. (Where the line must be drawn between decent and naïve will be discussed further in chapter 11, where decent is a positive quality and naïve is careless and often a certain way to problems.)

• Akin to the insurance sector, the banking sector also has many areas that are sources for service decency. One example is mortgage interest rates. In some countries, the predominant approach is fixed interest rates; in others most mortgages have interest rates that fluctuate with the market level. For a couple of years now, many countries have seen significant rate cuts from the central bank, normally stepwise cuts made to encourage economic activity and accelerate business development and private consumption. The general idea is that the banks should follow up these rate cuts and transfer the reductions to their customers, be they private or commercial. Many banks do, but since this is up to the individual bank, some drag their feet and either give smaller cuts to their customers, postpone the cut, or even practice a scheme where the cut is only awarded upon explicit request from the customer. Banks that have operated the latter way have seen a flux of customers transferring to competing banks, obviously because these customers think the decent approach is for the bank to initiate this rate cut and do so quickly after the central bank's cut.

• Different types of transport services, both privately and publicly operated, are run most easily and most profitably when there is an even and steady flux of passengers that require no special attention. Most passengers fit this description, but there are many that do not, for example, children traveling alone, people with different types of disabilities, grossly obese passengers, and so on. Being a decent transport organization, the services will be designed to accommodate these passengers, and without impatient or angry looks or clearly unjust extra charges.

• A similar issue is a current topic in many other types of service industries, namely the treatment of elderly customers or other customer groups with special needs. Many of these either require more time, attention, or assistance from the service provider or require entirely different processes to have their needs fulfilled. With the advent of Internet banking, for example, most banks quickly realized that making the customers do the work themselves by using their own computer was cheaper for the bank itself. Subsequently, Internet banking solutions have been rapidly deployed in parallel with a marked reduction in physical bank outlets with traditional counter service. Many banks have even gone so far as differentiating their prices and fees significantly; in many cases Internet banking services are completely free whereas counter services come with rather hefty fees attached. While there are many exceptions to the rule, it is a fact that most users of the traditional over-the-counter banking services are elderly people or others who do not own their own computer or have access to the Internet in other ways. These are most often the customers with less comfortable economies and are the same customers who are more or less forced to pay the fees that indirectly make it possible to keep the Internet services free. It is easy to see that this fee structure is intended as an incentive for everyone to switch to Internet banking, but it is not a realistic option for many customers. Decency in this case would involve taking care of all customer groups the way that would best suit them (or perhaps aiding customers currently without the possibility for Internet banking in becoming able to use it). The exact same issue is relevant in many other sectors, from restaurants with small-font menus to clothing stores with such tiny fitting rooms that only acrobatically inclined teenagers can use them. A decent, ethically founded approach means trying to facilitate all types of customers.

• When talking about product and service safety, risk was defined in terms of injury or damage to health or property. Financial risk for customers is another type of risk that most people like to avoid, but might not constitute a safety hazard, at least not directly. In services like banking, insurance, investments, and so on, the service provider gives advice that could cost clients much money. Quality, or decency, in such services means putting the interests of the client first and basing the advice on what is truly believed to be best for her or him. Stockbrokers like those mentioned in chapter 5, who give advice based on how they will earn the most money themselves, clearly do not subscribe to this ethos.

• In many different areas, the public sector is in a position where decency, or rather lack of, is a quality and ethical concern. One specific example is found in countries where most or parts of the healthcare system, especially the hospitals, are publicly run (which is the case in most European countries). People who are seriously ill with life-threatening diseases, for example, cancer, expect the hospital to do everything possible to either cure them completely or at least prolong their life expectancy as much as possible. From the hospital's point of view, a major and expensive operation that could possibly, but not likely, cure the patient, but might extend a cancer patient's life another six months can be deemed too expensive to be justifiable compared to the produced benefit. This is a rational assessment made in a system where there simply are not enough resources to treat everyone in the best possible way, but it is still devastating to the patient concerned. Other areas of the public sector facing similar dilemmas can easily be found, for example, traffic safety work, where expensive investments in road improvements may produce only a marginal effect of one or two fewer casualties per year, or drug addiction rehabilitation, where costly rehabilitation facilities and programs perhaps only postpone a likely overdose casualty by a year or two. The fundamental question in these cases is: Should a modern society subject such decisions to simple cost/ benefit assessments or are they so important they require other standards and criteria? Unfortunately, there is no obvious answer. Again, these questions will return in chapter 11, but there is probably a balancing point where expending any more money or effort on such services is practically a waste and impossible to manage due to strains on public budgets. The true challenge is determining where this point is, and figuring out how to communicate it in a way that the society understands and can accept. Still, for many parts of the public sector, such resource issues are a major source of decency or lack of decency in their services.

• Compared with the previous bullet point, this is perhaps a minor issue, but open hours are a component of service quality. From a customer's perspective, the ideal situation is open hours extensive enough for services to be available at any time the customer should decide they are needed. In some sectors, this is exactly the case, with grocery stores, pharmacies, restaurants, gas stations, and so on, open 24 hours year-round. And this is perhaps no coincidence; the private sector, where revenues are demand-driven, is typically not the area where short opening hours constitute low service quality. (As will be discussed more closely in chapter 11, perhaps the opposite is true: opening hours have become so extensive that they are a threat to employees and their chances for a decent family life.) In stark contrast, many institutions in the public sector, often so-called service offices, keep very short open hours. In the worst cases, they are open six hours from 9 AM to 3 PM, perhaps with closed doors during lunch break. Irrespective of whether it is the DMV, tax office, passport office, local planning office, or some other public institution, these are services we all need from time to time and for which there are no alternative service providers. As a result, many have to take time off from work to have their needs met, which does not constitute good service or decency toward the people these offices are supposed to serve.

Product quality is also about ensuring that your customers get the genuine article they believe they are buying. Many organizations are exposed to the temptation of purveying products that are either cheaper copies of brand products, products that have been smuggled into the country, or even stolen goods. It does not take a degree in business economics to understand that if a company can buy its products from dubious sources at half the price or less than regular suppliers would charge, profits will increase dramatically if the same selling price can be maintained.

Some sectors are particularly prone to this problem: restaurants and bars are frequently offered cheap meat or alcohol, cheap either because taxes have been evaded or because they are copies of the genuine products. Even if bars buy their beer or liquor legally, investigations often expose practices of watering them down to make more money (when caught, some bar owners even claim they did it for the good of their customers, to reduce their alcohol intake!). Copying products like clothes, electronic gadgets, furniture, and so on, is also a quite common "industry," and a large number of stores of different types can tell you about numerous attempts by criminals to sell them bootleg goods at a fraction of the normal price. Even more serious are organized systems in which fake or faulty spare parts for aircraft, trains, or other vehicles are sold at bargain prices. Such parts not only fool people, but jeopardize the safety of the users of such transportation. Needless to say, none of these practices can be condoned by an organization that subscribes to the ideals of business ethics.

A somewhat more far-fetched issue under product and service quality is related to the fact that one half of the business ethics framework is titled "remedial" (as opposed to the other half being "philanthropic"). By its very definition, remedial means "correction of faults" or something along those lines. It is a fact that many products and services, either by accident or as an inherent feature, inflict damage on property or health. Tobacco, guns, polluting vehicles, and so on, all share this capacity. It is perhaps more of a philosophical question, but under an ethical approach to business, should a supplier of products or services that do harm in some way voluntarily recognize this and be prepared to "make up" for these damages, either through "repairs" or monetary compensation? In serious cases, victims and their lawyers will make sure they are made to do so anyway by dragging them into court, for example, the tobacco lawsuits of late. Such cases always fuel public anger over the damage such companies cause and certainly have no positive marketing effects. Perhaps if the tobacco companies had acknowledged on their own initiative that their products cause health problems and offered to "settle the score" in one way or another, could they have avoided the negative publicity and even have received some positive press instead? In addition to this being the decent thing to do. . . .

CARING FOR THE ENVIRONMENT: MINIMIZING NEGATIVE ENVIRONMENTAL IMPACT

If product and service safety was an extensive subject, that of environmental impact is not much smaller. From being a marginal topic that only attracted the most hardcore "lefties" in the 1960s and 1970s, ecology, concern for the environment, and environmental management have become everyday subjects that concern absolutely everybody. As with quality management, there is an extensive library of literature available dealing with all possible aspects of environmental impact and how to minimize it. Equally, this book holds no ambitions as to providing you with a condensed abstract of this literature in general.

On the other hand, the environment and an organization's influence on the environment is obviously a vital concept when talking about business ethics. Most of the stakeholders listed in Table 5.1, page 171, are in themselves, or are represented by, people. At worst, the environment is an anonymous, intangible, and mute entity that can be ignored, at best, the environment as stakeholder is represented by relevant authorities, pressure groups, and individuals. This makes it a stakeholder that is often difficult to relate to, although in the long run, it is possibly the most important stakeholder for any organization. Similarly to many other stakeholders and their connection to ethics, unethical behavior toward the environment will have negative repercussions in the form of direct financial impact from fines and loss of business, and indirectly from loss of esteem from negative exposure, and in many cases from inflicting damage to the planet we all depend on to be in working order.

More interesting perhaps is that fact that responsible environmental management seems to pay. According to a study by Kurschner (1996), low organizational polluters outperform high polluters 80 percent of the time. Further, studies conducted by Stuart Hart at the University of Michigan–Ann Arbor on the impact of financial performance related to pollution cutbacks made at 127 firms listed on the Standard & Poor's 500 Index demonstrated that pollution reduction pays. Similar findings were reported in an analysis published in 1995 by the Investor Responsibility Research Center in Washington. Among other things, it found that firms with a relatively large number of environmental lawsuits, as compared with their industry peers, earn a lower level of return on assets and return on equity (Kurschner, 1996).

Having established that, the question still remains how to treat the environment and ensure that your organization does not cause any or any more damage to it than strictly necessary. This is no easy question to answer! Numerous attempts have been made to develop guiding principles for environmentally sustainable development. The best list of principles (nearly 100) has been compiled by the International Institute for Sustainable Development (IISD) (see http://www.iisd.org/sd/principle.asp). Some of the better-known items on the list are the CERES principles, the Ontario Round Table on Environment and Development, the Whitehorse Mining Initiative, and the Natural Step. Some are general, while others are targeted at specific economic sectors. More recently, attention is being turned to applying these principles to guidelines for corporate responsibility. It would take up too much space of this book to go into such principles in any detail, so again the coverage will be limited to listing some general issues to consider when relating environment to business ethics:

• When talking about environmental impact, most people first and foremost think of pollution, especially pollution caused by various manufacturing processes, for example chemicals released into a river or acid rain caused by huge smokestacks. Rightly so, perhaps, as discharges to sea and land and emissions to the air definitely represent an important environmental problem. Luckily, as technology has advanced, there are many ways to prevent altogether or at least dramatically reduce such pollution from a large number of different industrial processes. If your organization has problems of this type, you may find that remedying solutions might not be prohibitively expensive and most likely cheaper than the penalties you would have to pay in the future for damages caused.

• Pollution is certainly not only a problem for traditional manufacturing industries. In practice, every organization and its operations directly or indirectly cause some level of pollution: exhaust from vehicles, batteries being thrown away after use, paint remains poured down the toilet after repainting of an office, and so on. Even if such pollution rarely is as extensive or serious as that from heavy manufacturing processes, every bit counts and organizations should consider every aspect of its operations to identify any sources of pollution and ways of eliminating or reducing them.

• Discarded products, after their period of use has ended, are another serious source of pollution. People and organizations throw away electronic products and chemical substances, release gases, and so on, when getting rid of products that no longer work or have become obsolete. While those who physically discard them have their share of liability for acting responsibly, the suppliers of the products must carry much of the burden by designing products that will not be damaging when discarded or facilitating their return or recycling.

One approach to reducing emissions from traditional vehicles with combustion engines, used abundantly in business and the public sector, is a transition to electric vehicles or other types of environmentally friendly power systems. One major reason why sales of electric cars have been slow, especially among individuals, is probably their relatively impractical use outside city traffic. To promote the use of such cars, many states and countries have introduced legislation and practices to make them more attractive. Among other privileges, electric cars are allowed to park for free in public car parks and recharge for free at charging stations, use bus lanes in rush hour traffic, and do not have to pay toll charges.

Many companies and public sector institutions have fleets of vehicles that are mainly used for shuttle traffic inside limited geographical areas, for example, postal services, where the mail is delivered by truck in fixed routes, parking attendants who drive up and down streets looking for offenders, courier companies shooting back and forth between city addresses, and so on. To lead the way and prove the usability of electric vehicles, many municipalities and public sector institutions have purchased large quantities of such cars for this type of use.

Not only products that cause pollution to the environment after being discarded represent an environmental problem. The production of food for human beings is the single activity undertaken by the human race that puts the greatest strain on this planet. Estimates are that as much as 250,000 pounds of food per one million of population in Western countries are thrown out every year, much of it still perfectly edible. The waste of resources this represents is formidable, especially considering that there is a lack of food in many parts of the world.

National food and health administrations are quite clear in their assessment of the reasons for this waste. Partly to blame are stores that plan inventories and procurement volumes poorly and find it safer to overstock than risk running empty and thus annoying customers. The overstocked products are part of the amount of food discarded. Probably to blame are the manufacturers of food, who deliberately set expiration or best-by dates earlier than necessary. The result is that a large portion of the discarded food comes from households that fail to consume products before their expiration date. Having been taught to respect such dates, consumers throw away large quantities of edible food, a practice that of course increases stock rotation and sales for stores and manufacturers.

Some responsible players in this market have started taking measures to reduce the mountains of food being wasted, among other ways by consistently offering food approaching its expiration date at reduced prices, directing research efforts into increasing the shelf life of various types of food, or giving excess food to homeless people or other food aid programs in the local community.

• Environmental damage is also caused by depleting nonrenewable or endangered sources of raw materials or energy. The use of tropical wood in boats has already been mentioned as an example, others are the use of endangered plants from the rain forest, the making of food from tuna fish, practically any use of petroleum or petroleum products, and the use of electric power made by burning coal. In many cases, there are substitute raw materials or energy forms available, granted, sometimes at a premium cost, but in other cases even at lower cost. In any case, an ethically founded organization (and indeed every organization) has an obligation to look for alternatives that do not continue to deplete such limited resources.

• Wildlife and nature in general are other aspects of environmental impact an organization can cause, directly or indirectly. By their very nature,

Energy consumption is, and certainly will be even more so in the future, a paramount environmental issue. We surround ourselves with more and more products and infrastructure that require fuel or electric power. Satisfying the world need for power drives the development of facilities that destroy or damage the environment. Should larger parts of the world population reach a point where they consume as much power per capita as industrialized countries do today, the power supply system would simply break down. Thus, energy conservation is a global concern and obligation for any organization. There are numerous ways to save power, some that require investments, others that simply require better awareness and minor changes in practices. An example of the latter is the use, or rather abuse, of electric power in buildings. Drive down any street lined with businesses or public institutions in a typical city after dark, and you are guaranteed to see an abundance of lit offices, meeting rooms, stores, factory halls, and so on, even if they are not in use at the time. I cannot find the reference, but I seem to recall having seen an article estimating that all the power wasted in this way every day would be sufficient to supply the entire city of New York with electric power for a full day. Avoiding this waste can partly be achieved by installing motion detectors that switch off lights whenever a room is empty and partly by working with people's attitudes. There are shining examples of organizations that have managed to encourage employees to save power this way and have also achieved tremendous savings on the bottom line.

some sectors kill endangered animals or destroy endangered habitats, for example, certain types of fisheries, whaling, or tropical foresting. Others have the similar effect, but indirectly through developing birds' nesting places into real estate, offshore oil drilling that causes noise that disturbs whales and their mating rituals, or fishing for "acceptable" types of fish but accidentally harming endangered types in the process.

• While on the topic of wildlife and animals, many industries injure, torment, or kill animals, animals that may or may not be considered endangered species. By more and more people, this is also seen as a kind of overstepping of an environmental or ethical border, be it in the form of animal testing of cosmetics or other products, medical experiments with test animals, or purely for fur. Most people seem to draw a line between what is seen as unnecessary cruelty to animals, for example breeding and killing them simply for making fur coats, and a more holistic usage of animals for food and other products, for example traditional dairy farms. In the latter case, however, people are still of course concerned with the treatment and comfort of the animals.

• Unnecessary or excessive waste is another area of environmental concern. This can take on many forms, for example, serving such large portions to restaurant guests that much of it will be left uneaten and thrown away, packaging products in unnecessary layers and amounts of wrapping, or dumping the remains of opened cans or other packages of raw materials instead of resealing them and using them later. Most products contain some materials or components made from materials that are in short supply or cause damage to the environment when being produced, and failing to use these fully is a wasteful behavior. In addition, waste is in itself becoming a truly serious problem that threatens to drown us with its pure volume.

• Last, and perhaps a little more tenuous, noise "pollution" or "ugliness" are seen by some as environmental damage. Both contribute to making society more unpleasant and can also, in the case of noise, be dangerous to people's hearing. Some might argue that building ugly structures, putting up tacky signposts, or transforming a quaint little village into a commercial shopping mall is just as dangerous to people's eyesight. . . .

All of the points above are really different types and sources of negative environmental impact. The big question is of course how to prevent these in your organization. In some sectors, environmental problems are one of those inherent problems that can hardly be solved except for the terminal solution of closing down the organization; in others a solution can be extremely expensive or difficult to develop. Luckily, in many cases, environmental issues are simply a matter of carelessness or lack of knowledge about solutions or better alternatives. Some approaches to reducing or remedying environmental concerns in an organization are:

• First of all, if such an exercise has never been undertaken, to carry out a systematic assessment of the organization and its activities to uncover environmental problems of any of the types mentioned previously. Any problem areas identified should then be classified according to seriousness and solutions attempted, in the order of importance.

• For solutions to identified problems, there are an abundance of public, non-profit, or commercial organizations and institutions that can be consulted for help and advice. Many of them will offer help in reducing pollution or changing practices to reduce environmental impact.

• If the organization reaches a certain level of proficiency in the handling of environmental issues, different certification schemes are available to both document the organization's dedication to this topic and to improve its practices. By far the largest effort to develop a standard approach to environmental management is the ISO 14000 series, a family of environmental management standards developed by the International Organization for Standardization (ISO), one of the world's principal voluntary standards development bodies. The ISO 14000 standards are designed to provide an internationally recognized framework for environmental management, measurement, evaluation, and auditing. They do not prescribe environmental performance targets, but instead provide organizations with the tools to assess and control the environmental impact of their activities, products, or services. The standards are designed to be flexible enough to be used by any organization of any size and in any field.

• While ISO 14000, similar to ISO 9000 for quality management, is a very comprehensive standard prescribing management systems and processes within the certified organizations, there are other, less comprehensive types of certification available as well. Some of these are quite general, so-called *ecolabels*, which are given to products that can be documented to have been manufactured and will be used without any negative environmental effects. An example is the European ecolabel the EU flower (see http://europa.eu.int/comm/environment/ecolabel/); others focus on specific aspects of a product, for example the Forest Stewardship Council (FSC). All forest products carrying the FSC logo have been independently certified as coming from forests that meet the internationally recognized FSC Principles and Criteria of Forest Stewardship.

• Both ISO 14000 and ecolabels have in common some kind of external audit of the organizations or products that are approved. Even without being part of such formal standards or labels, such environmental audits can be helpful in assisting the organization in identifying problem areas and solving them.

• Organizations new to the thinking of eliminating environmental problems tend to focus on their own operations, as this is the section of the supply chain they can control themselves. For many companies, though, the greatest damage to which they contribute is through the use of their products by their customers over the life span of these products. Conducting lifecycle assessments of the products is therefore another approach that can be quite effective.

• Which brings us to the issue of end-of-life of products. Quite a few products are not very hazardous to the environment during either manufacturing or use, but can have extremely negative consequences when being discarded. Except for the relatively little electric power a computer uses, it has little impact on the environment during use. But if simply dumped on a landfill, it contains many materials and substances that are harmful to nature. Thus, return schemes that work and ensure that large shares of the harmful products are taken back for recycling or reuse by people qualified to do so is an important approach for many products. In many cases, legislation demands that certain percentages of products should be recyclable and that they must be manufactured in a way that makes it easy to do so, in others it is left up to the suppliers to see to this. For some products, a fee is added to the sales price to finance the return cycle, a fee that in some cases is given back to the customer when handing back the product (soft drink cans for example), in other cases public authorities take part in financing and marketing such schemes (paper recycling). End-of-life handling is relevant for products that are harmful or where it is feasible to a) reuse the entire product after a brush-up (car generators), b) disassemble the product and reuse components (copier machines), or c) disassemble the product to recover raw materials. In any case, closing the supply chain loop and implementing return cycles is an important environmental improvement approach.

• Recycling schemes are an example of mechanisms that individual organizations, entire industries, and governments can initiate and operate. Another effective avenue is really only available to governments and international bodies, namely quotas and penalties for inflicting negative environmental effects. The best known is the international system for trading CO_2 quotas, but others exist or are under development. Common to all of these is the principle that no one has a given right to pollute; it is a right that must be purchased and paid for. This way, companies that pollute are punished for it, which represents an incentive to improve, and the money generated through the scheme can be used to implement global improvements.

Let us move on to something a little more specific: your dealings with various external stakeholders in terms of supplying them with information, payment, reporting, and so on.

SUPPLYING EXTERNAL STAKEHOLDERS WITH TIMELY AND ACCURATE PAYMENT, INFORMATION, REPORTS, AND SO ON

While some of the practices discussed in this chapter apply mainly to one stakeholder, this section is general for all stakeholders. It deals with the attitudes and practices of your organization in affairs with external stakeholders.

Very often, different stakeholders require information, payment, or other types of input from the organization, and supplying this input in a timely and accurate manner is a matter of courtesy, quality, and decency that reflects the organization's commitment and attitudes. It gives a solid impression when an organization takes these things seriously and it gives an equally sloppy impression when it does not.

Essentially, the inputs in question are:

- Payments, for goods or services supplied by suppliers.

- Other financial dues, for example taxes, fees, and so on, to authorities or others.

- Specific reporting to various recipients, for example accounting reports, customs forms, employment figures, and so on, typically both to official institutions and other organizations.

- General information about incidents, trends, and so on, of relevance to the market, customers, suppliers, and so on.

Listed by stakeholder group, their main expectations typically are:

• *Authorities.* Public authorities expect to receive reports, forms, declarations, and the like, on time and as instructed (often imposed by laws or regulations), and any things such as taxes and fees are expected to be paid on time and in the correct amounts. Public authorities often have the most stringent requirements for such input and are generally also the stakeholders with the toughest sanctions in case of failure to meet deadlines or specifications, including fines, penalties, even legal prosecution. In general, ensuring that the organization has procedures of high quality for all such communication and payment to public authorities is crucial.

• *Shareholders and financial institutions.* Shareholders and potential shareholders (private investors, organizations, institutions, and funds) first and foremost expect the organization to provide the market with timely, accurate, and nondifferentiated information about earnings, sales, other financial issues, executive hiring, and so on. Many of the ethical scandals that have flourished in the media in recent years have been related to failures in this area. Sales have been unjustly inflated, financial problems kept under a lid, and accounting practices stretched to the limits of the law and beyond. In all cases, such practices backfire on the organization, and with the increased attention the recent problems have directed to such issues, there is every possibility that more breaches will be disclosed in the future. Shareholders also expect prompt payment of their dues in the form of return on shares, but this is rarely a problematic area. Financial institutions that lend money to the organization or handle its accounts are equally as interested in accurate information about the financial status of the organization and its predicted performance in the future as shareholders are. In addition, they tend to be concerned with upholding of payment schemes, loan obligations, and so on, but are usually more lenient than public creditors. Again, a practice of honesty and accuracy is recommended.

• *Suppliers and alliance partners.* It is tempting to assume that suppliers are mainly concerned with timely payment for goods and services delivered. Of course suppliers expect timely payment and this is important to them, especially in cases where the supplier might be in a situation of limited liquidity or there are concerns over the customer's long-term financial viability. However, most suppliers are equally, if not more, concerned about being kept up to date on expected future developments regarding likely demand from the customer, as precise prognoses as possible, early warnings about order changes and volume changes, any movements to evaluate alternative suppliers, and so on. While there are few laws that regulate these matters, experience clearly shows that organizations working closely with their suppliers achieve better overall supply chain performance than those keeping their suppliers in the dark. In addition, this is also a question of the same decency talked about earlier. Suppliers rely on their customers for business and predictability is vital for long-term planning. The same holds true for more formal partners in business, whose future prospects invariably will be to some degree linked to those of the organization itself.

• *Local community.* In cases where the organization is located in a smaller community or the organization is large enough to represent a significant employer in any community, local authorities, other businesses, potential future employees, and others all have a high vested interest in the organization. The authorities must base their planning of schools, roads, housing areas, and so on, on the plans and prospects of the organization, neighboring businesses downsize or expand in accordance with expected demand, people even move to an area in expectance of employment opportunities. Both to help all of these groups in making qualified decisions and to benefit itself from such qualified decisions, an organization should make a habit of sharing pertinent information with these players. Not being part of the formal supplier–customer network of the organization, they can be easy to overlook. Larger organizations have solved this by appointing press officers or local community liaisons, but this is often infeasible for smaller ones. Assigning the task of liaising with the local community to persons with other primary functions in the organization is usually a better solution in such cases.

• *Media and NGOs.* The organization has no formal obligations toward either of these two stakeholder groups, but their attitudes toward the organization and their "coverage" of it in public discourse can have a serious impact on the organization. Thus, being dismissive and less than helpful in supplying relevant and reasonable information to them is often an unwise strategy. To the extent that they do not ask for confidential or otherwise limited information and they seem to use what information they are given in a proper manner, the organization will usually benefit from being relatively open and forthcoming with both the media and NGOs. Again, larger organizations try to handle such issues professionally through appointing dedicated press officers while smaller ones might have to make do with key people assuming a special role toward the media.

The remaining two large groups of external stakeholders, competitors and customers, are quite different. Customers are in a singular position regarding their right to information, competitors equally so but without any real rights to information. In any case, both these will be treated in the sections to follow.

A singular industrial sector for which accuracy in the information supplied is a vital concern is the media. Media in this respect includes newspapers, magazines, journals, some types of books, television, radio, and Internet news services. The competition is fierce, the battle for attention is tougher than ever, and people seem to have less and less time for reading or watching news. A proven weapon in this race for customers is being first with the good stories, preferably sensational news. If beaten to the main story, leverage can be gained by supplying further details yet undisclosed. All in all, the media and their journalists are under extreme pressure to unearth new stories and headlines, providing all sorts of incentives for a number of questionable practices. Some resulting inherent ethical issues are:

• Inaccurate, exaggerated, or speculative reporting to reach wider audiences. Both more and less serious institutions can be tempted to twist facts or interpret them creatively to make "better" headlines.

• Overexposing individuals or organizations through continued and relentless media attention. Journalists have a tendency to build stories and stick with them till they are bled dry of any further interest, a practice that can wear down the objects of reporting completely (see the following sidebar).

• Overstepping of boundaries in obtaining information or pictures. Perhaps the grimmest manifestation of this are the notorious paparazzi journalists and photographers pursuing celebrities for pictures and stories, often climbing walls, hovering in helicopters, or sneaking in to closed-access

> The New York Times, one of the world's most famous and reputed
> newspapers, has been hit by a number of scandals in the last year. It is
> being accused of being in the corner of the government and of leading
> unfounded campaigns against individuals, and there have been
> revelations of fabricated articles. In June 2003, then editor-in-chief
> Howard Raines resigned together with CEO Gerald Boyne. Raines has
> now been replaced by the Pulitzer Prize–winning columnist Bill Keller as
> the new editor, whose main task ahead will be to restore the public's
> faith in The New York Times.
>
> The story of Jayson Blair, a former New York Times journalist, is per-
> haps the most extreme to be revealed in a long time about how jour-
> nalists succumb to unethical ways of getting their stories and headlines.
> For a newspaper with extreme demands for accuracy, owned by a fam-
> ily who sees it as its calling to publish a quality newspaper, Blair's way of
> practicing journalism is a low point in the paper's history. He blatantly
> stole from other newspapers, invented quotes from sources, and wrote
> articles from places he had never set foot. Half of the articles he wrote
> during his last six months at the paper contained such serious errors.

parties. More serious journalists, however, have also been known to rum-
mage through trash cans or unlawfully search offices.

   • Breaching the right to privacy, for example, naming victims or
alleged perpetrators of crimes, identifying suspects by name or photo, and
so on. Rules vary significantly from country to country in this respect; in
many countries this is still a problem even though technically illegal.

   • Source usage and protection. Journalists are dependent on sources to
uncover stories, and the ability of sources to remain anonymous (acting
effectively as whistleblowers, as discussed earlier in this chapter) is crucial
in allowing individuals to speak out against abuse of power. However, all
too often, news stories are attributed to "informed sources" or "unnamed
experts" when there really are no sources behind the allegations.
Unnecessarily shielding sources also makes verification of and defense
against allegations difficult or impossible.

   The sheer number and extent of these inherent issues suggest that jour-
nalism is a profession prone to ethical questioning. This is confirmed by the
fact that there exist a number of ethical codes and organizations overseeing
the industry. Although this might mean lower revenues, news providers will
in the long run probably benefit from an ethical approach.

During the last year, there have been two somewhat similar (but in important ways also different) cases where news organizations have played important roles in the tragic deaths of politicians. First, in Norway, the former minister for health, Tore Tønne, committed suicide just before Christmas 2002 after extreme media coverage became too much for him. The case took off when it became known that the former minister continued to receive payment of salary in arrears for his ministerial position while also having earnings from other sources for consulting work. After lengthy coverage in many newspapers, the National Authority for Investigation and Prosecution of Economic and Environmental Crime decided to press charges against Tønne. Following this decision, Tønne, who was known as a highly honorable person, took his own life. Shortly after, the Norwegian Press Association (with most newspapers, radio stations, and TV stations as members) formed a committee to investigate the media coverage of the case. Its findings were that the media conducted a one-sided campaign characterized by personal persecution and wild exaggeration. One of the largest newspapers in Norway especially was harshly criticized for its conduct for not letting Tønne himself see documents the case was based on, get a proper chance to comment on the story, or present his views, amongst other alleged infractions.

In the UK, the scientist and former arms inspector Dr. David Kelly committed suicide after raging news coverage for a few days over his role as a source for the BBC. Following the war in Iraq in spring of 2003, the BBC brought forward speculations that the British government had deliberately "sexed up" its dossier on Iraq to make the war more justifiable. At first, the BBC did not identify their source for their speculations, but claimed that the source said intelligence services were unhappy with the claim in the dossier that Baghdad could launch weapons of mass destruction within 45 minutes. After having read the transcript of the journalist's testimony to the Commons Foreign Affairs Select Committee on the affair, Dr. Kelly wrote to his manager to admit that he had met the journalist. Later on, *The Sunday Times* approached Dr. Kelly over the story but he denied being the source. Early in July, the Ministry of Defense (MoD) said that an adviser had admitted talking to the journalist and that this person was not a member of the intelligence services or defense intelligence staff and was not one of the senior officials in charge of drawing up the dossier.

continued

continued

> Richard Sambrook, the BBC's director of news, held "clear-the-air" talks with Geoff Hoon, the defense secretary. At the same time Mr. Hoon wrote to Gavyn Davies, the BBC chairman, asking if the corporation stood by its allegations about the dossier. He said that he was prepared to name the MoD adviser if the BBC would confirm or deny that that person was the source for the story. Mr. Davies was understood to have rejected that offer. As a consequence, the MoD named Dr. Kelly as the MoD adviser who admitted meeting the journalist. Later on, Dr. Kelly made his first public statement about the affair. He said that the Government's position on Iraq was "credible and factual," but admitted that the affair had played heavily on his mind. He also said that he was not reprimanded or pressured by his employers over the unauthorized meeting with the journalist but had been warned not to talk to the press.
>
> On July 15, the Commons Foreign Affairs Select Committee reconvened for a special meeting to question Dr. Kelly. He told them that he was not the main source for the story. Two days later, the BBC journalist gave evidence in private to the committee and again refused to name his source or the date of the meeting. The same day, Dr. Kelly went missing and was found dead the next day. In the furor following his suicide, the BBC journalist, the BBC executives, members of the government and defense department, as well as Prime Minister Tony Blair have been heavily criticized for their handling of the situation. In the case of the BBC, their usage of Dr. Kelly as source and subsequent behavior are certainly open to criticism.

A FRESH IDEA—HONEST MARKETING?

Chapter 4 outlined a general buying process, and the need every customer feels to obtain some confirmation after the purchase that the right decision was made was discussed. At that point, the wealth of the organization or its members was mentioned as one potential source of a sneaking suspicion that the buyer either paid too much or made the wrong choice. Another possible source for such disproof of the purchase decision is the very marketing of the product or service purchased.

All the marketing efforts expended to attract customers can easily go from being an asset to a liability if the performance or quality of the offering was exaggerated before the purchase. All marketing research clearly shows that creating realistic, albeit perhaps modest, expectations on the part of the customer and satisfying these is a powerful attraction, whereas creating exciting but unrealistic expectations and failing these is an equally powerful turn-off. Thus, as with most areas of the business ethics framework, an organization's motivation for being accurate in its marketing stems from several factors: exaggerated marketing is likely to cause dissatisfaction among customers, which in the long run diminishes revenues; dishonest marketing can become a legal liability; and untruthful marketing is unethical and will tarnish the reputation of the organization. There is also a risk in sending false or inaccurate messages to the marketplace in that chances of the "bluff" being called are constantly growing. There are so many different organizations out there conducting scientific, user, or other types of analyses of all sorts of products and services that it is likely your offering will be put to the test. In such tests, the resulting reports love to compare actual performance with what has been promised in marketing or on the packaging.

If you can have some faith in this tenet, the question is how to, in operational terms, approach marketing under an "honest marketing" label. Some issues of particular relevance to ethical aspects will be discussed.

There are some industries that sell products whose main effect, or at least an equally important side effect as the main one, is to create a sense of well-being and confidence on the customers' part. Cosmetics represent one example. When you buy shampoo, soap, or anti-wrinkle cream, you buy the effects of cleaning or smoothing that the products (hopefully) offer, but you also buy some satisfaction from the feeling that you are taking charge over your own appearance and acting to maintain or improve it. Anti-wrinkle cream is an excellent example of this: commercials with beautiful actresses claiming their good looks are owed to the cream easily sell the message that using the same cream will do the same for the viewer. Unfortunately, as science has progressed and new methods for testing such creams have been developed, there is much evidence indicating that these products have little or no effect at all in terms of smoothing. This leaves the customer only with the side effect of feeling somewhat in control over the aging process, which in itself has a value to the customer. Still, when commercials do their best to sell the smoothing effect of the product, this is not honest marketing.

First of all, consider your overall approach to marketing and indeed whether to undertake marketing or not. As consumers, the amount of advertising in all types of media, direct mail marketing, billboards, and so on, that we are exposed to is constantly growing. There is little doubt that people are growing tired of this. Furthermore, we all know this costs a lot of money (it is easy to tell simply by observing the style of the PR companies), money that the marketers need to recover one way or another. As payment from customers buying products or services represents the primary, often only, source of income for most companies, it does not take a PhD in business administration to figure out that part of the price we pay for what we buy goes into financing the advertising (which most of us hate anyway). In addition, many react negatively to the waste of paper and energy the production and distribution of advertisement represents. A reasonable question therefore seems to be: should you advertise at all? This is of course a catch-22 situation; if you never make what you sell known to potential customers, it does not matter that you keep prices lower by evading marketing costs, since no one will know it exists and therefore cannot buy it. Thus, the simple answer to the question is, yes, you probably need marketing (unless you are in the miraculous position where your products or services sell themselves).

Granted that you probably need to do some marketing, honesty about the features, qualities, and effects of your products and services is a key concept under an ethical business approach. There are, however, many different approaches to marketing that should be considered. Mass advertising is probably the approach most of us are familiar with, where ads in newspapers, magazines, on TV and radio, and so on, are supposed to create brand awareness and inform us of specific products and offerings. Clever marketers manage to obtain valuable marketing exposure through editorial coverage in mass media while others pay to have their products placed in movies or TV shows. From emptying the mailbox every day, we are probably also quite familiar with advertising sent by mail, either indiscriminately to all inhabitants in an area or addressed to selected recipients. If you use a computer to surf the Web or communicate via e-mail, you are bound to know very well the marketing approaches used there. Some companies send salespeople around the country, knocking on doors and demonstrating products; perhaps even cleverer is the home party approach, which in essence is the old traveling salesperson shtick but refined. Less known perhaps are approaches based on word-of-mouth, formal or informal, or networks of trusted intermediaries.

Deciding on the way or ways to market your products and services must be based on a number of complex assessments (there are expensive consultants that can be hired to help you with this). Documentation on the effectiveness of the different approaches is hard to find, but they should be assessed in relation to an ethical business perspective. Two key criteria to consider should be:

• *Cost recovery.* If you agree that costs incurred through marketing and advertisement must be recovered primarily through increased prices of products and services, this raises an interesting question about value for money. If the same amount of products or services could be sold without incurring these costs, prices could be lowered, often substantially, thus creating higher value for money (which represents high quality and decency toward the customers).

• *Image created.* The content of marketing and advertisement is aimed at creating an image of the organization, its products or services, even their customers. However, the mere fact that an organization engages in marketing and advertising also sends a message, namely that the organization is willing to spend money this way and transfer the cost to their customers. In an age where many customers are becoming ad-weary and see at least the most abundant marketing efforts as a waste, this can elicit negative responses and attitudes.

Combining these with the marketing professionals' analysis criteria, hopefully you can end up with a marketing approach that at least does not annoy those people in which you are attempting to instill positive attitudes toward your organization. A couple of marketing approaches were mentioned that are perhaps less well known, which could be alternatives to the traditional approaches:

• *Word-of-mouth marketing, also called referral marketing or networking.* Media advertising for businesses in the United States amounts to $200 billion annually, about 800 dollars per person. It has already been argued that the problem with this type of advertising is it drowns out each other's messages and besides, we tend to distrust the information conveyed this way. Word-of-mouth, that is, opinions of other people in our circle of friends and family, is much more likely to be trusted and presents a more concise message based on real customer experiences. As such, it is potentially much more effective in getting the desired message across, but making it happen can be more difficult than simply buying advertising space. The advertising industry itself has not been very helpful in facilitating this approach either, perhaps mainly because it involves little, if any, commission for them. Word-of-mouth is unique in many ways compared with traditional marketing: it really represents both the means of marketing and the ends of marketing (Cafferky, 1995), it is performed by customers for customers, and it is one of few methods where the marketing message does not originate with the supplier and thus tends to be perceived as more trustworthy than traditional advertising. There are several books and resources available on word-of-mouth marketing, one relatively recent addition being a book by Silverman (2001). Michael Cafferky claims to run the largest Internet resource on the topic, and lists the following as proven tactics under this approach:

– Involvement of customers in your business beyond the actual purchase transaction. Companies who involve customers have learned that an educated consumer is one of their best advocates, thus customers could be involved in the process of making or delivering your product or service. This can involve giving tours of your production facility to the public, to distribution companies, to your marketing company, or to champion customers; letting champion customers talk with selected suppliers so they can learn more about the value that you purchase and include in your product/service; or letting champion customers participate on a product review panel to give you feedback about improvements you are making for their benefit.

– Testimonials—a silent sales force that you have more control over (once you have them in your possession) than other forms of word-of-mouth.

– Active use of distribution channels (sales representatives, wholesalers, distributors, consultants, academic leaders, industry experts) adds to your reputation. Provide the type of information they would like to relay to others, for example, stories of successful customers and how you build quality into your work.

– Educate champions to allow them to be effective in spreading your reputation. Such educated champion customers increase their loyalty, good will is generated, and word-of-mouth is spread.

– Add pleasant surprises, which create the kind of delight that is likely to start word-of-mouth spreading. This can be done by adding unexpected value to the transaction or adding "entertainment" to the buying experience.

• *One-to-one marketing and tailoring of products and services.* There is not much coverage of either this topic or trusted intermediaries in traditional marketing literature, but the book *The Interactive Marketplace* by

Keith T. Brown (2000), essentially an e-business book, contains some fascinating perspectives on marketing and the concept of trusted intermediaries. Brown's tenet is that e-businesses, and conventional businesses, that try to sell something, usually based on the lowest price, have poor odds for success, whereas interactive B2B2C (business-to-business-to-consumer) chains of businesses offering service, availability, and reasonable prices are the future. The finer IT and e-business aspects of this theory will not be covered here, but at the core of this thinking is the use of computers to capture and store information about individual customers and their preferences and purchase history. Such data allow an organization to distinguish between perhaps 10,000 individual customers the same way the village shoemaker could when he had 100, and predict future needs the way the shoemaker could anticipate that a customer would soon wear out the left heel of his boot because of his limp. This can facilitate one-to-one marketing and so-called mass-customization that enables supplying two different customers with dedicated recipes for dietary supplements, stereo system configuration, or clothing design and size in a mass production setting. The advantage is that the organization and the customers are saved the trouble and costs of the mass marketing shotgun approach while it raises the threshold for changing suppliers.

• *Networks of trusted intermediaries.* This is to some extent a variant of word-of-mouth and one-to-one marketing, but with a singular spin on it. This approach can definitely be used in a noncomputerized setting and work perfectly, but as Brown illustrates with some examples, the potential is probably even higher when these networks take advantage of computing power and IT systems. The latter will typically consist of Web-based, calendar-run configuration and procedural-based control systems where alliances of innovative suppliers create networks of trusted intermediaries to offer one-to-one mass customization. Two examples outlined by Brown are:

– When a customer buys seeds to make a lawn, the seed supplier's system keeps track of when the lawn was established, local growth conditions, weather deviations from normal in the period, and so on, and automatically sends the customer information about fertilizing and lawn maintenance, offers for the right type of fertilizer, refreshment seeds, and so on, and offers from partners for the rent of a seed distributor or lawn maintenance performed by local teenagers on summer vacation.

– The supplier of office paper continuously estimates consumption of paper by the customer and can thus offer increasingly better timed automatic deliveries of paper, together with offers for copy machine service, toner, and access to a network of suppliers of office furniture, equipment, secretarial services, and so on, with discounts through the alliance.

As such alliances develop and attract more and more customers who are fascinated by this one-to-one mass customization (and avoid mass advertising), it becomes more effective and offers better service. In the best examples, this becomes a spiraling effect where the members of the alliance act as trusted intermediaries on behalf of each other. Such an example is found in Ohio where an alliance of forty-four construction companies with different areas of expertise offers almost every conceivable service to customers drawn to the alliance by word-of-mouth. Brown compares this concept to the rotational Wankel engine, which is quite inefficient at low rotational speed just after start-up, but is increasingly more efficient at higher cycles-per-minute and much more efficient than traditional engines at peak. The practice of referral (which was common in the village where our shoemaker worked) keeps the alliance growing as the trust among its members increases by "coming through" for one another. An important point to make is that true intermediary networks cannot fall into the two traps of either trying to force successful alliances onto customers as monopolies or revert to mass advertising for the alliance. Customers must initially come to the alliance by word-of-mouth and then be kept inside based on referrals to other members.

Ultimately, the strength of marketing approaches that are based on building trust, referrals, and offering true value for money lies in their ability to create a kind of society or family of customers and suppliers. The customer loyalty inside such societies is sometimes extreme ("Till the day I die, I will never buy anything but a Dodge from Dodge World on Lincoln Street!") and reduces the need for traditional marketing dramatically. As will be shown later on, in chapter 9, when adding the dimension of doing something good for others while buying a product or service, that is, the philanthropic dimension, such societies can grow even stronger.

To end this marketing section, a couple of warnings:

• There are some ways of marketing that can seem simple to accomplish, cost-effective, and with a great potential. This sounds too good to be true and usually is. Spam e-mail marketing is one current example of such. Figures on how much money such activity costs employers and individuals in time, bother, and protection software are constantly growing. Sending spam is so cheap, that only a tiny fraction of the recipients taking the bait is sufficient to keep this practice proliferating. But there can be no doubt that this is a highly unethical way of marketing. It is unsolicited, directed to your individual e-mail account, and creates massive problems for recipients and their employers and Internet providers. Beyond e-mail-based spam, the latest invention of these marketers is spam transferred via Short Message Service (SMS) messages to recipients' cellular phones, a practice that is both as annoying as e-mail spam and exerts a huge load on the telephone system. Under an ethical business approach (or indeed under any business approach), such marketing is not an option.

• Not as infernal as spam e-mail, telemarketing places high on the list of annoying marketing approaches. Callers with numbers that do not show up on your caller ID display, calling just after supper to sell you something, are likely to create hostility in most people toward the source of the call. Consequently, it is not very effective in terms of marketing and image building, and it represents a form of unsolicited marketing that is invasive of your personal sphere and not in line with an ethical marketing policy.

• Another marketing concept, also used to run entire distribution networks, that has become popular over the last couple of decades is the so-called multilevel marketing approach (often referred to as MLM). Before this was established as a legal way of selling products, similar methods were used to scam people in so-called pyramid schemes. In fact, quite a few such MLM schemes are even today deemed illegal and shut down by authorities, perhaps a testament to the fact that this concept still is a rather shady one. Granted, there are some of these that are genuinely set up as an alternative sales and distribution channel for legitimate products and which become long-term entities. For each of these, however, there seems to be one or two bogus ones that are set up to make the first entrants rich quickly. As enough levels have been recruited to reach this objective, the whole network becomes too large to manage or generate income for everyone and the whole thing collapses. With the reputation these schemes have, many businesses think twice before choosing MLM as an approach for a legitimate business.

• Finally, as discussed in chapter 5 in sectors with intrinsic ethical issues, quite a lot of the advertising we see today is powerful in transmitting and altering values and attitudes in people. When such advertising leads to eating disorders, a sense that drug abuse is acceptable, or violence, the marketers have gone too far in their measures to sell products or services. As an ethical organization, you will clearly have to decline such marketing approaches.

In the middle of the process of writing this book, my wife and I had our summer vacation. To make things easier, we ordered one of those all-inclusive travel packages of airline tickets, hotel accommodations, and even meal plans. The trip was found in a catalog containing tours to a large number of destinations across the globe. We fell for one that promised twenty-eight days of sunshine in the month of July and a hotel located in a quiet area. The pictures of the accommodations looked very nice, showing the hotel itself and a beautiful beach next to it. As a whole, the entire thing looked very attractive and gave a solid impression.

We soon found out the catalog was perhaps not telling the entire story. In ten days of vacation, we had four days of sun; the rest of the time it was cloudy with lots of rain. If this were but an anomaly that we were unfortunate enough to encounter, we would not have reacted that negatively. However, people kept telling us this was normal, quite different from what the catalog said. As for the hotel, it was quite nice, but the pictures and catalog description failed to mention the rather heavily trafficked road that passed close by. We even located the spot from where the catalog picture had been taken, and only with painstaking care had the photographer been able to avoid capturing the road in the photo. It is hard to say, but we might not have chosen this trip if the facts had been presented to us truthfully, so in that respect the tour operator managed to get customers where honest marketing might have not succeeded. However, it should be obvious that I will never again do business with this company, as I doubt will all the family and friends to whom I have told this story.

DOES YOUR SUPPLY CHAIN MAINTAIN THE SAME HIGH STANDARDS AS YOUR ORGANIZATION?

The heading says supply chain, but this is really a question that pertains to more than de facto members of the supply chain behind the organization. With the strong growth of supply chain management as a topic of its own over the last few years, one clear insight that has taken hold in most organizations is that industrial competition, more than a competition between individual enterprises, is a competition between entire supply chains. There are many ways to define the concept of a supply chain, for example: "A set of three or more companies directly linked by one or more of the upstream and downstream flows of products, services, finances, and information from a source to a customer" (Mentzer, 2001). As a consequence, you are in competition with other supply chains together with your suppliers of products and services, their suppliers, and your customers (provided you do not sell directly to the end customer), be they other manufacturers, wholesalers, retailers, and so on. The supply chain definition cited focuses on upstream and downstream companies, as such creating an image that a supply chain is a single, streamlined entity, see Figure 6.2.

In fact, what is popularly called a supply chain is more often than not a supply network with crossing lines of supplies of products, services, money, and information, as shown in Figure 6.3.

Irrespective of which view is taken of a supply chain, the point is that your image and reputation in the marketplace is a factor of your own performance and that of your supply chain partners (and vice versa). No doubt the contribution of your own performance is much higher than that of your partners in terms of building or breaking your reputation, but you would be naïve in assuming that it does not matter which partners you align with.

Figure 6.2 A tidy, linear supply chain.

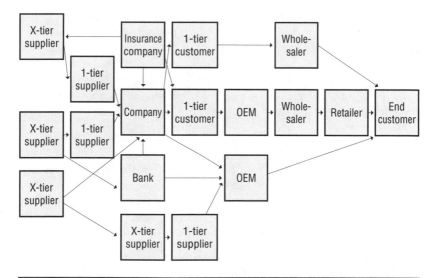

Figure 6.3 A more realistic, complex supply network.

Triumph International is a large manufacturer of underwear, and in advance of the Olympic Games in Salt Lake City in 2002, they won a contract with one of the national teams for the supply of underwear to the female athletes. After a while, it became public knowledge that Triumph had manufacturing facilities in Burma, a country where military forces claimed power after the party of Aung San Suu Kyi won a democratic election in 1990. She received the Nobel Peace Prize in 1991 for her struggle for democracy in Burma, but is still imprisoned along with hundreds of her fellow party members.

Humanitarian organizations soon launched campaigns against the choice of underwear supplier, calling for a ban on "dirty underwear." Receiving massive support from the public in the appeal, and from many of the athletes themselves, the sports team was soon on the brink of canceling the contract. Before this happened, Triumph decided to sell or close down the plant. According to Cathrine Long, press officer of Triumph International, the public debate about the plant in Burma became so heated that it created too many problems for the long-term planning of business activities in Burma. Since no buyer has been forth-coming, the company is gradually phasing out production while assisting the employees who will lose their jobs.

The less complex the supply chain or supply network is, the easier it is to maintain an overview of the activities and performance of its members. Unfortunately, industrial relations are often quite complex, and the fact remains that misconduct on the part of a distant member in the supply network can easily harm your organization. Thus, being conscious about the composition of the supply networks and their conduct is a vital concern. Some issues to consider are:

• Gaining an overview of the supply network, looking backward to the suppliers and their suppliers, looking forward to customers and their customers, and looking sideways to partners, service suppliers outside the main value-adding stream like banks, insurance companies, and so on. Try to assess each of the players with some impact on the organization's image and reputation in cases of misconduct and consider replacing unsuitable ones, to the extent this is feasible in the short term.

• Developing and imposing requirements on the players in the extended supply network in terms of broad ethical issues. Keep in mind that the power of the organization to impose such requirements will vary greatly from member to member in the network. For first-tier suppliers for whom the organization represents important business volume, the power is obviously much stronger than in relations with more remote players or players that the organization depends on. Nevertheless, varying degrees of power should not prevent you from at least presenting the requirements throughout the network—very often customers, banks, and so on, will welcome such an initiative. As for the actual requirements, the details can vary significantly between business and geographical areas. Main "headings" typically encompass guidelines or dos and don'ts on human rights issues, labor conditions, legislative adherence, environmental impact, and other areas of relevance and with strong presence in the organization's value system. Such requirements can also be included in contractual agreements as part of terms and conditions or as grounds for contract cancellation upon noncompliance. Some companies even demand that their suppliers transmit these requirements backward in their contracts with their suppliers.

• With complex supply networks, it is obvious that the organization cannot maintain a detailed overview of activities and developments of all the members in the network. Thus, setting such requirements, both general and preferably also specific ones where relevant, is a way to ease this job. However, imposing these requirements, even in contracts, is no guarantee they will be complied with. A proven approach in such situations is randomly conducted reviews or assessments. Most professional organizations of any size conduct some kind of supplier reviews to ensure that quality and other standards are upheld. Either undertaking dedicated ethical reviews or incorporating ethical issues into general supplier assessments is a logical approach to keeping the supply network members alert and gaining a periodic overview of their status.

• Arguably, a customer sourcing products or services from many suppliers cannot be expected to conduct costly assessments of these suppliers to ensure that they behave with the decency toward quality and ethics that the customer pays for as part of the package. This is the basic platform for the development of various certification or accreditation schemes. The ISO 9000 standard is probably the best known such scheme, certifying that the recipient of the stamp of approval meets certain requirements for a quality system. ISO 14000 is a similar standard, but related to environmental management, and there are others as well. The point is that instead of conducting assessments itself, an organization can with some degree of certainty source from suppliers certified by recognized certification auditors and assume that they have things in order. In an ethics setting, certification regarding environmental performance, human rights adherence, labor standards, and so on, are all relevant.

As mentioned in the introduction to this topic, equally important as setting ethical requirements for supply network members is choosing the right members in the first place. A key consideration should of course be to what extent the potential members have policies and practices in place that match the ethical standards and expectations of the organization, for the purpose of avoiding any negative exposure in cases of misconduct. However, the choice of suppliers and partners is also a matter of image and statement, on several levels:

• Choosing high-quality suppliers with strong brand names and good reputations reflects on the products or services the organization offers to the market ("Intel inside").

• Choosing suppliers from developing countries can be positive and negative. Negative if the key motivation for doing so lies in lower costs and leads to outsourcing and closing of home facilities, especially if the host country has a dubious reputation (like Triumph in Burma).

• Choosing suppliers from developing countries can be positive if this appears to be some sort of aid to a developing country where the organization helps in building industry and employment under decent conditions.

A particular type of risk is related to brand names and their image. Brand names play many important roles; they provide information and

Running shoes and trainers comprise one sector where revelations of sweatshops on the other side of the world from brand headquarters have shaken the manufacturers. That most of the major players have been exposed as running less-than-worthy facilities does not seem to have impacted the mutual competition among them, but some players are trying new avenues. The English shoemaker New Balance emphasizes strongly that their shoes are indeed made in England, with the following text on the label attached to the shoe:

> Thank you for purchasing a pair of New Balance . . . been making high quality performance footwear at our UK factory since 1882 . . . means years of experience and craftsmanship go into every single shoe we produce . . . that's why we don't let just anyone make them.

This is followed by a large "NB! Made in England" announcement further down. New Balance clearly tries to distance itself from the scandals of the industry and portray their shoes as positive exceptions.

security about provenance and content to consumers and they allow vendors an escape from detrimental price wars. Naomi Klein in her book *No Logo* (2000) reminded us of the problematic aspects of the modern "superbrands," which on one hand strive to promote a logo that portrays "high value" and related associations while on the other hand often producing the products under anonymous sweatshop conditions and low wages somewhere far away. This is a setup for a fall waiting to happen, which is what Klein really pointed out; when the associations of the brand no longer match the actual conditions under which it is being produced, revelations can be expensive. Choosing supply network members that stand the test of the expectations the brand name creates is paramount in maintaining credible brands.

On that note, let us move on to the often-controversial topic of pricing.

WHAT DO YOU CHARGE FOR YOUR PRODUCT OR SERVICE? FAIR PRICING

When discussing the issue of pricing with others, especially people with an economics education, this stands out as a hot topic. Some of them even claim that the prices you are able to command for your products or services have nothing at all to do with business ethics. My having included the topic in this book obviously reflects disagreement. There are a number of issues related to pricing that are a matter of ethics and decency on the part of the seller of goods and services.

First of all, the heading of this section refers to "fair pricing," which in itself relates fundamentally to how you regard your customers. There are many ways of calculating a price. Kotler (1988) mentioned the following, among others:

- Markup pricing; simply adding a percentage to unit costs and thus arriving at the price.

- Target return pricing; setting the price based on an estimate of the price that will yield the desired return on investment.

- Going-rate pricing; simply going with the flow and basing prices chiefly on those of competitors.

There are probably a number of variants of these as well, but common to all of them is the fact that the price to a lesser extent reflects the actual value delivered to the customer. A widespread practice not mentioned by Kotler is what can be termed "pain threshold pricing": figuring out how much the market will be willing to pay for your product or service before choosing another alternative or refraining from buying altogether, and quoting that amount or slightly below it as the price. Seen from a purely financial perspective, it seems to make sense to charge as much as possible for something it costs the least to deliver to the customer (maximizing the markup or the target return). In accordance with much of the argument of this book, this can only last for so long. As soon as customers realize they are paying for more than they are getting back, they will switch to other vendors. Thus, both from an ethical desire to avoid cheating anyone and delivering value for money and from a financial perspective of not losing customers down the road, a fair pricing policy makes sense.

Kotler included a pricing approach called perceived-value pricing, where the point is to convince the market of the value of the product or service and setting the price as the sum of benefits delivered, including durability, service, and so on. This is along the lines of fair pricing, where the main principle is to charge customers a price that reflects the value delivered and of course also the costs of delivering the product or service. Also under such a tenet, there will be many ways of determining the actual price level, but the important matter is the attitude behind the price setting. The calculations come out quite different when trying to squeeze as much as possible out of your customers versus trying to hit the "right" price. Some ways of calculating the fair price can be:

• Base the price on a calculation of the product's or service's worth in terms of manufacturing costs, subtracting a percentage for qualities inferior to those of competing offers and adding a premium for superior qualities. This is a variant of perceived-value pricing.

• Customer-determined pricing, where a survey of a suitable number of prospective customers are asked to estimate a value or price for the offer in question (Kotler refers to this approach as direct price-rating).

• Indirect perceived value rating, where again customers are asked to evaluate three or more competing offers (*n* offers) by assigning a total of 100 points to the offers to reflect the value of each. Based on a deviation from the mean of $100/n$, the price for your offer could be set above or below the average market price.

• Varying degrees of cost recovery. Normally, a price, regardless of how it has been arrived at, includes a smaller or larger gross margin beyond recovery of the direct costs involved in producing and delivering the product or service. Parts of this gross margin are used to recuperate indirect costs not directly involved in the production of the purchased object, but are still necessary to get the object to the customer, for example, supporting IT systems, office cleaning, conference participation, marketing, even R&D and product development costs. To a customer, some of these costs obviously seem fair to be included in the price, for example the product development

Kotler included an example in his book of the perceived-value pricing approach, citing Caterpillar, whose tractors are often priced higher than those of competitors. For example, in the case of a $90,000 tractor from a competing manufacturer, a similar-sized machine from Caterpillar can cost $100,000. When questioned about the premium price by customers, dealers show them a calculation as follows:

$90,000 is the tractor's equipment price, equivalent to the competing tractor
+ $7000 is the price premium for superior durability
+ $6000 is the price premium for superior reliability
+ $5000 is the price premium for superior service
+ $2000 is the price premium for longer warranty on parts

$110,000 is the price to cover the value package
−$10,000 discount

$100,000 final price

This price then reflects both a de facto discount compared with the competing tractor and a piece of equipment whose operating costs will be lower over its lifetime.

costs. For pharmaceuticals, these often represent the largest portion of costs, much more than the actual manufacturing and distribution costs. Marketing, on the other hand, in a society that is growing ever wearier of commercials, is a cost that many customers find outrageous to pay for in the price of a product or service. A fair cost-recovery pricing will consist of determining which indirect cost elements seem fair to burden customers with and including cost recovery of these in the price, while either recovering other indirect expenses through other means or slashing these altogether.

Ultimately, any organization must of course find the right balance between its prices and its costs, even if it spends very little money on extravagancies. It is no good setting prices so low that the company will run at a deficit year after year. Again, an ethical approach does not mean being silly or overly naïve, and fair pricing is to a large extent a matter of attitudes. Some other considerations to note under this heading are:

• Set and communicate prices in a manner that makes it clear and simple for prospective customers to understand the total end price. One could possibly write a whole book about tricks to use to conceal the true costs of a product or service until the customer has signed the contract. Some obvious ones include adding fees to the price that are hard to calculate, quoting the price of parts but leaving out the costs of the service or the other way around, setting cancellation or return conditions that make it very expensive to change your mind, composing offers of many components and giving a good price for the obvious element and charging a premium for the rest, and so on. These are (perfectly legal) ways of cheating customers that will do the company no good in the long run.

• Consider the value put on the brand name of a product or service. In the example of Caterpillar above, you could say the price difference of $10,000 is a brand name premium, but as the calculation shows, in this case the brand name actually comes with an added monetary value. In many other cases, there is no difference at all between a brand name product and a generic one, a fact that is clearly demonstrated by the proliferation of store brands in supermarkets. Very often, both the generic type and the branded product are made by the same manufacturer, from the same raw materials, using the same processes, and so on, thus for all intents and purposes being the same, but with the generic product costing much less. Where the brand means extra value through better quality or assurance that the product has been produced without child labor or exploitation of third-world suppliers, a premium price is warranted, but not where the only difference is the logo on the product and packaging.

• Using changes in currency exchange rates, interest rates, or other money market changes to justify unreasonable price increases is another popular tactic. When nine of the twelve European Union countries introduced the euro as their common currency in 2002, all purveyors of goods and services had to change their prices accordingly. Although a fixed exchange rate was defined between each of the old currencies and the euro, very few simply did the calculation and left it at that. Many took the opportunity to raise prices by rounding them off to €1.99 or €2.99. The same often happens when currency exchange rates fluctuate, at least when the fluctuation goes one way. Importers of products are quick to increase their prices when the exchange rates come out in their disfavor, but hardly quick to reduce them again when the opposite is the case. For an organization that subscribes to an ethical approach, such practices are of course unacceptable.

• Price guarantees are one approach used especially by retail stores to give their customers security that they will not pay too high a price. Such guarantees typically state that any difference between the price for a product in the store and a competing store with a lower price will be refunded, in some cases even with an additional markup of 50 or 100 percent. When designed properly and practiced as intended, these guarantees represent a good insurance for customers feeling uncertain about whether they are paying the right price or not. However, there are many examples where such a guarantee is more a marketing trick than a genuine price guarantee. One way to shirk the responsibility is to define that the guarantee applies only to the exact same product, down to the model number. Electronics stores are clever at this, where one chain sells a washing machine with a certain name, for example, WS-300 SP, whereas the exact same machine is sold in another chain under the name of VT-310 SX, thus making the guarantee invalid.

• Promoting so-called loss leader products is another common approach used especially by retail stores to attract customers. There is nothing wrong per se with having very good sales on certain items, but some stores exploit this practice even further in ways that are clearly unethical. For example, some advertisements for loss leader bargains make sure that fine print at the bottom informs the reader that the offer applies to a limited batch of products. When customers, who of course do not read the fine print, turn up to buy the product, the very small batch is gone and what is left is either another batch of the same product at regular price or an alternative product at a completely different price. Most people, even if they get annoyed, do not find it worthwhile to drive to another store to get what they came for and will therefore accept the higher price, for now; they might come back the next time they need something from this type of store.

• Price differentiation is another approach used by many vendors as a strategy to maximize profits. It is certainly a legal practice, and as will be discussed later on when dealing with philanthropic practices, in some cases even a means to do something good, for example, selling pharmaceuticals at reduced prices to developing countries and recovering the discount by charging more in markets that are better off. However, this practice can also be used in a way that seems unfair to the market. If a clothing company thinks it can get away with a higher price for a shirt in Toronto than in Rochester, New York, a few hours drive across the border, this is clearly a pricing strategy based on profit maximization and not value-based pricing. Once disclosed, customers are bound to react negatively to a practice they can only see as greedy.

• The next item is not related directly to fair pricing, but in many cases, retail stores, and indeed also other vendors, carry several different alternative products to what you are looking for, both from the same manufacturer and from different ones. Typically, depending on the agreements with the suppliers, the seller will have a varying profit for the different alternatives. Trying to steer the customer toward one with a higher profit

A mechanism similar to price differentiation can come into play in markets where the commodity being sold is in short supply and prices are very dependent on the balance between demand and supply. This is the case with oil products or electric power, for example. To an extent unknown to most countries, Norway has a large percentage of their power consumption produced by clean hydroelectric infrastructure. The country is not self-sufficient, but not far away either. A few years back, the electricity market was liberalized, seeing the power suppliers go from being owned by the state or local municipalities to becoming private companies, and the power market becoming an open Nordic one. Last winter, electricity prices skyrocketed in Norway, in many cases quadrupling, creating serious problems for many people, especially those traditionally worst off, that is, elderly or families with children. The dramatic price increases were a result of several compounded factors:

- A number of unusually dry seasons, both summer and winter, had led to a lower fill rate for the reservoirs than in a normal year.

- Power consumption increases, due to a cold winter and ever more houses and buildings being erected with each of these having more electric equipment in them.

- With the open power market, the suppliers were now free to export power to the highest bidder, leading to a depletion of domestic reservoirs.

The latter especially added to the other two factors. Electricity prices have traditionally been higher in the countries neighboring Norway (as they have produced power from coal, gas, or nuclear reactors). With the opportunity to sell power to these countries at premium prices compared to average domestic prices, the Norwegian power companies were more than ready to export. This mainly took place during summer and fall, but nonetheless eroded the fill rate of the reservoirs. With the onset of winter, which turned out to bring a little less snow than an average one and a bit lower temperatures, demand increased and the reservoirs did not fill up as expected. As a result, prices went sky high, turning the issue into the hottest news item for weeks. Having settled their accounts, all power companies showed record profit levels for this period, in addition to pleasant figures for the summer and fall due to the exports.

One of the largest chains of electrics and electronics stores in Europe was recently exposed in the media for having taken the practice of steering customers toward higher-margin products to the limit. A former employee in one of the stores told the media how this practice was deeply entrenched to the point that new sales assistants were given training in the procedure, which worked as follows: Several times a year, the chain would negotiate deals with suppliers to buy batches of some product type, for example, a vacuum cleaner or a DVD player, always at the low end and for a bargain price. Sales advertisements would prominently present these loss leader articles to bring customers into the stores. In the stores, all products had been very cleverly, but subtly labeled (of course not just for this sale, but year-round); the shade of green (the color of the logo of the chain) used as background on the price stickers varied in accordance with the profit margin of the products. This way, the sales assistants did not need to memorize which products the store (and themselves, as part of their wages was a commission based on the profits they made for the store) would make the most money from selling, they could clearly see it as they talked to the customers. Thus, as people came in to buy the loss leader they had figured out they could just about afford, the sales assistants would quickly tell them about all the shortcomings of that model compared with a slightly more expensive one next to it. Many customers would of course settle for the loss leader after all (which was fine, the store needed to sell the batch after all), but equally many would be persuaded to go for a "slightly more expensive" one, one that incidentally had a much higher profit margin.

margin, irrespective of the needs of the customer or the qualities of the product, is clearly an unethical approach to business.

So far, the discussion on pricing has been biased toward private companies selling products or services. However, the public sector is often as bad, if not worse, in its lack of decency in pricing matters. Public sector services like processing of permits, court services, public transportation, sanitation, kindergarten, connection to water, power, and gas, and so on, are normally monopoly services for which no alternative can be selected but the local public offering.

Depending on national and local regulations, the authorities are either free to set their fees at whatever level they deem necessary or they are restricted to pure cost recovery or certain maximum charges. In many cases, the fees paid for public services must even be considered a kind of additional tax that represents a budgeted income for the authorities, one that would create a deficit were it removed. For example, in many countries, there is a so-called "stamp duty" involved when buying property, often in the range of one to three percent of the buying price. The actual job done by the authorities is to change the name on the deed and stamp it, a job that takes a few minutes. The fee can easily be $6000, an unfair price no matter how much someone tries to argue the value of the service. While one can appreciate the difficulties states and authorities experience in making ends meet in their budgets, a much fairer approach to setting fees would be to charge such services at their actual cost and instead increase taxes. This way, those who happen to buy a property or use some other administrative service will pay the costs that service incurs and the population at large will chip in their share toward the balanced budget, instead of having those unfortunate ones who need a certain service pick up a much larger share of the total bill.

Before closing this section on pricing, remember that prices are a dual matter; you charge a price for what you sell, but you also pay a price for goods and services procured from your suppliers. When talking about fair prices on outgoing products, people tend to think of prices that are not unreasonably high. However, prices can also be unfair by being unreasonably low. Depending on the power balance between seller and buyer and other circumstantial factors, a buyer can often force a seller to accept prices that are certainly lower than the value of the product or service, sometimes even so low that the long-term viability of the vendor can be in jeopardy. Typical settings that are prone to such outcomes are:

- Where the buyer is substantially larger than the seller and thus can use its muscle to force low prices.

- In relationships where the buyer is a key customer accounting for a large portion of the seller's revenues, or even all of it, and as such represents so important a customer the seller cannot afford to risk losing it.

- Longer-term sourcing contracts, often in the form of frame agreements, in many cases contain clauses governing annual price reductions or volume-dependent discounts that can in the end send prices very low.

- In markets where there are many alternative suppliers, perhaps coupled with excess supply compared with demand, it is a buyer's market and buyers can push prices down.

- When goods or services are procured from low-cost, developing countries, the local cost levels are much lower than in Western countries. For a Western customer, a fair and acceptable price would often be much higher than what is actually possible to obtain in such countries.

From a buyer's perspective, as from the seller's earlier, it makes financial sense to pay the lowest price possible, thus incurring the least costs. But from both a practical and an ethical point of view, this can be detrimental in the long run. Practically speaking, a supplier forced to accept rock-bottom prices will perhaps not be able to keep on developing their products or services to offer you better deals in the future, it might even come into financial trouble, leading to unstable deliveries and ultimately its bankruptcy, and a supplier pushed to the wall in price negotiations will hardly be eager to give you the best possible service. Ethically speaking, forcing prices unreasonably low to maximize your own profit looks bad if made public knowledge. The motivation is the same as when Western brand names use sweatshops in developing countries to produce their products; such revelations always turn people off. No matter how you look at it, showing a sense of moderation in price negotiations with suppliers should be a wise approach.

During recent years, prices for coffee beans have remained unusually low, due to overproduction and price pressure. Low in the sense of the price the coffee farmers are paid—prices to consumers have remained relatively stable. The result is that around 25 million coffee farmers, most of them in poor regions of the world, are facing severe financial problems. Some earn as little as ten dollars a month, are heavily in debt, and are thus forced to sell to generate some income even when prices are low. Profiles of some of these farmers have been shown on TV and tell the story of families having to send their children away or take them out of school to work on the farm.

In sharp contrast, the middlemen arranging the sales of coffee beans to Western manufacturers of brand name coffee put some of the markup in their pockets; the rest is shared between the manufacturers and their distribution channels. As an example, last year's profits of the global coffee manufacturers increased sharply: Nestlé by 15 percent, Kraft Foods by 80 percent.

MARKET RESPECT: ARE YOU EXPLOITING YOUR MARKET POSITION?

In markets where organizations are able to achieve full monopoly dominance or an oligopoly position, chances are they will exploit such a position by raising prices (which is also an issue of fair pricing treated earlier). Most countries have developed, and reinforce, strict antitrust laws, but in many cases it is simply not feasible to avoid questionable situations. Major players go bust leaving only one or two real contenders behind, sellers pull out of certain market segments with the same effect, quiet mergers and takeovers are allowed to move forward until a giant is formed, and in many markets, there is even an intrinsic monopoly setting, usually in cases where the public sector is responsible for service delivery.

Antitrust laws have been designed for the purpose of avoiding the negative effects that often come from near-monopoly dominance: inflated prices, poor service, low innovation rate, supply shortages, and so on. These effects occur because it simply is so tempting to raise prices when there are no competitors that most organizations in such a position fail to resist the urge, and because there is no pressure to constantly improve and innovate. Even if such practices do backfire in terms of bad publicity and even downright hostility toward the monopolist, consequences are small since there is no alternative. However, most monopolies have a tendency to topple, either through regulation or new entrants, and in the aftermath, a poor image in the market can be a serious liability. Thus, both because it is unfair toward customers to exploit monopolies and because it can backfire in the long run, being decent enough to not exploit your position should you find yourself in a monopoly or oligopoly market is the right thing to do.

Even in markets where there are a number of competing players present, it is still possible to exploit the market in ways that are both unethical and illegal. The most common approaches are price-fixing and market sharing. In price-fixing, two or more competitors secretly agree to stick to a certain price level to increase their profits. This practice can be used both in tender situations and regular over-the-counter sales and is typically more effective when more sellers are involved. This is of course an illegal practice, but one that can be hard for authorities to detect and put a stop to. As such, it is obviously a tempting avenue; a few phone calls or discussions over a beer one night and the problem of being undersold and low profit margins is gone. Still, if found out, the price can be high, both in fines and in loss of goodwill and sales (see sidebar).

In market sharing, two or more competitors agree to a certain division of the market. Each partner involved agrees to stay away from the others'

In 2001, a federal jury found Mitsubishi Corporation guilty of aiding an international price-fixing cartel for graphite electrodes used to make steel. Investigations eventually led to convictions of six companies and more than $300 million in criminal fines, in addition to a $134 million fine to Mitsubishi. Prosecutors said the cartel had secret meetings in luxury hotels around the globe and code names for the conspirators in a plot that almost doubled the price of electrodes from 1992 to 1997. During the trial, the chairmen of two of the other companies in the cartel testified that they convened at a May 1992 meeting of cartel participants in London to formally begin the arrangement. Afterward, the pair met for years with top executives of their competitors to set prices. The clandestine meetings were held in hotels in London, Paris, Zurich, Vienna, Singapore, and Tokyo, the prosecution witnesses said. Conspirators gave each other secret code names, such as "Emperor," "Caesar," "Mustache," "Wave," and "Cold."

The price-fixing scandal spawned a flood of other civil suits by steel-makers seeking triple damages for overcharges during the five-year conspiracy in which United States sales of graphite electrodes totaled $1.7 billion. Many of the U.S. lawsuits have been settled out of court for more than $100 million. Besides paying a $110 million criminal fine, Nashville, Tennessee–based UCAR reached a $40.6 million settlement in 1999 with shareholders. It has since sued Mitsubishi for inducing its participation in the cartel.

turf, thus reducing competitive pressure and normally allowing higher prices, even if no fixed levels have been defined. This is a practice that is just as unacceptable as price-fixing, and both are of course not an option to serious organizations.

A related matter pertains to services that traditionally have been public sector responsibilities, at least in many countries, for example public transportation services, primary and secondary schooling, healthcare services, and so on. Perhaps truly gaining momentum with former UK Prime Minister Margaret Thatcher, a wave of privatization of such services has swept most Western countries the last couple of decades. In many cases, this has represented a move away from monopolies to deregulated, free markets with competition. At least that is the idea, and in many cases the result. Many countries have for example seen a marked improvement in road standards by allowing private companies to build, own, and operate highways as toll roads.

However, many of these public services have been exactly that, public, for a reason, namely that they represent the kind of services that can be difficult to operate under regular market conditions. If public transportation is left solely to private enterprises, chances are that the most inhabited and profitable routes will be serviced while rural areas will lose their service. In some countries, postal distribution has been privatized into incorporated companies operated as commercial enterprises, albeit usually wholly owned by the state. The result has sometimes been differentiated rates depending on the population density; people in cities get their mail cheaper than people living in the countryside. There are many more examples, but the point is that the exact opposite mechanism takes place as in the unjust exploitation of monopoly situation mentioned above. When the public sector handled such services, the monopoly was a guarantee of full service coverage and homogeneous prices. The pendulum is starting to swing and some privatized services are indeed being reclaimed by the public authorities, an indication that not all areas of a society can be left to private actors. Being a responsible and ethically oriented government, services that will face problems in the hands of private players should not be privatized this way.

Loyalty programs or cards are another concept that is hard to pigeonhole within the business ethics framework, but one that still deserves some attention. They are used by airlines, video rental stores, gasoline stations, supermarkets, clothing stores, and many others to give their customers incentives to stay loyal. These incentives range from progressive discounts to special offers for members to the possibility to exchange points for goods or money to status upgrades (to many, holding a gold card in an airline frequent flyer program has some status).

There is of course nothing wrong with these programs per se. Brandenburger and Nalebuff (1996) even called loyalty programs a genius invention that allows a company to create long-term customer loyalty and at the same time allow their competitors to do the same, thus reducing the worst peaks of war. The drawback is that as these programs proliferate, many customers join all of them and thereby dilute the effect.

Most such programs are designed so that the customer has a "bonus account" with the company, one that often comes with an electronic card used when registering purchases and thus being awarded bonus points. In an ethical setting, this design of loyalty programs is the possible questionable aspect. As the technology gets better and better, it becomes easier and easier for companies to register the entire buying history of their customers, storing their preferences for products and services, when, where, and how purchases are made, and so on. Customers realize that in order to claim their bonuses, their purchases must be registered, but few realize the extent to which they are actually being monitored. Companies with sophisticated systems can easily extract vast amounts of data about their customers and use it to target them personally with dedicated offers. If you shop for next week's groceries on a regular basis on Thursday afternoon in the same store week after week, the store can send you direct mail offerings on Wednesdays for certain products. If you usually buy steaks for Sunday dinner, some beer, and a low-priced brand of ice cream, the store might make you aware of a certain barbeque sauce that will enhance the steaks, persuade you that it is nicer to drink a good red wine with the steaks, and that another, more expensive brand of ice cream is a much better treat for your Sunday dessert.

Again, there is nothing explicitly wrong with this widespread practice; in fact, it is in some ways similar to the trusted intermediary concept discussed earlier. The thing is, there is a line somewhere that should not be crossed. In any case, the main objective of the company is obviously to generate more revenue, but under the trusted intermediary concept, there is a belief that the customers are better taken care of by pointing them to other service or product providers that they might need, providers that the company knows are trustworthy and deliver quality. In the most elaborate loyalty program schemes, many customers would probably feel that they had to some extent been victims of cheating had they known how their purchase registrations were being used, especially since no one tells them the data will be exploited this way. A piece of advice is therefore to either restrict the use of loyalty programs to their main objective, namely to give incentives to your customers for staying loyal or at least be completely open with them if you intend to use the data the program generates more extensively.

Finally, having respect for your markets and customers also means choosing your customers carefully. When discussing requirements poscd to suppliers, it was mentioned how this is a way of using your power as a customer to demand ethically sound practices. Turning the tables, the same is to some extent true for your customers. Any organization selling products or services will typically have a large number of customers, be they consumers or professional organizations. The latter especially use your products and services in their own businesses, and just like your suppliers, these customers can operate in ways that are below your own ethical standards and that could backfire on your organization. The same way revelations that an organization has used a supplier that is actively destroying rain forest will tarnish its reputation, media attention to the fact that a manufacturer of forestry equipment sells the machines required for this destruction to this company will be damaging.

There are many reasons why a particular customer can be an undesirable one: from inflicting environmental damage to having questionable practices toward its customers to being engaged in downright criminal activities to being a regime that is criticized for its politics. Companies that make generic parts, parts that can also be used in the manufacture of land mines, have suffered demonstrations from pressure groups over their sales to land mine companies. Being a key player in the Middle East conflict, Israel is seen by many as an aggressive and brutal nation, and companies conducting extensive business with Israeli companies have also been targeted by demonstrations. In addition to falling victim to demonstrations and smear campaigns that will damage the organization's reputation, dealing with questionable customers can also directly impact revenues. In cases where attention has been brought to such cases, other customers of the organization have been known to switch suppliers to avoid being connected to the questionable supply chain. All in all, choosing your customers carefully can be as important as choosing your suppliers.

WHEN SOMETHING GOES WRONG— HANDLING COMPLAINTS

Perhaps the most reliable way of telling whether a supplier is a decent, ethically minded organization is to test their practices for handling complaints. Whereas most organizations are more than happy to help you buy their products or services, not everyone is equally helpful when there is something wrong with them afterward. This is, however, a crucial point of interaction with customers. A negative experience in trying to get a broken product replaced or repaired can completely overshadow the positive impression generated during the period when the product worked as intended.

On the other hand, while products breaking down never will be an asset, careful after-sales handling of such incidents can be an opportunity to reinforce the positive assessment the customer made when buying from you in the first place. As such, complaint-handling is an area that needs to be taken seriously by any organization. For one trying to portray itself as ethically oriented, it is even more crucial. Attempting to shirk responsibilities and evading the cost of making up for things gone wrong is certainly not behavior worthy of such a profile.

Complaint-handling is really a collective term for a number of different situations and their respective procedures. The most important ones are:

• *Returns of products working properly, but not meeting the expectations of the customer.* Many companies have a policy for accepting such returns without any questions asked within thirty days after the sale, as long as the product is returned in working order and in its original packaging. Others have shorter or longer acceptance periods, some demand that the package must be unopened, while others refuse to reverse the sale. The preferred option for both customer and company seems to be a policy of accepting returns within reason; it gives the customer insurance that a product that fails to meet requirements can be returned, and the company stands out as a decent partner to do business with.

• *Complaints about products or services not working as intended, either from the outset or after some time.* This is perhaps the most common situation, where typically a product either has a fault when it is sold or breaks down after a period of time. How such situations are handled depends on a number of factors: is the warranty still valid, is the fault obviously due to a manufacturing or design problem or something done by the customer, can the problem be traced back to poor maintenance, is the fault an expected wear-and-tear issue, can the problem be corrected through service or repairs, or must the product be replaced? It is impossible to outline proper responses to every permutation of these factors, but in general a company must also strike a balance here. Being overly naïve and offering to replace or repair any broken product, no matter what caused it or for how long after the sale, is just being stupid. This will cost a lot of money and the company is guaranteed to be swindled by ruthless customers. However, when a complaint is valid, within the warranty period and for a problem that falls within the responsibilities of the seller or manufacturer, being forthcoming and helpful is the best approach. From a customer's perspective, a replacement product is often much better than having to wait for a repair. Especially if the repair will take some time or will likely not fix the problem properly, replacing the product will in the long run ensure better goodwill than insisting on trying to repair it. This type of complaint is normally well regulated in consumer law, which of course must be complied with.

• *Compensation for poor products or services.* In some cases, a customer suffers damages beyond the inconvenience of being without a product when something breaks. In the worst cases, such breakdowns cause damage to other property or injury to people; often they will lead to financial losses from the inability to use the product in the customer's own business. Also in such situations, there will in many cases be laws dictating if and how much compensation a customer is entitled to. Again, an organization will normally benefit from a forthcoming attitude. If a customer who has bought three dozen vans from you loses two days of revenues on one of them because it will not start, chances are this customer will buy the next generation of cars from you as well if some compensation is awarded for the loss. With admittedly smaller figures involved, some supermarkets have adopted practices whereby customers are refunded twice the price they paid if they find spoiled or bad fruit or vegetables in their groceries.

• *Recalls of products for replacement or repair.* This is not a case of customer complaint as such, but situations have become more and more frequent where the manufacturer of a product, after a period of sales of the product, realizes that it has some faults. Sometimes the fault can be repaired, especially for expensive products, but often the product must either be replaced or returned and the customer refunded for the purchase. With increased pressure to constantly launch new products, product development times have been reduced dramatically over the years, including shorter time for testing of new products. The result is that many products display faults that deteriorate over time or have weaknesses that could lead to breakdown in certain situations. The automotive industry is a good example of this, where a large portion of new cars are recalled by the manufacturer to undergo repairs or part replacement at local dealers' repair shops. Such recalls are, however, expensive, no matter what action is taken, so manufacturers are naturally reluctant to issue unwarranted recalls. This is a defining difference between a decent and caring organization and one that tries to get away with things. A decent organization does not undertake calculations as to whether a recall will be more expensive than a possible trial following accidents with non-recalled products; it does the right thing and absorbs the costs involved.

In 1999, in a case against General Motors Corporation, a jury awarded a record penalty of $4.9 billion to six passengers severely burned in an accident in 1983 in a Chevrolet Malibu. In the accident, the Malibu was hit from the rear and the gas tank exploded. The Los Angeles Superior Court jury focused on GM documents that the plaintiffs' lawyers said showed the carmaker knew its gas tanks were unsafe, but was unwilling to pay for a recall of the vehicles. A key piece of evidence was a 1973 memo that said deaths from fires cost GM only $2.40 per car while fixing the tank in a Malibu would cost GM as much as $4 to $12 per car.

GM appealed the verdict and pointed out that the accident was by any standard a severe one, with the car hitting the Malibu being driven by a drunk driver and striking the vehicle at 70 mph, and the Malibu sitting still at a stoplight. In the appeal trial, a judge reduced the original $4.8 billion punitive damages portion of the jury award to $1.09 billion, saying the original amount was excessive. He let stand $107 million in compensatory damages awarded to victims of the crash.

• *Product take-back after discarding.* Most products reach a point in their lifecycle where they are poised for discarding by the customer. For many types of products, this is merely a matter of dropping it in the trash can and having it removed by the regular waste disposal service. However, increasingly, products contain materials or substances that make them a hazard for the environment if disposed of this way, for example most electronic products, refrigerators, paint, car tires, and so on. Legislation is in place or emerging that instructs manufacturers or dealers to put in place end-of-life take-back regimes, but in many areas these do not yet exist. An ethically oriented organization should help their customers in disposing of products in a safe and environmentally friendly manner, by accepting discarded products and handling them properly. In many cases, innovative manufacturers have demonstrated that reuse of old products can make good business sense as well, so such an arrangement need not be an expense. Xerox copiers have been hailed as paving the way for this insight. There are very often only leased, not sold, to customers and taken back by the manufacturer when they become obsolete. Here it is disassembled and parts reused to make new machines, at a cost advantage compared with discarding the old machines.

RESPECT FOR COMPETITORS: FAIR COMPETITIVE PRACTICES

Although perhaps one stakeholder many organizations would rather do without, competitors are entities most of us simply have to live with. And no matter how enticing it might be to try and get a leg up by turning to unfair competitive practices, it is another inadvisable solution. The argument is the same as for many other unethical practices: the punishment if caught can be severe and the loss of goodwill from customers reacting negatively to such practices can be even more serious.

What is meant by unfair competitive practices, then? There is a large selection of ways to treat competitors that qualify as unfair. Most of these also qualify as illegal and have as such been covered by the appeal to comply with all relevant legislation. Still, a few typical ones will be mentioned, some that are illegal and some that only qualify as unethical:

• Plagiarism, formally defined as using someone else's words or ideas as if they were your own, is an old and widespread way of coming up with new products, designs, features, and so on. It can be difficult to detect, and plagiarism can be as much an involuntary act as a deliberate attempt at fraud. We are so exposed to commercials, catalogs and manuals, all kinds of information on products as well as the products themselves that we are bound to accumulate ideas and insight into how things work and can be designed. When a product designer develops a certain product, it is impossible to tell where the specific impulses come from that dictate the end result. Thus, borrowing inspiration from someone else can easily happen, even if it should be avoided in an ideal world. The real problem is deliberate plagiarism, where entire products are copied exactly or specific features or designs of products are transferred to other products (but there is a line between common design features [is it plagiarism to use airbags in a car?] and singular traits that have been copied). Plagiarism is also a matter of patents and design and trademark protection. Unless the original designer or manufacturer holds a patent for the technical solutions used or trademark rights to designs or logos, the legal obstacles to copying them are less formidable.

• Whereas patents apply to technical designs and trademarks to distinctive names, symbols, or mottos, copyrights are used in the case of text, lyrics, music, pictures, and similar "products." Copyright infringement (that is, copying such material and publishing it as one's own) is of course just as unethical as plagiarism.

• Industrial espionage is perhaps more common than you would like to think, if not perhaps in the form of hired spies in long dark coats forcing their entry into the CEO's office. Reliable statistics are hard to find, but the FBI and CIA told U.S. businesses two years ago it was on its own with regard to such crime. The federal agencies admitted there was no way it could protect American business from itself or foreign agents. Industrial espionage can take on many forms, from downright breaking and entering to stealing documents or other objects to infiltration by consultants or temporary staff to information gathering through IT systems, and so on. Unlike plagiarism, gaining such unlawful access to information can hardly be anything but deliberate.

• Reverse engineering and benchmarking are two other ways of gaining insight into products and processes of competitors. The former consists of acquiring products made by competitors and disassembling them to determine how they have been designed and produced, and how they function, for the purpose of gaining inspiration. Benchmarking, which sometimes is combined with reverse engineering, is a method for comparing your own organization with others to learn from exposed differences. Being one of many tools available for improvement work in an organization, benchmarking is of course a perfectly legal and acceptable approach. However, there are ways to conduct benchmarking that are more sensitive to scrutiny, for example, obtaining data without consent from the benchmarking partner, using concealed cameras to videotape facilities, or relaying information gained through benchmarking to other parties. In fact, there are sufficiently many ethical pitfalls in benchmarking to have induced the International Benchmarking Clearinghouse to define an ethical code of conduct for benchmarking. Thus, both reverse engineering and benchmarking are perfectly acceptable concepts as long as they are undertaken within certain boundaries.

• Negative comparative marketing is, on the other hand, a line of attack that must be deemed clearly unethical and which in many regions also is illegal. In some countries, comparative marketing per se is prohibited by law, negative competitive marketing even more so. The difference lies in the comparisons made; if they are accurate and fair, they are "safe" with regard to prosecution for negative comparisons. James and Hensel (1991) identified negative advertising as "a particularly malicious strain of comparative advertising." Negative advertising is differentiated from regular comparative advertising in that it focuses on damaging the image or reputation of a specific competitor through inferences and other subtle techniques, often in a manner that is perceived by consumers as snide or "hitting below the belt." Positive comparative advertising attempts to persuade the consumer that the sponsor's product or service is superior to the competition, and claims are typically more objective and factual in nature.

As for plagiarism and copying of products of competitors, in most cases the organization doing the copying or breaches of patents is the one with ethical issues to answer for. However, in some cases, the patent holder can come under criticism, especially in cases where patents are used as a means to create a monopolistic situation where almost indecent prices can be commanded. A very good and current example of this can be found in the ongoing debate about the costs of AIDS medicine for those countries most badly affected, that is, typically poor African nations. International pharmaceutical companies are protected under patent laws that allow them a 20-year monopoly to produce and set the prices of drugs they have developed, and since most antiretroviral drugs are relatively new, their patents still have many years to run. In 2001, 39 pharmaceutical companies filed court action against the government of South Africa over its attempts to buy inexpensive, generic AIDS medicine, but even though the suit collapsed, very little has changed in terms of costs for the country. The Medicines and Related Substances Control Amendment Act does not allow generic versions of medicines still protected by patents to be imported (called parallel importation) nor will it enable South African companies to make cheap local generic versions of patented drugs.

In further attempts to relieve the poorest AIDS-inflicted countries of these prohibitive costs (and indeed those of sufferers of other diseases like malaria, TB, and a few others), the World Trade Organization took charge of negotiations to establish a global deal to provide cheap drugs to poor countries. The negotiations culminated in late 2002 after Dick Cheney, the U.S. vice-president, blocked the deal. This decision followed intense lobbying of the White House by America's pharmaceutical giants. The argument by the industry is that it spends billions every year on drug research and that if companies can override their patents and manufacture copycat drugs at bargain prices, research will dry up. This is of course a relevant point, but counter-arguments show that the sales to such countries account for a very small portion of global sales (sub-Saharan Africa accounts for only 1.3 percent of total global sales of AIDS medicines. Some drug companies may decide to donate certain drugs to African countries, as Pfizer has done (fluconazole) and Boehringer Ingelheim (nevirapine). The question is, wouldn't these companies benefit after all from allowing these unfortunate people the opportunity to buy the drugs they so sorely need at reduced prices? There seems to be little doubt this would be the decent thing to do, at least in light of how small a portion this would account for compared with global revenues. As of late, there seems to be further movement on this issue that might lead to a breakthrough in discussions involving both the United Nations and the World Trade Organization. Canada plans to be the first G8 country to relax its patent rules to allow generic copies of anti-HIV drugs to be manufactured and shipped to pandemic regions in Africa and other southern nations might be snagged in a web of domestic political changes. Prime Minister Jean Chretien promised the patent law changes at September's World Trade Organization (WTO) meetings in Cancun, Mexico. He planned to bring in the changes as part of his "legacy" agenda before his retirement scheduled for early February, 2004.

The remedial aspect of competitor treatment will be concluded with an appeal to simply promote fair and free competition. As the extensive work of Michael Porter (1980, 1985, and 1990) has shown, strong competition in home markets is a determinant of competitive advantage. Having little or weak competition does not inspire an organization to keep improving, fierce and fair competition does. Undermining the competitive mechanisms of your markets only undermines your incentives to becoming better. Perhaps the Biblical approach of "do unto others as you would have others do unto you" is a suitable attitude.

LOCAL COMMUNITY PRACTICES AND BEHAVIOR TOWARD OTHER STAKEHOLDERS IN GENERAL

Being the last section of this chapter on remedial and operational issues concerning the outside world of the organization, this is to some extent an odds and ends section of items that were difficult to fit elsewhere. Even local community practices are somewhat "loose" compared with the rest of the chapter, although these refer to a specific class of stakeholders.

Specific is perhaps not a very good choice of word; the local community of an organization can mean anything and everything. In this context, it typically includes entities like the population of the immediate area that either directly works for the organization or makes a living off those that do, local authorities with the responsibility for coverage in terms of school, daycare, healthcare, housing, and so on, local suppliers of goods and services to the organization, cultural, sports, and other ideal organizations and institutions in the vicinity—in short, all those people and institutions that make a local community. In a large city, the concept of local community is perhaps not as well defined as in smaller towns where one or a few companies represent the main sources of employment. Still, cities also rely on employment and suffer for every job that is eliminated or moved elsewhere.

What kind of responsibilities does an organization have with regard to its local community, then? Beyond its obligations to pay taxes and follow current laws and regulations, very few in fact. A company can up and leave to relocate whenever it likes, it can lay off people, it can live a secluded life without engaging in local life at all, and no one can force it to do otherwise. However, most organizations realize that they benefit from a well-functioning local community and thus dedicate time and energy to uphold and even further develop it. Since such efforts are really of a philanthropic nature, more extensive local community practices will be presented in chapter 10. For now, the focus will be on the few remedial practices there are:

• First of all, the introduction to this section talks about organizations present in the local community as a positive asset. In most cases, they are, but not always. Many towns that have hosted various types of industrial corporations suffer negative consequences from lack of free space, pollution, parks that have been turned into parking spaces, struggling local economy due to investments in schools and other types of infrastructure required by the employees of the companies, and so on. Even years after such companies have gone bust or moved elsewhere, the local community is showing the effects of their operations years earlier. In these and other less extreme cases, where the presence of an organization is predominantly an asset but also entails some negative effects, the question is whether the organization should volunteer to rectify any such negative effects. It is not unheard of; some larger corporations have procedures for, for example, replacing green areas put to use with equally sized areas of park or forest elsewhere in the vicinity. Others build up funds of money to clean up and convert any area that might be affected by inevitable pollution during operations. In such cases, the expenses are covered by the organization, and these initiatives are normally made by the organizations themselves, not due to outside pressure. Of course, it is impossible to keep score of positive and negative contributions stemming from the organization being present in the local community and asking it to pay for any negative balance. Thus, such an approach must be based on voluntarily making up for any direct damages caused, either environmentally or otherwise, as a favor to the local community.

• A form of indirect damage or negative effects on a local community can come from the negative reputation of an organization associated with that community. Usually, the real situation is the other way around—many cities and towns are positively associated with leading organizations. When I spent a year in Rochester, New York, I saw clearly how much the corporate office of Eastman Kodak meant for the image of Rochester. On the other hand, steel towns in the United States and other countries have been prone to cornerstone companies closing the facilities, with ensuing loss of jobs and local prosperity. Many of these are well known national tragedies and any mention of such a town will spur negative associations, for example Allentown, Pennsylvania and Flint, Michigan. The same goes for companies that have been depicted negatively in the media or involved in scandals of some sort—hometowns of such companies are unavoidably marked by their links to them. While an organization of course has no clear or legally binding obligation to act in a manner that creates positive images of the local community where it is located, it should keep in mind how such communities can be affected by behavior that is unethical or illegal. The best insurance against creating such negative ripple effects for others is probably to adopt the business ethics framework of this book and stay clear of any negative exposure.

• Talking of abandoned steel towns, rapid growth or decline of organizations, especially ones that represent substantial employment in an area, is another problem for many local communities. On the one hand, growing pains related to companies taking on more and more employees and creating an influx of inhabitants cause challenges in terms of developing the local infrastructure at the same pace. On the other, decline, especially following a period of rapid growth, is perhaps even harder to handle, rendering infrastructure investments superfluous and causing budget deficits. In general, the shorter the notice given and the more surprises such important employers spring on their local communities, the more difficult the situation is to cope with. A caring organization concerned with how its presence affects the local community should strive to include local authorities in their long-term planning and at least make sure these are warned sufficiently early of any major changes to accommodate for these in their plans. Best practice in this area seems to be achieved by those organizations that appoint dedicated liaisons to work with local governments and planning offices to make sure there is a positive two-way discussion that benefits both parties in their plans for the future.

One particular type of behavior toward local communities stands out as an offense to those affected, namely raiding of companies for various reasons. There are numerous examples of investors and other businessmen that buy out entire companies or certain facilities, very often with proclaimed good intentions of carrying on the current operations. Once the required permits have been issued and the deal made, the true intentions are revealed: some divide the company into pieces and sell it off for much more than the original buying price, others see the real value of the company in its property and close the company altogether to sell the land.

There was an example of this recently in a medium-sized European city. A shipyard with a long tradition for building anything from small boats to frigates for the national navy was located virtually downtown, at a prime site. A young property tycoon set his sights on the company and managed to buy it for a substantial amount of money, always with firm reassurances that the company would be run like it always had. Shortly after, the yard was declared bankrupt with creditors losing around $50 million and 411 employees losing their jobs. Having settled the fate of the old company, the property was sold for close to twice the original price paid by the tycoon. The buyer intends to redevelop the area into housing and shopping facilities, expecting to make record investments. In the wake of the raid, the city has lost more than 400 full-time employees, many more in indirect employment surrounding the yard, and tax revenues, and faces the major job of processing the entire planning application for the redevelopment.

The last issue to be mentioned at the conclusion of this rather extensive chapter is that of bribery. Bribery can take on many forms and shapes. To many, the word sparks only thoughts of Western companies operating in foreign cultures and there "degrading" themselves to locally accepted practices of bribes to have decisions and progress made. Bribery is far from a problem only in non-Western countries, although bribes may take on other forms in Western countries. They may be kickbacks as a percentage of certain revenues ("if you include our hotel in your itinerary, you can bring your wife for a lovely weekend here"), return purchases, or support for controversial plans or decisions. All forms of undisclosed payments, information supplied to unauthorized parties, or even membership in privileged yet limited networks, constitute, in effect, bribery.

The problem with bribery, except for the fact that it is illegal in most countries, is that those organizations not operating this way will find themselves at a great disadvantage compared with their competitors. In the end, the damage is transferred to the consumers, competitors, or both. The direct cost of the bribe is passed on to the consumer, either in the form of higher prices or in inferior goods or services. Firms that cannot afford the illegal payment will not be able to compete. This results not only in reduced sales and profits for them, but also a loss to consumers who will often have to bear the cost because of the reduced competition. Of even greater importance than the economic effects on consumers or competitors, is perhaps the moral effect on all involved parties. On a national or global level, corruption weakens democracies, distorts investment decisions, and disrupts economic growth. Yet until recently, bribes by companies were accepted as a tax-deductible expense in many countries. As a result of initiatives developed within the framework of the Organisation for Economic Co-operation and Development (OECD), many governments are now making determined efforts to combat corruption and to achieve a stronger culture of accountability, including within their own administrations.

In cases of bribery, both the briber and the recipient of the bribe are equally to blame. And most organizations will at some stage find themselves in a position where making a bribe to make headway is tempting, or where a bribe is being offered, however innocent it may seem. To counter all these negative effects, direct or indirect, from bribery and corruption, ethical organizations, indeed any organization, must do its part to avoid such acts. Specific issues to think about are:

• The obvious, direct, and unveiled bribes given or taken to public sector officials or business partners. These represent an obviously illegal form of bribery and must of course be refrained from.

• Giving or receiving of gifts, which may often seem insubstantial, can still be intended as some form of bribe. Giving away anything of value to people external to the organization may raise questions about its integrity. The decisive factor is whether such gifts are intended to influence, or even could appear to influence, business decisions. However, ordinary and reasonable business entertainment or gifts of nominal value that are customary and legal in the local market should not be deemed improper.

• Kickbacks and other forms of improper business arrangements that in effect represent bribery should also be considered carefully. The type of loyalty programs discussed earlier, which mainly apply to private consumers, can in relationships between professional organizations be considered improper. For example, frequent flyer miles that are awarded to individual airline passengers are very often awarded based on travel paid for by the individual's employer. While the frequent flyer miles can in no way be construed as bribery to the employer, there is no doubt they influence the individual's decision with regard to airline, even though there may exist cheaper alternatives. There are many other business practices where purchases or other decisions in one way or another trigger benefits that could be deemed dubious.

• Targeting the shadow needs of individual decision-makers is another way of interpreting such schemes as the frequent flyer miles example. Any decision made by an organization is made by one or more employees acting as representatives on behalf of the organization. When presenting offers for decision, the offering party will obviously target the specific needs and requirements of the organization. In addition, the representative making the decision will have some personal needs, often termed shadow needs, which involuntarily can impact the decision. Given the choice between a supplier close by or one located in a sunny spot, where the contract requires the representative to conduct inspections of the supplier's facilities, catering to her or his desire for a sunny weekend could be the deciding factor. Using such shadow needs to achieve favorable decisions is on the border of bribery.

> The Swedish telecom giant Ericsson faces tough allegations over corruption. Ongoing investigations indicate that as much as $400 million may have been used to bribe decision-makers into awarding Ericsson telecom contracts. Both the Swedish and Swiss police are looking into

continued

continued

accounts in the major Swiss bank UBS that might have been used as transfer points for extensive corruption using false invoices.

Lengthy investigations have also been conducted into related corruption at TotalFinaElf. Magistrates have filed a report that names close to forty Ericsson executives, politicians, and middlemen that were part of a network that took nearly three billion francs in kickbacks from Elf in the early 1990s. Investigative judge Eva Joly, who presided over the case in 1994, has written a book on the trial since her retirement last year. In extracts published in the French press she speaks of the case being hampered by government resistance and claims she received death threats; she is now protected by bodyguards around the clock. The book, which was due out June 19 this year, was the subject of a temporary ban until July 7 when the defense were due to present their closing statements in the trial. The book, *Is This the World We Want to Live In?*, argues that France is institutionally corrupt.

Total originated as Elf Aquitaine, founded by General De Gaulle. Elf Aquitaine was privatized in 1994 and merged into TotalFinaElf. It has routinely served as a cover for secret French governmental operations, which included the bribing of African leaders and money laundering in Latin America. Elf's activities in Africa were organized in the 1950s by President Charles de Gaulle and his adviser, the late Jacques Foccart. France used a series of networks as a way of accumulating oil wealth, via Elf, from newly independent colonies in West Africa. Elf used a system of split commissions as a way of maintaining French influence and later subsidizing Gaullist political activities.

This work was carried on by Charles Pasqua, 74, a Gaullist who was twice interior minister. Evidence presented in the court case showed that he used Elf corporate planes on more than seventy occasions. It has been alleged that the trips were for political and personal reasons. The court case has exposed the links between top levels of the French state and a shadowy network of middlemen, corrupt businessmen, and outright crooks. Elf former chief executive Loik Le Floch-Prigent has been accused of using company money to pay his divorce settlement, with the permission of the late French President Francois Mitterrand. Le Floch-Prigent was convicted in 2001 in an earlier trial. That case also brought convictions in May 2001 for Roland Dumas, France's former foreign minister, who was jailed for six months for receiving illegal funds from Elf from 1989 to 1992. The entire case has been called France's biggest postwar financial scandal.

IMPLEMENTATION SUMMARY

In implementing external, remedial, and operational practices based on ethical principles, some advice follows:

• Reaching a state where the organization on the whole adheres to relevant laws and regulations is imperative. This is closely related to the development of an ethically based organizational culture, the culture being the platform for the organization and its members' behavior. The approaches of storytelling and refining tacit knowledge are relevant here. More traditional training is of course also a key element at this stage.

• Improving product and service safety is a task directed toward the organization's customers. Some tools for identifying and eliminating safety hazards were already mentioned in this chapter, and should be combined with general product or service development approaches.

• Minimizing negative environmental impact is another extensive job at this stage. Unfortunately, there are few specific tools to be used for this job; it is basically a matter of systematically scanning the organization's operations to uncover problem areas and then trying to improve them. This again is an area where the general problem-solving tools will come in handy.

• Improving practices for supplying external stakeholders with the various output they require is another extensive area. This is mostly a matter of developing or improving business processes that efficiently and effectively deliver what they are supposed to. This is another area where the quality management movement has refined tools and approaches that are quite powerful, whether geared toward more radical changes, as in the case of business process reengineering, or targeting minor improvements. A useful selection of these tools have been described in books like *Business Process Improvement* (Harrington, 1991), *Understanding and Applying Value-Added Assessment: Eliminating Business Process Waste* (Trischler, 1996), *Mapping Work Processes* (Galloway, 1994), or *Business Process Improvement Toolbox* (Andersen, 1998).

• Improving complaint-handling principles and practices is another area that is mostly about business process development. Thus, the same tools mentioned above can be applied here.

• Upgrading the supply chain to acceptable ethical standards is perhaps even more difficult, as this is about encouraging change in not only your own organization, but others as well. As was mentioned earlier in this section, one approach to this task is lending your own experience and expertise to your partners and trying to replicate things that have worked well in your own organization.

That finally concludes the remedial half of the business ethics framework. By nature, this half is more extensive and has thus taken quite a lot of space to cover. On the other hand, the perhaps most innovative and rewarding practices are found in the philanthropic half, so please read on for the rest of the framework.

7

Pampering
the Organization?
Philanthropic, Internal,
and Strategic Policies

C hapter 3 dealt with remedial policies pertaining to internal stakeholders, that is, mainly employees at all levels of the organization,
remedial meaning "setting things right" in terms of acceptable working conditions and fair pay levels. As will be discussed further in chapter 11,
fulfilling the remedial requirements is really all that can be expected of an
organization; there is no obligation to go any further in order to subscribe to
an ethical position. Many organizations do, however, find that moving into
the philanthropic half of the framework is a natural progression once the
remedial aspects have been mastered.

Being internally focused, this inevitably means providing even better
working conditions or benefits to the employees than could reasonably be
expected. The one warning that is warranted in this respect is the risk of
pampering the organization and its employees into conceit and parochialism.
If compensation levels and other benefits bestowed upon the employees are
perceived as excessive compared with the effort expended and results
achieved, the important cause-and-effect link between performance and
reward is weakened or severed and can lead to "spoiled" employees that fail
to earn their reward, but come to expect or demand it anyway. To avoid this
dilemma, any philanthropic benefits implemented should either be designed
to come across as extraordinary rewards or it should be made clear that long-
term philanthropic offers can be abolished if performance drops.

By the nature of the business ethics framework, the remedial half is
more extensive than the philanthropic one. Thus, you will see that these
next four chapters are shorter than the previous four, but as mentioned at
the end of the last chapter, the ideas that are brought forward are perhaps

more innovative and inspiring. In this chapter, the focus is on philanthropic human resource management policies, the relationship with trade unions, and the use (or lack thereof) of so-called sweatshops in low-wage countries.

SPURRING THE ORGANIZATION ON TO HIGHER LEVELS OF PERFORMANCE— PHILANTHROPIC HUMAN RESOURCE MANAGEMENT POLICIES

In theory, it should be possible to improve conditions or benefits beyond what is reasonable to expect for any of the areas representing human resource management (see Figure 3.1, page 59 for an overview of these). In reality, it is neither feasible nor desirable to attempt doing so. The most relevant areas for extending the organization's offers toward its employees are listed in Table 7.1 along with relevant examples of philanthropic policies.

Table 7.1 Areas of human resource management with philanthropic policies.

Human Resource Management Subarea	Policy Element
Physical work conditions	Policy for providing supreme physical facilities regarding comfort, equipment standards, space, and so on.
Organizational work conditions	Policy for offering kindergarten facilities for employees.
	Policy for enabling employees in supporting or engaging in philanthropic enterprises.
Compensation structure	Policy for profit sharing and bonus schemes linked to performance levels and that go beyond average compensation levels.
	Policy for allowing employees to receive products or services supplied by the company at reduced prices or for free.
Access to information and decision power	Policy for practicing a more extensive organizational democracy than strictly required.
Competence and career development	Policy for providing extensive training and career development beyond reasonable levels.
	Policy for recruiting people with disabilities and helping these in developing a career.

The common denominators for all of these policies (whose practical design and implementation will be dealt with in the next chapter) is either offering more benefits to employees than the norm or supporting employees in aiding good causes on their own. If the negative effects of pampering are avoided, the intention is of course that such more-than-fair treatment will inspire employees to yield their very best and go the extra mile for the organization. There is much evidence to support the hypothesis that content employees perform better than ones that hold a grudge of some sort; following up such policies with real-life schemes seems worthwhile.

HELPING TO ESTABLISH A CONSCIOUS WORK CULTURE BY WORKING WITH TRADE UNIONS

In Western countries, we take it more or less for granted that trade unions are there to represent employees in matters pertaining to work conditions (even if this is in fact not the case in every sector or company, this is not really the issue here). The role such trade unions play today is quite different from the role they had in the beginning of the industrial era or even some fifty years ago. Work life in Western democracies is so regulated by laws and regulations that the labor force no longer needs trade unions as watchdogs to ensure that its basic rights are respected and upheld. Most unions engage most actively in pay negotiations, discussions related to training and continued education of employees, joint insurance schemes, and other less controversial matters.

In developing countries, with less tradition for work life development and industrial organization, conditions today are often much more like they were a hundred years ago in Europe or the United States. When, as a Western company, you establish new or buy existing facilities in such countries, there is no legal obligation to actively stimulate the development of improved work conditions and trade union traditions. Any organization in such a process is of course free to leave things as they are and "exploit" the lower costs involved in both wages and the facilitation of adequate working conditions. The decent thing to do, however, is to use the knowledge and power held by the organization to induce changes toward a more worthy work life for employees in third-world countries.

One particular way of promoting better work-life conditions is through cooperation with trade unions, whether already existing or needing to be stimulated or downright initiated from scratch. Traditionally, the attitude of the employer has been one of relief if the employees never get around to organizing themselves in unions, but this is again one area where opting for maximum short-term profits can create severe backlashes. Counting your blessings and your money over the fact that the workers in your new manufacturing facility do not know about trade unions and only demand 45 cents an hour can be a short-lived bliss. Increasingly conscientious consumers are aware of where products have been produced and under what conditions. And for the unaware, there is help available through organizations such as the Fairtrade Labeling Organization (see sidebar) in avoiding products made under questionable conditions and finding acceptable alternatives.

In addition to the very likely possibility of reduced revenues from failure to sell products that have been manufactured under less than acceptable labor conditions, there will of course be negative consequences in terms of lower productivity. Workers operating under "the whip" will have few incentives for contributing their best, and such workers will certainly not engage in creative thinking about how to improve performance. There is, however, also a need to mention again the discussion from chapter 3 about global versus local labor standards—higher than average standards in one facility might not do any good to surrounding facilities not operated by the same organization.

The Fairtrade Labeling Organization (FLO) is an international standards organization working with local marketing organizations in member countries to ensure that a wide range of products sourced from developing countries adhere to certain minimum standards for labor rights and environmental impact. The standards apply both to products imported from producers in developing countries and products made by Western companies using facilities and workers in these countries. Products that meet the standards are allowed a fair trade label, in some countries this is the Max Havelaar label, in the United States the label is Fair Trade Certified. This way, consumers in any FLO member country can easily find products that they can trust have been brought to the market in an ethical manner.

The requirements that must be met to gain approval for such labels are wide-ranging, covering many different aspects of labor conditions and other issues. In this chapter, the labor conditions are of most relevance, but the entire set of requirements for situations involving hired labor follows:

continued

1 SOCIAL DEVELOPMENT

1.1 Fairtrade Adds Development Potential

Fairtrade should make a difference in development for workers.

1.1.1 Minimum Requirement

1.1.1.1 The employer can demonstrate that FT revenues will promote the social and economic development of the workers.

1.1.2 Progress Requirement

1.1.2.1 A monitored plan should be developed under which the benefits of Fairtrade (including the Premium) are shared based on a democratic decision taken by the beneficiaries.

1.2 Nondiscrimination

FLO follows ILO Convention 111 on ending discrimination of workers. The Convention rejects "any distinction, exclusion or preference made on the basis of race, color, sex, religion, political opinion, national extraction, or social origin, which has the effect of nullifying or impairing equality of opportunity or treatment in employment or occupation" (art. 1).

1.2.1 Minimum Requirements

1.2.1.1 There is no distinction, exclusion or preference made on the basis of race, color, sex, religion, political opinion, national extraction, or social origin in recruitment, promotion, remuneration, allocation of work, or other activities.

1.2.2 Progress Requirements

1.2.2.1 Programs related to disadvantaged/minority groups are in place to improve the position of those groups, particularly with respect to recruitment, staff, and committee membership.

1.3 Forced Labor and Child Labor

FLO follows ILO Conventions 29, 105, and 138 on child labor and forced labor. Forced or bonded labor must not occur. Bonded labor can be the result of forms of indebtedness of workers to the company or middlemen. Children may only work if their education is not jeopardized. If children work, they shall not execute tasks which are especially hazardous for them due to their age.

continued

258   *Chapter Seven*

1.3.1 Minimum Requirements

1.3.1.1 Forced labor, including bonded or involuntary prison labor, does not occur.

1.3.1.2 Children are not employed below the age of 15.

1.3.1.3 Working does not jeopardize schooling or the social, moral, or physical development of the young person.

1.3.1.4 The minimum age of admission to any type of work which, by its nature or the circumstances under which it is carried out, is likely to jeopardize the health, safety, or morals of young people, shall not be less than 18 years.

1.3.1.5 Employment is not conditioned by employment of the spouse. Spouses have the right to off-farm employment.

1.4 Freedom of Association and Collective Bargaining

FLO follows ILO Conventions 87 and 98 on freedom of association and collective bargaining. Workers and employers shall have the right to establish and to join organizations of their own choosing, and to draw up their constitutions and rules, to elect their representatives, and to formulate their programs. Workers shall enjoy adequate protection against acts of antiunion discrimination in respect of their employment.

1.4.1 Minimum Requirements

1.4.1.1 Management recognizes in writing the right of all employees to join an independent trade union, free of interference of the employer, the right to establish and join federations, and the right to collective bargaining.

1.4.1.2 Management allows trade union organizers to meet all the workers, and allows workers to hold meetings and organize themselves without the interference of the management.

1.4.1.3 Management does not discriminate against workers on the basis of union membership or union activities.

1.4.1.4 If one or more independent and active trade unions exist in the sector and the region, FLO expects that the workers shall be represented by (a) trade union(s) and that the workers shall be covered by a collective bargaining agreement (CBA) within one year after certification.

continued

1.4.1.5 If no independent and active union exists in the region and the sector, all the workers shall democratically elect a worker's committee, which represents them, discusses with management and defends their interests. This committee negotiates with the management an agreement on the conditions of employment, covering all aspects normally covered by a collective bargaining agreement (CBA). Such an agreement must be in place within two years after certification.

1.4.2 Progress Requirements

1.4.2.1 The representation and participation of the workers is improved through training activities. These are also aimed at improving the workers' awareness of the principles of Fairtrade.

1.4.2.2 If no union is present, management and the workers' committee get into a process of consultation with the national union federation(s) for the respective sector and the International Alliance of Trade Union Federations (or appropriate International Trade Secretariat) about improvement of the workers' representation and implementing a collective bargaining agreement (CBA).

1.5 Conditions of Employment

FLO follows ILO Conventions 100 on equal remuneration and 111 on discrimination as well as ILO Convention 110 in case of plantations. All employees must work under fair conditions of employment. The producer organization must pay wages in line with or exceeding national laws and agreements on minimum wages or the regional average. FLO expects that the progress requirements will annually be dealt with in the collective bargaining process.

1.5.1 Minimum Requirements

1.5.1.1 Salaries are in line with or exceeding regional average and official minimum wages for similar occupations. The employer shall specify wages for all functions.

1.5.1.2 Payment must be made regularly and in legal tender and properly documented.

1.5.1.3 Regarding other conditions of employment like maternity leave, social security provisions, nonmonetary benefits, and so on, at least the provisions as laid out in the collective bargaining agreement or the

continued

agreement signed between the workers' committee and the management must be fulfilled.

1.5.1.4 After two years of certification all workers are employed under legally binding labor contracts.

1.5.2 Progress Requirements

1.5.2.1 The employer works toward all permanent workers having the benefits of a provident fund or pension scheme.

1.5.2.2 An adequate sick leave regulation is put in place.

1.5.2.3 A working hours and overtime regulation is put in place, with maximum normal working hours not exceeding 48 per week or local law if lower. Overtime should not exceed 12 hours per week averaged over the year.

1.5.2.4 Salaries are gradually increased to 'living wage' levels above the regional average and official minimum.

1.5.2.5 Differences in the conditions of employment for casual, seasonal, and permanent workers are progressively diminished.

1.6 Occupational Health and Safety

FLO follows ILO Convention 155 which aims "to prevent accidents and injury to health arising out of, linked with or occurring in the course of work, by minimizing, so far as is reasonably practicable, the causes of hazards inherent in the working environment."

1.6.1 Minimum Requirements

1.6.1.1 Workplaces, machinery and equipment are safe and without risk to health. FLO may require that an inspection is carried out by a competent authority or independent inspection agency.

1.6.1.2 Among the workers' representatives, a person must be nominated who can be consulted and who can address health and safety issues with management. They should be given time to consult workers and investigate issues.

1.6.1.3 Those who are handling hazardous chemicals are adequately trained in storage, application, and disposal of these. They are actively

continued

informed of all relevant information on the product they are handling by the company. This information is provided in the local language.

1.6.1.4 Adequate personal protective equipment of good quality is available and appropriate, especially for the use of hazardous chemicals. Workers handling hazardous chemicals must use it.

1.6.1.5 The following persons are not allowed to work with the application of hazardous materials:

- Persons younger than 18 years, pregnant or nursing women,

- Persons with incapacitated mental conditions;

- Persons with chronic, hepatic, or renal diseases, and persons with diseases in the respiratory ways.

1.6.1.6 Workers are not allowed to bring clothes or protective equipment used for spraying to their homes.

1.6.1.7 All finished goods, inventory, and storage materials are placed in a hazard-proof manner, uncluttered, and easily accessible. Floors and aisles have to be kept clean.

1.6.1.8 Fire exits are provided for every workplace, properly marked, and kept clear of obstructions, allowing swift and safe exit during emergencies. Workers are drilled in evacuation procedures regularly.

1.6.1.9 All workplaces where open chemicals or inflammable materials are used, maintain acceptable air-quality levels through adequate ventilation.

1.6.1.10 All workers have continuous access to clean drinking water, and proper toilet facilities that are cleaned regularly with suitably covered drains and pipes.

1.6.1.11 All workplaces have acceptable lighting and ventilation according to local weather conditions.

1.6.1.12 Electrical equipment, wiring, and outlets are properly placed, grounded, and professionally inspected regularly for overloading and leakage.

1.6.2 Progress Requirements

continued

1.6.2.1 Workers' capability and awareness of the chemicals they are using, relevant health protection and first aid are improved through training.

1.6.2.2 Establishment of an occupational health and safety committee with the participation of workers.

1.6.2.3 Collective risk assessments are carried out regularly.

2 ECONOMIC DEVELOPMENT

2.1 Fairtrade Premium

The price paid for Fairtrade products includes a Premium. This Fairtrade Premium is to be used for improvement of the socioeconomic situation of the workers, their families, and communities. Workers and management decide jointly about the use of the Premium. Procedures, roles and responsibilities are laid down in a separate guidance document available at FLO. The employer must have the commitment and capacity to administer the Fairtrade Premium in a way that is transparent for workers and FLO.

2.1.1 Minimum Requirements

2.1.1.1 Management clearly commits itself in writing to set up a Joint Body in line with the requirements laid out. The Joint Body has to be established immediately after certification has been granted but before the first FT money flows.

2.1.1.2 The workers' representatives must be chosen through a democratic process. Workers' representatives can at all times invite external support persons to assist in the meetings of the Joint Body.

2.1.1.3 The Joint Body should strive to reach decisions by consensus. Failing this, no decision can be approved if the majority of the workers' representatives does not consent.

2.1.1.4 All the spending of the Fairtrade Premium and related issues are decided exclusively by the Joint Body.

2.1.1.5 The Fairtrade Premium can not be used for the running costs of the company and for the costs of the minimum requirements, for example such as those in the Conditions of Employment section.

continued

2.1.1.6 The spending of the Premium is separately accounted for and FLO and the workers are able to check the relevant books.

2.1.1.7 The Joint Body is responsible to inform the workers and FLO on a regular basis, but at least once a year on the planned use of the Premium and on the progress of projects carried out with the Premium.

2.1.1.8 The Joint Body prepares a yearly premium work plan. The premium work plan contains a reasonable budget based on expected premium income, which sets priorities for premium use. In the course of the year the work plan can be adjusted if the premium earnings are other than expected.

2.1.1.9 The Joint Body, including the management representatives, is to account to FLO for the administration and use of the premium.

2.1.2 Progress Requirements

2.1.2.1 The composition of the Joint Body shall reflect the gender, cultural, and other makeup of workforce.

2.2 Export Ability

The producers must have access to the logistical, administrative, and technical means to bring a quality product to the market.

2.2.1 Minimum Requirements

2.2.1.1 Logistics and communication equipment are in place.

2.2.1.2 The producer organization proves that it meets current export quality standards, preferably through previously exported products, which were accepted by importers.

2.2.1.3 Demand for the producers' Fairtrade product exists.

3 ENVIRONMENTAL DEVELOPMENT

3.1 Environment Protection

Producers are expected to protect the natural environment and to make environment protection a part of farm or company management. The Management shall implement a system of integrated crop management

continued

continued

(ICM) or equivalent in nonagricultural settings, with the aim of establishing a balance between environment protection and business results, through the permanent monitoring of economic and environmental parameters, on the basis of which an integrated cultivation and protection plan is devised and permanently adapted. FLO encourages producers to work toward organic certification. ICM minimizes the use of fertilizers and pesticides, and partially and gradually replaces them with organic fertilizers and biological disease control.

3.1.1 Minimum Requirements

3.1.1.1 The company conforms to national and international legislation regarding the use and handling of pesticides and other hazardous chemicals (storing, filling, cleaning, administration, and so on), the protection of natural waters, virgin forest, and other ecosystems of high ecological value, erosion, and waste management.

3.1.1.2 Pesticides in WHO class 1 a+b, pesticides in the Pesticide Action Network's "dirty dozen" list and pesticides in FAO/UNEP's Prior Informed Consent Procedure list (respecting updates, see appendix) cannot be used.

3.1.2 Progress Requirements

3.1.2.1 The management shall implement a system of integrated crop management or equivalent.

3.2.1 Environment Sustainability

3.2.2 Minimum Requirements

3.2.2.1 The company has procedures in place to dispose of wastewater and other hazardous liquids minimizing the environmental damage.

3.2.3 Progress Requirements

3.2.3.1 The company takes measures to separate hazardous waste (like waste from print screening, dyes, ink, and chemicals in the case of sportsballs production), from nonhazardous solid waste; wastewater and other hazardous liquids are treated before disposing of and solid waste is recycled.

Companies not adhering to these standards will subsequently not be eligible for such fair trade labels and can thus be singled out by aware consumers.

Many refer to production facilities in developing countries with dismal work life conditions as sweatshops. This is a term that brings about associations of children locked away in a dark and dirty room for hours making cheap products to be sold to Western customers, one that should perhaps not be mentioned at all in connection with decent, ethically minded organizations. Nevertheless, it is a fact that such sweatshops are not only the domain of backyard carpet weavers of dubious origin or other organizations that we would never deal with in our everyday lives. According to Ferrell, Fraedrich, and Ferrell (2000), it has been alleged that for each $14.99 pair of JC Penney Arizona jeans produced, a worker earns 11 cents, and that for each $12 Victoria's Secret garment made, an employee earns 3 cents. In addition, Wal-Mart, Kmart, and Nike have been accused by the National Labor Committee of outsourcing production to countries with low wages to boost profitability.

Concern for domestic employees and their work life conditions is of course commendable, but far from sufficient if an organization strives to be construed as decent and caring. Moving production to low-wage countries to make more money is one thing, exploiting the lack of a tradition of labor standards to pay rock-bottom wages and save as much money as possible on facilities is not acceptable. Experience from the 19th century when the industrial traditions were developed in Europe and the United States and from recently developed countries show that active cooperation with a solid body of trade unions is an effective way of elevating labor standards. This will not only impact the facility in question, but contribute to a general improvement of awareness and standards for work life in the region or country. Consequently, organizations establishing facilities in developing countries with a lack of trade union infrastructure are encouraged to:

- Establish relationships with existing trade unions and assist their development, or even initiate the formation of trade unions if none exist.

- Actively cooperate with the trade unions on setting standards for labor conditions and improving them.

- Promote organizational democracy and employee representation in suitable forums to allow the employees to develop insight into overall views of the company and its link to markets and the parent organization.

Ultimately, such improvements might come at a cost disadvantage, but certainly at an advantage in terms of development of the area and its people, in some cases even to an extent where a functioning industrial sector,

including trade unions, paves the way for more extensive societal changes
toward democracy.

CLOSING DOWN, OUTSOURCING, OR
ALLOWING EMPLOYEE BUYOUT?

The establishment of sweatshops is usually the end result of a process of
downsizing and ultimately closure of existing facilities. The direction of this
flux is often from Western countries with higher wage and cost levels to low-
cost developing countries, but there are many examples of facilities being
closed for other reasons as well. During consolidation of smaller units into
one or a few large ones, operations are frequently shut down, and the same
is of course true in cases where companies struggle financially and either
scale down their activity or go bankrupt altogether. No matter the circumstances, the consequences for those employees, at all levels of the organization, that are affected are severe and usually involve either moving with the
job or being fired, laid off, or quitting to find employment elsewhere.

Except for cases of serious financial trouble or failing markets, the case
is very often that the unit being closed is currently making profits. The move
to somewhere else might increase these profits, but the facility per se is in
good shape. Some companies have realized that there is an alternative to
simply closing down such units and laying off people, namely to allow the
employees the opportunity to buy out the unit and take control themselves.
There are (at least) two variants of such buyouts:

- Management buyout, where an organization sells a business or part
  of a business to a team led by its existing management.

- Employee buyout, involving the owners of a company selling a
  majority of their stock to their employees.

In both cases, ownership of a business changes hands, but these two
lead to slightly different end results. In a management buyout, there will still
be a small portion of the employees owning the company whereas all or a
large share of them takes on ownership in an employee buyout. Employee
buyouts especially have shown a capacity for inducing significant changes in
a company, in the most extreme cases turning around failing ones, increasing the cash flow of already good companies, motivating employees to out-
perform their competition, and reducing or eliminating corporate taxes for
years and thus providing a tax-advantaged investment for employees. This is
also a mechanism for transferring wealth in a free market transaction to the
employees who have spent their lives building the company.

In any case, both variants of buyouts represent a strategic alternative to closing down the unit or facility. For some organizations, such a sale of a business unit will represent a welcome way out of a tricky situation where it is withdrawing from that particular market segment or scaling down its presence. If the alternative is bankruptcy, a buyout is also normally a welcome relief. However, there are certainly situations where closing of facilities are part of a consolidation or outsourcing strategy. In such cases, allowing the unit planned for closing to stay in business under new ownership can be problematic, creating a new competitor not taken into consideration during the planning of the shutdown. This is perhaps the true test of the moral fiber of an organization and its senior management—if it has the courage to allow the employees the opportunity to avoid losing their jobs and take over the company even if this can mean more competition, it is truly dedicated to its employees. Since increased competition can be good in terms of spurring a company on to higher levels of performance, such a development need not be altogether negative either. There have been cases where such buyouts have created a new supplier or customer instead of a competitor, mainly from targeting different market segments or adjusting the product or service portfolio.

Management or employee buyouts are also an option in cases where the company or unit in question is not poised for closing. This can be relevant, for example, for:

• Public sector service organizations, such as public canteens, homes for the elderly, X-ray units of public hospitals, or the IT management department of a public institution. Many such units are relatively autonomous and provide services for which there are no requirements that they be undertaken by an organization operated by the authorities at some level.

• Separate business units in a larger corporation, typically ones with their own market focus and with relatively few interconnections to other business units.

• Various support functions of an organization, such as custodial services, building maintenance, IT system support, or accounting.

Most of the same benefits listed above for employee buyouts can be achieved in such cases and a means is provided for the employees to become owners of a business, to take part in strategic direction-setting and management of it, and to share profits made. As the unit being acquired already is established as a running business, the risk involved is typically much lower than for entrepreneurs starting businesses from scratch. An employee buyout can as such represent the best opportunity many people will ever have of realizing the quite common dream of becoming business owners. When such a sale of a unit does not represent a threat to the strategic plans of an organization, agreeing to it is a nice gesture that shows concern for the employees.

IMPLEMENTATION SUMMARY

Having reached the philanthropic, strategic, and internal area of the business ethics framework, some issues to keep in mind during implementation are:

• Similar to when developing remedial internal policies, the formulation of philanthropic internal policies can be guided by the suggested elements in Table 7.1. And again, this is typically a task that the executive team of the organization must take charge of, headed by or with significant contributions from the human resource manager.

• Establishing or supporting the establishment or development of trade unions in areas where this is not a common practice is an important philanthropic aspect. As for many other ethical dimensions, this is however also an aspect that it is virtually impossible to provide more specific guidelines for.

• Implementing a principle and regime for a decent decision-making process related to the closure, moving, or outsourcing of units of the organization. Organizations that have moved in this direction already have chosen quite different ways of doing so, but a common factor has in many cases been the establishment of a dedicated board for conducting this type of analysis and making recommendation to the real board. This analysis board contains cross-representation from various groups of employees, middle management, and senior management, and holds powers ranging from making recommendations to laying down veto.

In the next chapter, the philanthropic and internal policy elements outlined will be described in more detail through a conversion into operational practices.

8

Developing Philanthropic Internal Business Practices

A s mentioned at the start of the previous chapter, the business ethics framework, by its very nature, displays a philanthropic side that is less extensive than the remedial one. Furthermore, in the philanthropic half of the framework, the internally focused items are fewer than those benefiting external stakeholders. This is not surprising as there are typically many more stakeholders in need of good deeds outside the organization than those inside, who already hold jobs and presumably lead normal lives. However, in line with the internally focused philanthropic policies of the previous chapter, there are some specific business practices to consider.

INSTILLING DELIGHT IN YOUR EMPLOYEES

What contributes to making a happy and content workforce? This is a key question that has been researched probably at least the last hundred years. While there are numerous theories around to explain cause-and-effect relationships between various work life conditions and contentment, it seems fair to say that this varies highly. Exactly what one person is looking for in a job can be of little meaning to another, and there is usually not one single thing that dictates happiness or discontentment. Even though theories such as Maslow's hierarchy of needs try to structure the expectations an employee holds toward work, job conditions are a complex and compounded matter that is difficult to optimize.

Still, there are some basic elements that need to be in place, typically issues that are covered by laws and regulations (termed remedial in the business ethics framework) and elements that go beyond what any employee could reasonably expect or take for granted. The ideas presented in this chapter belong to this latter group, and are presented under the belief that adding some of these will lead to gratitude on the part of employees, gratitude that will translate into extra effort and higher performance. A selection of this kind of human resource management practices is presented below.

First of all, most people are more comfortable in their surroundings when these are clean and tidy, with sufficient amenities, and maintaining a certain standard. That places of work are satisfactorily cleaned and maintained goes without saying; standards in terms of materials used or equipment quality can be a tricky area. Moving beyond these two aspects of physical work conditions, one way of adding extra care for employees lies in the facilities offered on the premises:

• On-site daycare is one service to employees that has become popular. In many areas, daycare capacity is limited and finding an opening in a daycare of good standard and in a location that makes it convenient to deliver and pick up the kids can be a real challenge. In addition, many daycares stay open only during core working hours, making it even more difficult to manage for people working odd hours. Having an on-site daycare at the place of work eliminates most of these problems. There is no extra driving involved for delivery and pick-up, the open hours are usually adapted to the working hours in the organization, and the employer represents a kind of quality stamp for the daycare. Such an on-site facility can either be owned and operated by the employer or independently operated in facilities leased from the employer. Depending on the ownership model, prices can be set at average levels or even at a cost recovery level and payment can be arranged as a direct deduction from wages, all in the spirit of simplifying this aspect of life for the employees.

• Company school is a concept tried by some larger organizations, where the idea is the same as for staff daycare, namely to provide a good quality service that simplifies life for parents and their children. It is unfortunately a fact that in many areas, schools have budgets stretched to the limit, gang problems, poor maintenance resulting in poor facilities, and the school location can involve a lot of driving for parents bringing their kids to and from school. If an organization is of a sufficient size to enable a separate company school, obtaining authority approval for establishing such a school need not be a very difficult obstacle. Once established, the benefits for employed parents are about the same as for an on-site daycare, and such a school also gives the organization an opportunity to provide training suited for a future job with the company. In this way, a staff school can even function as a recruitment aid.

• Fitness facilities for employees are another service that can be offered, one that has already been mentioned. Many organizations do indeed have small gyms, a pool, or the like on the premises, but these tend to be used fairly infrequently. Organizations that have really been successful in stimulating their employees to exercise have added organized workout sessions facilitated by a coach of some sort. Others have made company bicycles available to their employees, sometimes instead of company cars, sometimes as a means of doing small errands inside or outside the organization's premises. I have even seen a small company rowboat moored on one side of a small bay separating two buildings owned by the same company, a boat used by employees to go back and forth between the buildings. The possibilities are endless, but the point is to encourage employees to get exercise one way or another.

• Other services that some employees are fortunate enough to have access to at or close by work can be restaurants, banks, post offices, hairdressers, and so on. For people working in cities, popping out during lunch to take care of errands is simple, but for organizations located some distance away from such services, this can be a problem. As a result, some, typically larger, organizations have made arrangements with such service suppliers for the establishment of an outlet on or close by the organization's premises. In my own case, the Norwegian University of Science and Technology has made sure there is a bank, post office, and a small selection of stores on campus, which makes the use of their services much easier than when they were only located downtown.

None of these services can really be defined as compulsory, but represent ways in which an employer can make life easier or better for its employees. With life constantly picking up pace and with most people trying to cram as much as possible into it, time is one thing few people have enough of. Aiding employees in saving time is one effective way of helping them become less stressed and more content.

Another way, which incidentally often means spending some time, is facilitating employees in supporting good causes. Volunteering for various causes is a very common practice in the United States, probably largely out of tradition, but certainly also because it gives people extra meaning in their lives and makes them feel good about doing something to help others. Many people use their own spare time to do volunteer work on their own initiative, but employers can help their employees in seeking such rewards. There are several ways to do so (which of course represent benefits for external stakeholders, but in this chapter the main effect sought is the reward for employees through facilitating such efforts):

• *Organizing volunteer work or other charitable efforts on behalf of the employees.* In this case, the organization is active in setting up such volunteer work opportunities, but the actual work is done outside working hours, thus being time donated by the employees themselves.

• *Donating employees' time to charitable causes.* In this case, the employer goes further and allows employees to spend part of their working hours on such efforts.

• *Facilitating donations to good causes by employees through direct deductions from wages.* Many companies offer employees the opportunity to donate a certain amount every month to one or more good causes simply by having it deducted from their paycheck and transferred to the charity organization. This saves time and effort for the employees and can often be the initiative needed to give regular donations.

As opposed to facilitating employees' aid to charitable organizations and other people, an employer can offer some aid to its employees as a nice gesture. Although most people employed by decent organizations in the Western world are fortunate enough to afford all things required to lead normal lives, there are certainly many people in other parts of the world worse off. Even holding regular employment, wage levels are in many areas so low that it is hard to support a family, and there are certainly also employees in Western countries earning minimum wage that find it hard to make ends meet. One way of helping employees to a better financial situation is of course simply to pay them better, but this is an approach that has many facets. It will of course cost more for the organization; it can introduce differences in pay levels within an industry that seem unfair; and simply raising pay levels beyond the norm without linking them to achieved results or performance levels is usually not wise.

However, to the extent that it is feasible, allowing employees to buy the products or services supplied by the organization at reduced prices is an alternative way of helping them to stretch their money further. If the organization manufactures industrial pumps or constructs roads, this is probably not a worthwhile idea. On the other hand, if the employer is in the business of food supply, clothing, consumer electronics, cars, insurance services, housing construction, or any other line of business where the products or services are targeted toward end consumers, this concept can work. There are many different ways of designing such a scheme, from giving away a certain quota of products or services for free per year per employee to selling to employees at cost recovery prices to setting a discount percentage for an unlimited amount of products or services. Depending on the extent to which these are relevant for the employees and in what volume, such schemes can represent anything from a small and infrequent "bonus" to a substantial annual savings for the household budget, without costing the employer much or even nothing at a cost recovery price (except perhaps for lost sales through ordinary distribution channels).

Especially for companies supplying food, medicines, or medical care, such a scheme can be of vital importance to some employees. The availability of certain medical care services or drugs can be very limited or extremely expensive in some parts of the world. For employees that depend on these items to get well or stay well, allowing them easier access to them can mean more than simply a price discount.

Time often being in short supply for most "modern" employees, especially time outside work, time to pursue leisure interests or spend with family and friends is a benefit employers can offer more of than what is required. Time can be awarded basically in two ways: as more vacation and days off than minimum requirements or shorter working hours. Both of course come at a cost to the employer, either in the form of having to hire more people to do the same amount of work or from having to automate work previously performed manually. If such costs are acceptable, there is much research to indicate that more time can often be of far greater benefit to employees than more money. This is also an area where there are vast differences from country to country, both in terms of legally imposed working hours and vacation days and practices. Europe in general has shorter work weeks and much more vacation, by law, than the United States. Most European countries have as a standard four or five weeks of vacation annually, whereas American workers often earn only two weeks off after five or more years in employment.

The practices mentioned so far aim at giving employees more money or more time, two key "needs." A third need is the ability to develop oneselves further, certainly both as humans and as professionals. The right to training and continued education is in many countries governed by regulations, in others in agreements between employers and unions, and does to some extent represent a basic right (the issue was therefore also treated in chapter 3 as a remedial practice). There are, however, great differences in the extent of such career development aid offered by employers. Most organizations know very well the expenses involved in recruiting and training new employees to the point where they really become productive members of the organization, and would very much like to avoid incurring these costs as a result of people leaving or changing jobs internally. Thus, many provide training that will help the employees in performing their current job more efficiently.

Of course a lot of organizations go further as well, enabling employees to qualify for other positions inside the organization or even outside it, and this is perhaps a crucial issue: will employees who feel they are being held back remain loyal employees of the organization and will those that are given good opportunities for personal and career development be the ones that leave it? Perhaps, but I know from own experience with employees in organizations that I have worked with that the most loyal ones are normally those that have been supported in their struggle to increase their qualifications and subsequently feel gratitude. On the other hand, those that feel they have a potential for better jobs, but are persuaded, convinced, or forced to remain where they are out of convenience for the employer often hold a grudge that can transpire into seeking new challenges elsewhere. Investments of time and money in career development of employees will yield returns in many different ways and should be an institutionalized practice of a decent organization.

To make this a philanthropic practice instead of a remedial one, the deciding factor is the extent of investments made in terms of time off to pursue training or education, fees and tuition for such training paid by the employer, the time spent by superiors or the human resource staff in arranging such training, and the attitude with which such career development is encouraged and discussed. Active support and a willingness to invest in high school diplomas for employees lacking them, university or MBA courses in cases where this is the next logical step, or night classes or technical on-the-job training where deemed suitable are key components. Qualified assistance in deciding what is the suitable means to career development for the individual employee is also important. Should you still be worried that once the training or education has been paid for and completed, the improved mind will walk out the door and take up a position with the competitor, there is always the possibility of including a clause specifying a non-transfer period of some duration during which the employee is not allowed to leave the organization.

The last issue to be presented in this chapter concerns the organization's practices regarding employees with disabilities. This is not an equal opportunity issue per se: employees of minority race, creed, sexual orientation, or other factors do not require any special arrangements to work in an organization. Most persons with disabilities, be they physical or mental, do require such arrangements, to varying extents. There are no obligations for an organization to employ disabled people, but it is certainly a sign of decency to do so. A large number of people with disabilities suffer from inactivity, loneliness, lack of a sense of worth to society, poor financial conditions, and so on. At the same time, there are a great number of examples that demonstrate that they make excellent and productive employees when given the chance in jobs that are suitable for their abilities. In many cases, there are also schemes that involve a sharing of costs between the organization and the authorities, meaning the organization does not pay full wages. In this way, extending an open hand to this group of (potential) employees can be both a kind, philanthropic gesture and an investment that in many cases yields a reasonable return.

Exactly how to approach a position where disabled people are welcome as employees of the organization can vary quite a bit from country to country and situation to situation. Very often, there are national or local chapters of special interest organizations for people with disabilities, either in general or with specific types of disabilities. Contacting such organizations and cooperating with them is one obvious way of making it known that the organization welcomes disabled employees and is recruiting suitable candidates. Regular advertisement of job offers in classified sections is another way of attracting applicants, so is working with the local employment office or other recruitment agencies. Once the organization is established as an employer of disabled workers, the availability of applicants is usually not the problem.

Before charging right into advertising, though, there are preparations that need to be undertaken. Many organizations employing people with serious disabilities find it necessary to have an in-house staff person with experience in adjusting and adapting workplaces and conditions to different types of disabilities. Identifying jobs that are suitable for varying degrees of disability is another important task. There is often a need for more extensive training and on-the-job follow-up than with regular employees, and in many cases, close cooperation with authorities and possibly hospitals or other medical care institutions is necessary. For some types of disabilities, especially in cases of mental disabilities and where the authorities cover a substantial part of the costs for wages and other cost elements, there is a procedure for approval of an organization as suitable for such employees. To take on disabled employees, the organization must understand what it entails and be prepared to expend the extra effort and costs required. Not in the least, be prepared to maintain the employment in the long term, as taking on an employee with special needs only to reverse the decision when things get difficult is worse than not offering work in the first place.

Adaptation of equipment, desks, computers, and so on, might be required to allow, for example, a person without arms or with only one leg to function properly. This is a highly technical area for which you will be referred to more specialized literature. In the case of mentally disabled persons, depending on the degree of disability, there might also be a lack of reading and writing skills (often in addition to physical disabilities). Such employees require even more special arrangements to function in a job setting. As a result, most mentally disabled persons that do hold jobs are employed in special organizations that offer sheltered employment and have the skills and facilities necessary to take care of them. There are also, however, good examples of "regular" organizations taking on people with mental disabilities and with good results. To the extent that an inability to read or write is the main problem, this is not a problem that applies only to people with such disabilities. Dyslexics can suffer the same problem, as do many people who have come from foreign countries and have yet to learn the native language or people who simply failed to learn to read in school. No matter what the cause, it is clear than any organization employing people who cannot read or read well enough to function in jobs that require good reading skills must make other arrangements. This chapter concludes with an anecdote about a company called Prima, which has taken this issue very seriously.

This concludes our presentation of a selection of philanthropic internal business practices that you can implement to extend your ethical position beyond the remedial sphere. These should be seen merely as examples and not an exhaustive list. Virtually all areas of human resource management, as outlined in Figure 3.1, can be transformed into philanthropic elements by extending benefits further than what is strictly necessary or by "overdoing" things. The examples presented can hopefully serve as inspiration for other practices.

IMPLEMENTATION SUMMARY

The area of philanthropic internal business practices is not as extensive as the remedial counterpart, and as such will rely on less implementation support. For the most part, these business practices take the remedial ones one or more steps further. This is usually achieved by either building or installing facilities with more or better services for employees or changing business practices to encompass elements that go beyond what can reasonably be expected. Undertaking such a job thus becomes a matter of systematically identifying areas that can be turned into philanthropic elements and then using previously described tools for business process change. In the next chapter, attention is turned to strategic philanthropic issues with respect to external stakeholders.

Prima is an organization of about 300 employees, of which a large number are mentally disabled. To be able to offer jobs to such a large group of people with special needs, Prima has entered into a number of different business areas: operating canteens, delivering catering, performing maintenance of bus stop shelters, restoration of furniture, packaging of electrical cables, and much more. The company is partly owned by the local municipality, partly by the local chapter of the Red Cross, and has status as an approved organization for various sheltered employment schemes.

Traditionally, Prima has organized jobs in a conventional manner for this type of work situation, with a nondisabled foreman, often specially trained in supervision of disabled workers, directing a small team of employees. The employees have usually been examined and tested to identify tasks they can perform and, once determined, they have often stuck to this task for a long time. The tasks have normally been quite simple and isolated jobs, for example, filling a cardboard box with electric switches and closing the lid with tape.

These practices have helped move many mentally disabled people into work life who would normally sit at home, but have rendered many of the jobs boring and with few opportunities for progress. Lately, Prima has tried some new, and successful, approaches including:

• First and foremost, a realization that our natural propensity to put everything in writing hampers the performance of both people who cannot read and those who can. Product or article names or identification terms are usually combinations of letters and numbers, procedures are written text, signs on walls and shelf labels are text-based, and so on. This (perfectly understandable) practice makes it virtually impossible for someone who cannot read well to function in the organization, and in many cases it takes people who can read perfectly well more time to understand the meaning of a piece of communication than if it were designed differently. Thus, Prima started experimenting with symbol-based communication. Food recipes now have pictures of the ingredients in addition to their names in text, measurements are given both in numbers and by showing the number of boxes or items, procedures are designed as symbol-based flowcharts, products are labeled "dragon" or "bear" by using drawings instead of words, and so on. This has clearly made life much easier for those with reading disabilities, but also the "regular" employees say they have grown so accustomed to the ease of

continued

continued

understanding the symbols and drawings provided that they get annoyed when faced with complicated text where symbols could have been used.

• Self-directed work groups are a new attempt at workshop organization, where the employees themselves take charge of planning their day or week and prioritize jobs based on demand. This is of course not a practice that is suitable for absolutely everyone, but the challenge it represents seems to inspire a good number into taking more responsibility.

• The traditional risk that jobs become boring is counteracted by conventional job rotation where each person is trained to master at least three different jobs, in many cases more. With varying frequency, people are then switched between these jobs to enjoy some variation.

• In line with symbol-based signs and documents, paint has been used to clearly indicate flow patterns of products on the floor of the workshop. Symbols and arrows outline the flow from inbound raw materials and packaging through assembly and out into finished goods stock. This makes it much easier for the employees to see the natural progression of the production processes, and themselves move goods in various stages of completion along to the next step.

• Kanban ordering, that is, using small cards that appear when a box or a shelf has been emptied as a signal that new units must be ordered and also using that very card as the order form that is sent to the supplier, be it an external supplier or the preceding step in the production process. The basic logic of kanban ordering is extremely simple and the only tool used is the card, which of course uses symbols instead of text. Once a shelf of packaging material (the second-to-last remaining before the supply runs out) has been emptied, the card appears and the employee manning that operation at the time simply puts the card in the fax machine and sends it to the supplier to order more. Previously, this needed the intervention of a foreman.

As a result of these and many other improvements and novel ideas, most mentally disabled employees at Prima can now perform much more complex tasks than before. The employees have become more content with their jobs, and operations have become more efficient, thus making the financial situation easier for the company. This helps ensure the viability of Prima and the jobs of 250 mentally disabled people who would otherwise simply sit at home and wait for their benefit check.

9

The Most Visible Ethical Elements: Philanthropic External Strategies

The title of this chapter refers to the fact that organizations reputed for their ethical profile and corporate social responsibility have often achieved this status through strategic involvement in charities and other good causes. As the chapters covering the remedial half of the business ethics framework have clearly demonstrated, there are plenty of things to clean up before an organization vigorously pursues such philanthropic causes. However, being associated with reputable humanitarian organizations or profiled as supporters of sports, the arts, or important charities tend to be effective in creating an image in the public's mind that this organization does good beyond making profits. A survey by the Conference Board covering 463 U.S. companies found that companies are increasingly taking a more businesslike approach to charity, an approach that results in a better image, increased employee loyalty, and improved customer ties (Schwartz and Smart, 1995). Whether philanthropic activities should come only after a clean bill of health in the remedial sphere or not was discussed in chapter 2, so suffice it to say that the kind of strategic philanthropic pursuits fitting this chapter are often visible and highly "marketable."

This chapter will mainly focus on this very strategic question of whether or not to engage in philanthropic or charitable activities and, if so, with a low profile or using active marketing of the fact. Further, a discussion barely hinted at in chapter 1 regarding the creation of a "community" of customers will be elaborated on before the chapter is closed by running through possible philanthropic policies directed at different external stakeholders.

MARKETING CHARITY OR CHARITABLE MARKETING AND SUPPORT?

This heading, being perhaps somewhat cryptic, refers to the paramount decision an organization faces when moving into the philanthropic half of the business ethics framework: should you silently and/or anonymously take on the role of a good citizen corporation and support good causes or should you offer such support and make it well known to the rest of the world that you are doing so? In a way, the latter is similar to kids that stay off the lawn where signs tell them to only when their parents are around to witness this good behavior and possibly reward it. Along this line of reasoning, an organization contemplating engaging in philanthropic activities could argue that: "Unless I get to tell the world about how much good I am doing, there is no point in doing it. I would not benefit from it so it would simply be a waste of time and money." Ultimately, this comes down to the key question of whether an organization supports good causes primarily to benefit others or primarily to gain goodwill and profits itself.

While the ideal, altruistic answer to this question is that the main motivation is doing some good for others, this is probably rarely the case. From a wider perspective, the ideal answer is probably not viable in the long run. If you think back to the discussion about why you and your organization should adopt an ethical approach to business (see chapter 1), the benefits to be achieved encompassed improved customer loyalty, better-motivated employees, ultimately even better financial performance. As will be discussed further in chapter 11 about the negative effects of an ethical approach, corporate social responsibility will only be a viable concept if it simultaneously brings benefits to the organization itself and the beneficiaries of its good citizen way of doing business. If corporate social responsibility (CSR) benefits only various external stakeholders and brings increased costs or other competitive disadvantages as primary results to the organization, it will be a short-lived experiment.

It thus follows that silent and/or anonymous philanthropic pursuits, although doubtlessly of much benefit to their beneficiaries will do very little good for the benefactor, beyond producing the warm feeling of knowing one is doing some good for others. Taking this argument even further, the continued benefits produced by an organization through philanthropic activity are dependent on its making sufficient money to be able to afford it. Making sufficient money hinges on a healthy balance between income and expenditures and sufficient sales of its products or services. Sufficient sales in turn comes as a result of enough potential customers both knowing of the organization's offerings and not in the least the fact that purchasing from this organization will not only generate revenues for it but also contribute to one or more good causes. This renders the entire question of whether or not to "market" an organization's charitable support and good causes as somewhat of a catch-22.

Ultimately, with the perspective of business ethics being primarily an approach targeted at increased competitive advantage of organizations, the best advice is probably to adopt a strategy of "exploiting" philanthropic engagements in image building, marketing (if the organization has strategically decided to advertise), and linking such a profile to the topic of the next section—creating a community of customers. If the organization can afford it or feels strongly about being an anonymous benefactor, then it should by no means feel obliged to follow this advice, but in general the preferred option will be to make use of a philanthropic profile this way. If you think of famous/important business figures, be they Carnegie, Rockefeller, or Gates, they are well known for their contributions, in line with this advice.

The decision whether or not to use philanthropic contributions as part of a strategy for image building and profiling is, however, a decision that succeeds a prior decision to be present on the philanthropic stage in the first place. This is in an equally important question to answer, one that depends on a number of factors:

• *Prior history and tradition regarding philanthropic contributions or efforts.* Deciding on-the-fly to convert to a business ethics approach and revving up such activities from scratch will normally be more difficult than in cases where experience in these matters already exists within the organization.

• *Expected benefits to be achieved.* Going for a business ethics approach will generally have more impact the more thought-through and consistent such an effort is, and benefits will be achieved by a concerted effort to clean up any ethical issues the organization struggles with, to develop a public profile as an ethical organization, and possibly reinforce these with a targeted set of philanthropic pursuits that match the overall ethical profile; a haphazard pursuit of a helter-skelter selection of good causes will rarely produce the same benefits in terms of improved competitive advantage. Thus, a somber estimation of benefits, in terms of employee motivation, customer attraction and loyalty, and financial gains should be made in terms of a consistent plan for an ethical profile. If philanthropic support seems to fit and reinforce this profile, the decision is easy to make, and equally so if not.

• *Expected costs and efforts required.* There is no doubt that philanthropic support involves time, energy, and expenses to establish and operate.

These can vary significantly depending on the level of commitment and extent of the activities, but they should be estimated before the decision is made. There is equally little doubt that moving beyond a remedial approach and into the philanthropic half of the business ethics framework means sticking the organization's neck out even farther. The more ambitious the ethical profile an organization attempts to develop and maintain, the more credible behavior it needs to sustain and the harder the fall should it be caught straying from acceptable behavior.

If a careful assessment of these factors gives a positive indication toward moving ahead with philanthropic support, this is an important strategic decision, with potential and pitfalls. The possible philanthropic policies this decision can be translated into are presented later in this chapter and operational business practices in the next chapter. Perhaps the greatest potential for benefits from this decision lies in the opportunity for creating what have so far a little inaccurately been termed a community of customers. This is the focus of the next section.

A PHILANTHROPIC PROFILE CAN TIE YOUR CUSTOMERS TOGETHER IN A COMMUNITY OF CUSTOMERS

In the introductory chapter outlining potential benefits of an ethical approach to business, achieving superior customer loyalty through appealing to something more "noble" in customers than merely price or quality consciousness was discussed. This is the main idea behind the concept of a community of customers.

Using a particular organization as supplier of a product or service can represent something more than a convenient way of obtaining that item, something that renders switching to a different vendor an unlikely decision. Normally, where competing offers are mainly differentiated (or rather not differentiated) by minor price variances or packaging or minute design differences, switching vendors is easy and done without much careful deliberation. In contrast to this, some companies have succeeded in developing a philanthropic structure for their business that ensures most customers know that part of what they spend buying from the company contributes to a good cause. The most successful ones have even come to a position where supporting this good cause seems to have replaced acquiring the product or service as the primary objective for the custom brought to the organization. We personally buy our wall calendars from a company that started out just as a calendar company, but has now turned more into an animal protection organization with calendar sales as a side activity. Certainly our main motivation for being their customers is not any longer the calendars, but the good they do with our money. In such circumstances, the loyal customers are people who care about the same values and are willing perhaps even to pay more or experience minor inconveniences in performing their purchases to support these values and causes. At this stage, the body of customers develops from separate individuals coincidentally using the same vendor into a more integrated community of customers who share values, common support for a good cause, and a supplier that helps them in supporting this cause. Being a member of such a community creates a feeling of belonging, gives more meaning to the business done than merely acquiring an item, and can instill a powerful loyalty to the organization at the center of the network tying the community together.

Some product types and/or manufacturers of certain brands have been able to achieve some of the same community effects even without adding a philanthropic dimension. There are many motorcycle owners (or rather enthusiasts) who would never consider buying anything but a Harley-Davidson, who wear clothes adorned with their logo, are members of Harley-Davidson owner clubs, who even, like the owners of a house I sometimes pass, paint the logo on the largest wall of their house. Apple computer owners have been renowned for their near-religious belief in the superiority of their Macs over "Wintel" PCs, to the extent that otherwise peaceful chaps have ended up in fistfights defending their beloved machines. Saturn owners share not only ownership of their Saturn cars, but visits to the plant, family picnics and outings where they bring along their cars, and many other activities facilitated by the manufacturer and its dealers. When you see how powerful customer loyalty can be to such brands, think of what it could be when the dimension of buying a good product or service is combined with the possibility of doing some good for others.

If you agree that for organizations with products and services where this is feasible, reaching a state where you indeed have such a loyal community of customers is desirable, the question of course is: how do you get there? Sadly, there is no single recipe for this challenge, but some elements that can help are:

• First of all, ensure that you offer a product or service that holds a general high level of quality, is safe to use, and that has no inherent ethical issues connected to it or the processes required to produce and bring it to market.

• Define and implement a "powerful" philanthropic dimension that can be added to the product, service, or the organization in general. This is of course the tricky part! Powerful means several things: that the philanthropic dimension in one way or another seems logically connected to the product or service, that it is a cause that people find important and will be willing to support, that it is apparent that doing business with the organization not only generates a few dollars a year toward some charitable event but truly contributes to the cause in question, that channeling support to the good cause does not involve any/many additional steps or burdens for the customer, that the entire scheme is perceived as credible, and that the philanthropic involvement can be used as part of image building or marketing.

• Keep reminding customers, existing and potential new ones, of the fact that their custom goes beyond lining the pockets of the organization and its owners and management. Use the philanthropic dimension to build and reinforce the public image of the organization and its products or services as something different than traditional pursuers of maximum profits.

• Nurture the sense of community and belonging among the customers by publishing a newsletter, arranging events of a social nature (for awareness creation, to demonstrate how the money contributed does good for others, or events where customers can directly take part in charity work), or in other ways bring the members of the community together.

At the end of the day, the crux is to make the link between a customer's purchase from the organization and some philanthropic benefit to others as clear as possible, require as little extra cost or inconvenience as possible from your customers for being part of this chain, and nurture the feeling each customer has of being part of something greater than themselves. Some examples of such philanthropic elements organizations have added to their primary offering to achieve this community effect are discussed in the following sidebar.

The Body Shop is to many an excellent example of the philanthropic business approach. The primary products of The Body Shop are cosmetics, an industry that has been strongly criticized for animal testing of products, its use of ingredients that have questionable origins in terms of environmental damage, and its negative effect on women's self-esteem through marketing. By turning all of this around, The Body Shop has designed its products around a strategy of no animal testing whatsoever, fair trade with third-world suppliers of raw materials, environmental concern in product development and packaging, and "no

continued

nonsense" products that keep their promises and whose prices reflect their contents and manufacturing costs more than inflated brand name prices. In addition, The Body Shop donates parts of its profits to various causes and idealistic organizations. All of these elements have been successful in creating a type of cosmetics store that sets itself apart from the rest (granted, there are stores that have copied the concept, but at the time of its launch, this approach was completely different) and attracts the type of loyal customers that would never consider buying a pricey branded lipstick that might have been tested on a rabbit.

Avon is perhaps representative of the more traditional cosmetics company, although it labels itself as "the company for women." Women are thus obviously the main target group for Avon's products, consequently, Avon has decided to target an area of high concern to women as a good cause to back, namely breast cancer. The Avon Breast Cancer Crusade is the name of the campaign, which from 1993 through 2002 reached its 10-year goal of $250 million net in total monies raised worldwide to fund access to care and finding a cure for breast cancer. In addition to the United States, Avon now supports programs for breast cancer and other vital women's health issues in fifty countries around the world. The goal of the Avon Breast Cancer Crusade is to benefit all women through research, clinical care, support services, education, and early detection, but there is special emphasis on reaching medically underserved women, including low-income, elderly, and minority women, and women without adequate health insurance. Through this effort, Avon contributes to this important medical issue and gets a clear message across to consumers that buying Avon products helps directly fight a disease all women are afraid of.

The philanthropic dimension does not have to be as altruistic as in these cases to work. Previously, a large European brewery was mentioned that made the mistake of believing its customers would not react negatively to its campaign to buy and later close local breweries to centralize all production at one site. In a few of the cities that lost their traditional brewery and their brand (breweries that were operating at a profit!), grassroots initiatives have established small local breweries. A couple of these have been successful in making a beer that is similar to the lost one and have been successful in attracting customers. Part of their approach to marketing has been to donate portions of their revenues to a fund for workers who lost their jobs when the old brewery closed and to guarantee that no matter what happens, the brewery will stay put

continued

continued

where it is. Given an opportunity to both give the large brewery a reminder about how to behave and to support local initiatives, customers have welcomed the new beers and even formed clubs that celebrate them. Again, a community has been formed that stays loyal to the company partly because it sells a good product and partly because it supports local employment and loyalty to the city and the region.

PHILANTHROPIC STAKEHOLDER POLICIES

In this last section of this chapter, the same as in the other strategically focused chapters, a set of possible strategic policies will be presented, in this case of a philanthropic nature toward external stakeholders. The list of policies is shown in Table 9.1. Again, these serve in part as a menu of ideas from which others can be developed and in part set direction for the operational practices presented in the next chapter.

IMPLEMENTATION SUMMARY

As was mentioned at the outset of this chapter, external philanthropic strategies are probably the most visible element of an ethical business approach. Formulating such strategies is then a very important task, but the approach for doing so is not any different from the other policy formulation tasks:

• External philanthropic strategies can be based on the ideas presented in Table 9.1. When defining these policies, the executive team must make sure that they are in line with the organization's traditions and overall strategy. Trying to convert the organization completely and make a sudden U-turn is rarely successful.

• Conducting the policy formulation in a structured manner is important. A more structured process for stakeholder analysis can help in doing so.

• As with remedial external policies, and indeed any strategy of the organization, various validation approaches are useful tools in stimulating the desired behavior of the organization and its members.

This concludes the philanthropic, external strategic policies chapter, leaving only one chapter to go before the entire business ethics framework has been presented.

Table 9.1   Philanthropic policies toward external stakeholders.

External Stakeholder	Policy Element
Suppliers	Policy for taking on suppliers with special needs or disabilities.
	Policy for taking an active role in developing good quality of work life conditions and democracy in countries from which products or services are sourced.
	Policy for assisting "regular" suppliers in developing an ethical business approach through good business mentor programs.
Local community	Policy for contributing to local community development programs, either on your own or through already established programs run by charitable organizations.
The environment	Policy for establishing or taking part in environ-mental improvement programs that go beyond minimizing or cleaning up damage that is inflicted by the organization itself.
	Policy for eliminating or minimizing pollution caused by the organization, and especially "unnecessary" pollution caused by profit-maximizing strategies.
Competitors	Policy for attempting to pursue a co-opetition approach to business where feasible.
	Policy for showing leniency to competitors in times of crisis.
Charitable/idealistic organizations and other types of nongovernmental interest organizations	Policy for participating in or supporting philanthropic work performed by charitable organizations.
	Policy for donating funds to sports or the arts.
Customers	Policy for differentiated pricing to deliberately allow less fortunate customer groups the opportunity to purchase products or services.
	Policy for no-profits pricing.
	Policy for offering more than the minimum required for after-sales service and complaint-handling.

10

Supporting Good Causes: Philanthropic External Business Practices

W hen organizing some of the previous chapters, the difficult part has been the multitude of various elements that could be included in each chapter, for example all the human resource management practices presented in chapter 4. If anything, this final chapter, dealing with the business ethics framework, is just as diverse in the variety of ways an organization can support good causes. As you probably have become accustomed to by now, the bulk of this chapter will go through a selection of these ways, categorized by the stakeholders they benefit. There are, however, a few more fundamental questions that should be posed initially.

DESIGNING PHILANTHROPIC BUSINESS PRACTICES

Some of these questions might border on being strategic decisions, but have been included here if for no other reason than for its proximity to the treatment of the actual practices following. There are probably even more such key decisions, but these three are important to consider when designing the operational practices that will bring to life an external philanthropic activity in the organization:

• Should we support "any good cause" or only causes closely linked to the business area of the organization? As was discussed in the previous chapter, reaching the position of having a community of customers is easier when the philanthropic element of the organization is logically linked to its business area and customer groups. Computer companies can help schools by donating computer equipment, pharmaceutical companies can help less fortunate patients by donating medicines, food manufacturers can help homeless people by giving away food, and so on. In all these cases, there is a clear connection between what the company does "for a living" and how it supports a good cause. For many other organizations, finding such obvious ways to aid external stakeholders can be difficult. Turning to one or more charitable organizations of some sort may be the only way to channel support into good causes. A management consulting company can donate one percent of its profits to the Red Cross or the employees of a local municipality can work the lunch shift at a soup kitchen. Such approaches can be just as beneficial as those linked to the company's business area. Where possible, linking an organization's philanthropy to its core business has some advantages over general support of more or less arbitrarily chosen good causes. It makes understanding why the organization supports this cause in particular much easier, which in turn makes image-building easier; it can be less expensive than cash donations as the organization can often use its products or services as support; and being within the general area of expertise of the organization, it is often easier to design philanthropic practices that have a real impact. Thus, if possible, you should attempt linking the aid given to what the company does.

• Should we develop independent charitable activities for the organization or participate in existing programs or organizations? This question is in some ways linked to the previous one; in cases where the organization finds it difficult to provide aid within its business area, the most logical approach is usually to cooperate with existing charitable organizations or programs. This of course has the advantages that the support channels are already established, they may have developed a solid reputation, and it can save the organization time and money that otherwise would have to be spent on establishing its own program. A possible negative aspect is that the image effect can be weaker this way as the cause supported will be known in its own right and will not necessarily be linked to the specific organization. It is, however, possible to establish a new charitable program or organization. This can be difficult, though, and it is generally recommended to consider this approach only when you can work inside the business area you already know. In this case, having "your own" charity can be an advantage in that it reflects more clearly back on your organization; you can design the scheme, its beneficiaries, and other details the way you see fit; and you are more flexible in terms of making changes in scale or operational mode. The drawbacks can be that such a newly established charity can take years to amass sufficient credibility and trust to have much effect, and that running such a scheme yourself will normally incur costs.

• Should we give support in the form of cash donations or in the form of time, effort, or equipment? This question is also linked to the previous two, but can to some extent be decided independently. No matter whether the good cause is within the organization's business area or is run by the organization itself or not, there is always the choice between the two, both of which have their pros and cons. Donating money will normally set the organization back more as these funds will have to come from pre-tax profits and thus fairly directly impact the bottom line. Administering cash donations is usually simpler than involving employees' time and/or equipment, though, and direct funding to good causes renders them more flexible in putting the support to good use. If there is an opportunity to donate employees' time (during working hours) or equipment, products, or services from the organization, it is usually easier to demonstrate to the outside world the logical link between the organization and the charities it supports. In terms of expenses, donating time or products at incurred costs will usually be less expensive than direct cash transfers, but can require more administrative effort.

When posing these three questions, you might get the impression that an organization can only support one good cause, in one way. This is of course not the case—most organizations find ways to benefit many different good causes, obviously some more than others. Some of these can be aided by limited donations of money, others through participating in charitable events, while at the same time the company may run a separate philanthropic organization of its own. This is perfectly all right, but an organization trying to develop an image as a caring good citizen organization should really focus a major share of its support on one cause. Having one main cause will again give the best opportunity for promoting the philanthropy and gaining the positive side effects such support potentially can lead to.

SELECTED PHILANTHROPIC BUSINESS PRACTICES

Since there is truly such a plethora of ways to channel support to various good causes, it is impossible to present an exhaustive overview over all the possible approaches. Consider this chapter a set of examples that can be copied or be used to create other approaches. The examples are presented in the order of the policies presented in Table 9.1. It should also be pointed out that, as these examples will demonstrate, good causes or charitable organizations are not the only possible targets for philanthropic activities. Related to the business ethics framework, philanthropic in this respect is the counterpart of remedial, that is, any practice benefiting any stakeholder, that goes beyond remedying any "damage" inflicted by the organization or beyond minimum or reasonable standards. Paying more than average market prices to a third-world supplier is a philanthropic practice as relevant for this half of the framework as donating money to United Way.

Treating Suppliers with Extra Care

The relationship between an organization and its suppliers is to some extent characterized by both love and hate. Having a business relationship, the logical inclination is for the supplier to obtain as good prices as possible for its products or services and for the buyer to push prices as low as possible. Also, for sourcing conditions other than price, for example, delivery times, ordering horizon, contract duration, and so on, the two parties are naturally at odds with each other. This is only apparently so, as the massive research that has been conducted on industrial procurement and sourcing has revealed that the most successful supply chains are those that consider themselves integrated partners who cooperate, where one link benefits from the success of the others. Consequently, arms-length supplier treatment practices where prices and other conditions are squeezed to the limit are rarely beneficial for either party. There are, however, ways to treat suppliers in a philanthropic manner other than being moderate in contract negotiations:

• *Accepting poorer purchasing conditions.* This is perhaps being moderate in negotiations and involves agreeing to pay better than rock-bottom prices or accepting a longer lead time than was ideally specified. Moderate in this respect means renouncing demands to an extent that really makes a difference to the supplier. In normal supplier relationships, dealing with suppliers that are not experiencing difficulties or have special needs of some sort, this approach is not really recommendable. Beyond being reasonable in negotiations with such "normal" suppliers, there are no real motives for taking such a position. Granted, "being kind" to a supplier might involve some extra effort on the buyer's part, but there is no reason for giving extraordinary treatment to regular suppliers. However, for suppliers experiencing temporary hardship (financial, lack of human resources, loss of competence, and so on) or for other reasons unable to fulfill their obligations, a temporary agreement to relinquish the toughest demands to tide it over may be warranted. Provided the supplier actually survives and recovers, they will usually be a loyal and solid partner for the future.

• *Taking on suppliers with special needs.* An organization is of course free to choose the suppliers it would like to do business with, and most organizations source the products and services they need from regular suppliers. Regular in the sense that the supplier operates under normal competitive

A fairly large consumer electronics equipment manufacturer had used the same supplier of packaging for a few years, a much smaller company compared to itself. Following a slump in demand, the packaging supplier faced financial problems, especially in terms of short-term liquidity, and received little help from its bank. After pleading with the electronics manufacturer, the buyer agreed to pay substantial advances on future deliveries. This was enough to keep the company afloat; a company that increased sales significantly during the next three years and today is alive and well.

Two years later, the electronics company developed a completely new type of operating panel for its products, with a display that would light up at a touch and change appearance depending on the function accessed at the time. Being a highly innovative product, the company felt it needed to offer customers a chance to easily see how this control panel worked before deciding to buy the product. The best idea they came up with was a type of packaging that would simulate the control panel without having to power up the unit inside. Power for this test panel would come from a small and inexpensive battery inserted into the cardboard. Such a packaging solution was certainly also innovative, but not very complex to make; it simply required a new machine to make a few special operations. Having approached larger packaging suppliers and been turned down by all of them due to claims of the risk being too high, the supplier the company had saved two years earlier agreed to give it a try. Granted, this would be a risky move for a fairly small company, but it was prepared to return the favor. A couple of months down the road, the packaging was ready and the product launched—and became a big hit.

conditions, employs regular human resources, is located in countries that promote free competition, and so on. A gesture beyond what can be reasonably expected from an organization is using suppliers that for some reason are facing special conditions, special in the sense of making it difficult to compete on regular terms with normal suppliers. Such suppliers may include those hiring employees with disabilities, even sheltered employment organizations; suppliers located in countries or regions with difficult conditions, for example, developing countries or nonindustrialized regions; or "suppliers" that consist of individuals working from home, but able to deliver what the organization needs. In all of these cases, chances are that the buyer will have to pay a premium of some size compared with regular, professional suppliers, and buying from such suppliers with special needs might involve

Kalikå is the name of a toy store that first opened in Sweden twenty-seven years ago. Their first toys were quite unlike the traditional toys sold at that time, with an emphasis on incorporating pedagogical values into their design. Many Swedish children have grown up with these toys and many of the original models still exist today. From the start, the soft, velvety creatures have been produced in an ethical, environmentally friendly way. Today, many of the children who had Kalikå toys when they were young are bringing their own kids into the store to buy toys for them. What many of them do not know is that many of the finger puppets are made in St. Petersburg, Russia. There, they are sewn by mothers of disabled children as part of the so-called Fair Play project started in 1996. The aim is to help some of the estimated 600,000 abandoned children in Russian orphanages, children that often are not orphans at all, but disabled children whose parents the authorities have discouraged from taking care of at home. So far, the project has offered 38 mothers and two fathers of such disabled children the opportunity to work from home and thus both support their families and take care of their children. The project equips each family with a sewing machine and includes them in a network of parents in similar situations. In return, they produce puppets professionally and with care, delivering every other month as they are supposed to. As an added bonus, each one adds a personal touch to the puppets by making unique eyes, noses, or whiskers, a special feature greatly appreciated by the customers.

other disadvantages as well compared with traditional suppliers. However, there is often a deeper sense of satisfaction from aiding disadvantaged suppliers, and developing lasting relationships with these kinds of organizations can be an asset in terms of developing an image as a caring organization.

• *Aiding suppliers in developing an ethical approach to business.* Setting requirements of suppliers for compliance with certain minimum standards, which really is a remedial element, has been mentioned earlier (see chapter 6). Going further, a customer organization can take an active part in helping its suppliers to become good citizen organizations themselves. This is much more than asking suppliers to avoid breaching labor rights or environmental protection principles; this is about "converting" other organizations into active supporters of an ethical approach to business. This is again beyond the call of duty, but an initiative that can pay off in terms of profiling the entire supply chain as an ethical engine. In practice, this can involve several different activities, from describing to suppliers how

Baxter is one company that has implemented wide-ranging practices for developing ethical supplier relationships. These include external ethical education of the same standard as internal ethical education. The training is first offered to key suppliers, mid- to small-size suppliers of components and services, and suppliers with performance concerns. A business practice standards help line also is open to suppliers, and Baxter runs a mentor program for suppliers titled "Partners in Good Business." This encompasses a toolkit for creating and maintaining a business ethics program along with various other resources and access to Baxter's Business Practice Team, a team of internal consultants.

your organization made the change to offering training in operational business ethics to actively working with suppliers as consultants.

• *Actively supporting the development of good work-life conditions and democracy in supplier countries.* This might sound like an overwhelming task for an organization to take on, especially if your organization is a smaller one. It might not be as impossible as you may at first think, and it is an important job. There are a large number of countries in this world where basic democratic rights of the people are ignored and where work is a matter of coercion and force, not a chosen profession where ambitions can be fulfilled. The rights to freedom and work are fundamental in global human rights standards, and being deprived of these is a serious attack on human dignity. Most countries are, however, dependent on some sort of economic relations with the outside world to stay alive, normally through selling raw materials or semi-finished goods to other countries. Usually, the customers of these goods are private companies without the influence large countries might have to encourage changes in such countries. Still, a small business buying products from a company, be it privately or state owned, in a country lacking democratic and work-life standards can in its own small way encourage changes. By including in contracts the right to assessment visits, requirements for work conditions, and so on, some leverage can be applied to make small changes. In the short term, these might not have a major impact, but could start to change some attitudes. Going further, when contracts are up for renegotiation, the right to help employees of the supplier to organize trade unions could be added. Teaming up with customers of other companies in the region, cross-company unions can be established that hold more power. Combined with the continuous pressure such countries usually are under from democratic governments, the UN, and other organizations to change their ways, the efforts are often crowned with success some years down the road. Granted, some countries revert to their old ways after a while, but the general trend is an increase in countries operating under democratic principles, and more can be achieved. Again, this is an effort that could cost both time and money to be involved in, but one that brings the organization and its representatives into a movement that has much more important goals than mere profit generation.

Suppliers, at least those close to the organization culturally or geographically, are fairly well known entities that can be targeted through specific initiatives. The next external stakeholder to be dealt with, the local community, can be harder to get your arms around.

Helping to Develop the Local Community

The term local community can be construed as a single entity. This is of course not the case; it is a collective term covering elements like the local authorities, schools, homes for the elderly, roads, parks, the inhabitants of a region, social organizations such as the Boy Scouts, marching bands, sports teams, and many, many more. Common to all of these is the fact that they make up the fabric of the community that the organization is invariably part of by virtue of its location. While there are no formal obligations

---

In Norway, there is a national program whose title translates literally into Night Raven, but is basically a Neighborhood Watch program. It has a chapter in most cities and towns of a minimum size and focuses not on preventing burglaries but rather violence in the streets, drug abuse, and underage drinking. The program recruits adults who volunteer to patrol the streets at night, especially during weekends. They have no right to search kids, seize alcohol or drugs, or make citizen's arrests, but are meant to function as stabilizing elements through their presence. Experience shows that their patrols have a very positive effect on disturbances and violence, and the entire program has come to be seen as a very positive initiative among the population in areas where it is active. While the adult patrols are mostly individuals recruited through sports clubs or other organizations, some businesses have also found it worthwhile to support the program with manpower. Under this scheme, companies either allow employees to use part of their working hours for patrolling or at least help recruit volunteers from the company who patrol on their own time.

for an organization to contribute anything to the development of this community beyond taxes and other law-imposed elements, most organizations realize the value of a good local community and good relations with it. Employees live in this community and their happiness is in part dependent on its quality; the security and safety of the organization and its facilities is improved by having a caring and well maintained local environment; and the kids who grow up in the area are potential employees a few years down the road. Thus, not only obliging in terms of imposed contributions, but actively supporting the local community is an investment that usually pays off. And as usual, there are many ways to offer such active support:

• *Participate in or support with time and/or money already established local community development programs.* Depending on the level of such activity in your area, there can be programs targeting schools, sports activities, infrastructure improvement or development, financially disadvantaged people, recreational areas, and so on. Offering such support is perhaps the most obvious way of helping to improve different aspects of life in the community.

• *Establish local community development programs.* In cases where there are no suitable programs already in operation or where an area the organization would like to support is not covered by existing programs, the organization can itself initiate or establish a program of its own. Referring to the discussion in chapter 2, there are many considerations to make when contemplating setting up your own charitable program instead of supporting existing ones. However, in some cases, that can be the best

---

GTE, now merged with Bell Atlantic, ran a foundation that in 1999 distributed more than $30 million nationwide. One of the main focuses of GTE's philanthropic activities was the fight against illiteracy, resulting in the establishment of the GTE Family Literacy Program. The program funded 44 technology learning centers nationwide. With an estimated 40 million U.S. citizens classified as illiterate, GTE saw this as an opportunity to influence the quality of life for customers as well as employees. Part of the program has been continued under the new company name, Verizon. Verizon Foundation also includes a program titled Verizon Reads, which has a wide variety of programs and a network of collaborative literacy partners to reach illiterate adults and children across America.

course of action and help ensure that the support given is truly channeled to causes the organization deems important.

• *Deliberately source locally where possible.* Like it or not, it is a fact that local communities thrive better when there is a viable industry present, with companies that provide employment, tax revenues, and activity in general. Subscribing to the tenet that vibrant and active local communities also benefit the companies located in them, one way a company can contribute is by sourcing goods and services from local suppliers when this is possible. There has been a tendency lasting recent years to source globally whenever an organization needs to acquire something, a practice that most certainly does not stimulate the local community and one that also has environmental consequences related to increased transportation needs. If there are suppliers available locally that maintain acceptable standards of quality and price, they should be considered. In addition to supporting "neighbors," there are also benefits from having suppliers close by, such as enabling tighter follow-up and making it easier to get together to resolve any problems that might occur.

• *Employing chronically unemployable people.* Sourcing locally is one way of stimulating employment and thus fighting one of the things that really negatively impact a local community, namely unemployment. Still, all statistics indicate that even in periods of high economic activity and correspondingly low unemployment, there will always be a certain small portion of the potential workforce that remains unemployed. Some for reasons of disability, others because they fall between the cracks or find it hard to function straightaway in "normal" jobs. Helping these people into gradual employment is a philanthropic deed that truly benefits both the individuals assisted and the local community (by reducing benefit spending and reducing petty crime often perpetrated by the chronically unemployed).

The local community certainly encompasses the dimension of local environmental health, be it related to pollution levels, the existence of forests and parks, or traffic and noise disturbances. Philanthropic practices related to the external environment are, however, a topic of its own.

Days Inns of America, the hotel chain, has a practice of hiring homeless people as reservations sales agents and allows them to stay in hotel rooms until they can afford their own housing. Some of Days Inns' formerly homeless employees have used the skills they learned there to go on to better, higher-paying jobs.

Not Only Avoiding Inflicting Environmental Damage, but Helping Clean Up

As should be evident from the earlier treatment in this book of environmental practices, the environment is a diverse concept that can be difficult for an organization to relate to. Especially when talking about philanthropic practices, most organizations find it hard to figure out how they can actually contribute. Reducing discharges or emissions from processes the organization is completely in charge of itself is, if not easy, at least something that is possible to control in some way. Taking on the seemingly impossible task of not only minimizing one's own impact but improving the environment and repairing damage done by others can certainly be a frightening prospect. Again, there are ways of contributing that are perhaps less monumental than taking on the entire world's environmental problems, yet still effective:

• *Supporting environmental protection organizations.* This is perhaps not the most active philanthropic part an organization can take, but is a start. There are a large number of various organizations of this type out there, ranging from the familiar and rather "harmless" ones like the World Wildlife Fund and its like to equally well-known, but more aggressive organizations like Greenpeace to smaller, less recognized, and often highly aggressive activist organizations. Many of these also specialize in researching, protecting, or lobbying certain aspects of the environment, for example, endangered species, the rain forest, or fighting desertification. Depending on the business area of your organization and any particular environmental concerns it might hold, it is most certainly possible to find an environmental protection organization to support that seems suitable. This can be a small and good start.

• *Supporting more specific environmental improvement programs.* There are both temporary and permanent programs that target specific areas in need of cleanup or measures to improve damage done. After large oil spills, there are usually cleanup teams being organized that remove oil, help seabird victims of the spill, and so on. Of a more permanent nature, there are active programs in place to replant trees to fight desertification. Such programs require funding and they require manpower to do their work. Supporting such programs with funding or employees' time is a more active form of support that can make a visible difference.

• *Setting up repair teams locally.* Some companies have been acclaimed for establishing small task forces of employees who are supported by the company in both scanning the "neighborhood" for environmental problems

A fairly small supermarket in a small town has followed the environmental task force approach. Having grown tired from seeing streets, walking paths, and industrial backyards being littered with everything from household garbage to industrial waste, the owner and manager decided to make a difference. He slowly started making his employees aware of the problem and how ugly it looked, and after a while had many of them motivated to chip in on the effort to clean up some of the mess. In the beginning, a group of employees would spend an hour per week after closing time to clear away trash from various public sites. After seeing pictures of the "before and after" type hanging in the store, some customers started inquiring whether there was any way they could help. A few months into the initiative, there were regularly between 40 and 50 people out two or three nights per week looking for "ugly spots" and removing messes. The local newspaper got interested and started writing small pieces about parks, stretches of highway, or other areas that had been cleaned up and made nice again. From all the interest in this program, the store manager claims he could easily have made it a full-time job managing the program, but this was not the intention. The point was to give some of his and his employees' time to make a difference, thus he has capped the effort at a moderate activity level. Needless to say, other businesses in the area are following suit and cleaning up neighboring towns.

and finding ways to rectify these. Such teams need not require much money or effort and can often do a lot of good without much prior expertise, training, or equipment.

There are certainly other ways an organization can contribute to environmental repair, and if you are looking for some that suit your organization better than those mentioned, please get in touch with local environmental protection organizations. They can usually advise you on local possibilities. Next, our focus will be on a group of stakeholders that you might not immediately appreciate should be made subjects of philanthropic attitudes or behavior: competitors.

Mercy in Business—There Are Times When Even Competitors Deserve a Break

As has been talked about earlier, war has often been used as the dominant metaphor for industrial competition. War and philanthropy are quite opposite terms, but there are situations where a different treatment of competitors than trying to squash them can be a wise approach. There is even a business concept based on a different outlook to competitors than trying to get rid of them.

Novell founder Ray Noorda first coined the term "co-opetition" in 1993, a concept that has been warmly embraced by many scholars of business strategy. Brandenburger and Nalebuff (1996) published a book bearing this title, claiming that business is about cooperation when making the cake and competition when sharing it. The basic idea is that if competitors conduct so much warfare that all or parts of the cake are ruined, there is nothing left to conquer, a typical lose/lose situation.

A basic concept in co-opetition thinking is complementors, that is, a product or service that by being complementary increases the value of another product or service. There are numerous examples: computer hardware and software, cars and car loans, TV and TV Guide, and so on. Very often, there are different actors in the market that supply these complementary products or services, and the absence of key complementors can be fatal. Downtown stores without access to parking spaces will fail in the competition with suburban malls.

Brandenburger and Nalebuff used game theory to highlight various aspects and examples of business relationships among competitors and complementors. Reciting the details of this thinking is not apropos in this book, but a combination of cooperation and competition, (co-opetition) can be a fruitful approach in many cases. Brandenburger and Nalebuff have certainly gained a supporter in Ed Freeman at the Darden School of Business: "What America needs is not to be more competitive, but more cooperative."

Other specific philanthropic methods include:

• *Being considerate in mergers, buyouts, and takeovers.* Although showing clear cycles of activity levels, mergers and takeovers are frequently popular business strategies. Such moves are used to gain entrance into new market segments, strengthen one's position, eliminate a competitor, or acquire more capacity. In some cases, ownership simply changes hands and all units involved remain virtually the same. Equally often, such acquisitions are founded on a potential for synergies and cost reductions, usually creating an overcapacity and a corresponding need for downsizing. As has been treated already, downsizing situations are stressful times for employees and say quite a lot about the attitudes of owners and executives in terms of their handling of people (see chapter 4). When downsizing follows a merger or acquisition, this becomes even clearer. Such takeovers usually have a "winner" and a "loser," respectively the active party and the reluctant one, and the winner gets to dictate many of the rules for the ensuing restructuring that will take place. The "winner" in such dealings frequently gives clear preference to their own employees, preparing them better and earlier, or being much more open with information with them. This creates frustration and despair for those on the "losing" side that eventually are let go, often with many harsh words and often with good media coverage. While the "winner" often is in its rights legally speaking, the negative press and customers' reactions to what seems like unfair treatment can often backfire badly. Thus, showing some consideration toward former competitors being acquired and their employees can avoid some of the ugly scenes seen in takeovers.

• *Showing selected "mercy in business" when called for.* Given that you believe in the hypothesis that competition in general is healthy, it follows that grasping any opportunity to get rid of a competitor is perhaps not your best option. It happens now and then that a competitor is in serious trouble, trouble that jeopardizes its entire existence. Such trouble can arise from temporary loss of orders, problems with manufacturing equipment, loss of key personnel, accidents, and so on. Generally speaking, these events are out of the ordinary (if serious trouble is caused by a general decline in performance, sales, or other factors over time and seems to be leading to an inevitable slow death, this is no situation where mercy is called for). In such cases of extraordinary problems, it can be easy and tempting to deal the competitor the final blow by announcing big discounts, going aggressively after the competitor's customers, or trying to attract key people to leave the organization, from a motivation that one less competitor will automatically mean a higher market share for your organization. This is where you should perhaps think twice; there are examples of companies that have actively pushed a competitor over the cliff and into bankruptcy only to find that the diseased competitor's customers would rather live without this particular product or service than to become a customer of the "killer." In the town where I live, I recently saw this happen. A large, powerful chain of pizza restaurants after much pressure was able to take over the site of a small, independent restaurant acclaimed for making the best Italian pizza in town. Even if the new restaurant sits in a prime location, business here is much slower than other comparable restaurants in the chain, much due to people protesting againt the way they closed the old restaurant. This kind of industrial euthanasia can cause animosity in customers, other competitors, analysts, and other stakeholders. On the other hand, showing mercy, even offering a hand to help, can have the opposite effect, eliciting sympathy and positive reactions. This is of course an assessment that must be made on a case-by-case basis, but leniency in times of crisis is a philanthropic practice that can pay off.

There have traditionally been two major airlines in Norway: SAS, the Scandinavian Airlines System cooperation between Sweden, Denmark, and Norway, and the entirely Norwegian company of Braathens. To some extent, these two have competed fiercely and split the market between them, allowing the other to operate freely on some routes. Following the general problems in the airline industry over the last few years, SAS finally put in a bid to take over Braathens altogether. Both employees of the two companies, especially Braathens, and Norwegian competition authorities were skeptical, but after it became quite clear that no other buyers were available and that Braathens would most likely disappear altogether if continuing on its own, the deal was allowed to go through.

During negotiations, the Braathens unions were greatly concerned about their members' jobs, but seemed to get reassurances from SAS executives that seniority would to a large extent dictate who would have to go during the restructuring. When the deal had been finalized, SAS announced that at least 1,000 people had to be laid off, at least in the first round (following the continued difficulties in the industry, more people have been laid off since). During the restructuring, 350 ground crew employees from Braathens had been transferred directly to SAS's ground crew. To the surprise of these former Braathens employees, when layoffs were being decided, general seniority was not the deciding factor. As it turned out, a Braathens employee with fifteen years of service could lose against an SAS employee with only five years.

As of August 2003, proceedings are starting in a lawsuit filed by the unions of the Braathens employees against SAS. This follows months of disgruntled Braathens employees complaining to newspapers and other media about their treatment, public scholarly debate among legal professionals about rules and regulations applying in this case, and low motivation among employees waiting to be laid off. All in all, the sweet prospect of buying the main competitor has turned sour and has contributed to making life hard for SAS in these troubled times.

The last approach that could be mentioned under this heading refers not directly to competitors, but more to alliance partners, or complementors to follow the terminology of the co-opetition concept: acting as so-called trusted intermediaries on behalf of partners' products or services your customers might be interested in (this practice was discussed under the topic of marketing, see chapter 6). The main objective is to provide your customers

---

The Wilh. Wilhelmsen Group spans a number of different companies all related to shipping and ship management. After a joint venture with the Wallenius shipping company, the resulting unit is in fact the largest car carrier in the world. Being an old company, times have not always been as good as of late. In particular, the company came close to extinction in 1989. In connection with the launch of a new vessel built at a shipyard in Germany, half the management and staff from the head office in Oslo was flying down to the yard in a privately chartered aircraft. On September 8, the Convair plane crashed outside Denmark, killing all fifty passengers and the crew of five.

In this crash, key people from all areas of the organization were killed. Important management functions were all of a sudden gone, tacit knowledge disappearing immediately, and leaving behind a company in shock and grief. Shipping has been termed a gentleman's business, something that became apparent in the trying times following the tragedy. For at least a year after, competitors refrained from attempts at capturing clients or attacking the weakened competitor. Some even offered their help by seconding personnel to the company and helping out in other ways.

---

with easy access to products or services of a guaranteed quality at a fair price, which in turn is a means to attract and keep more business for a coalition of partners offering complementary products and services. As such, it is ultimately aimed at generating more revenues for the organization itself, but it has a philanthropic trait to it. The philanthropic dimension, however, is a lot clearer in an organization's support of charities and other good causes, the next topic.

Ways to Support Charitable Organizations and Good Causes

Philanthropic organizations and charitable programs are one group of external stakeholders a good citizen company should relate to. These organizations are not themselves the target of good deeds from the company, but vehicles that help the company in aiding less fortunate groups in society. Some principal decisions regarding support to such organizations have already been discussed, that is, whether to give money or time, whether to link support to the business area of the organization or not, and so on. This topic will be wrapped up by giving you some examples of mechanisms some organizations have used to give their charitable support:

• *Financial donations*. This is the most obvious way of supporting charities, requiring the least administration and effort. Some define a fixed percentage of pretax or bottom-line profits that is donated to one or more programs, others decide on an irregular basis how much and to whom will be donated. The Dayton Hudson Corporation has followed the first approach and said that it will donate five percent of its pretax profits to charities and social causes. The company feels that this is a part of its culture and that success emerges from aligning the corporate philosophy with worthwhile causes.

• *Employee time donations*. Also an often-used mechanism where employees spend part of their working hours, paid by the employer, to help out various social programs. Twelve hundred volunteers from 50 companies in the Boston area donate time to community service projects throughout the city. Totaling more than 6000 hours of service annually, volunteers build playgrounds, clean parks, paint schools, and plant crops.

• *Equipment donations*. Many organizations provide support by donating equipment or products to suitable causes or organizations. In many cases, these are products the company produces or sells (in which case the support also doubles as positive marketing), in others an organization can use its bargaining power to acquire needed equipment or products at lower prices than if the charities themselves were buying them. Often, donated products are brand new, but many companies are in situations where new models replace old ones, making selling the old model very difficult. Instead of scrapping such obsolete products, donating them to people who would not be able to buy them in the first place can be a nice gesture. SmithKline Beecham pledged a $1 billion commitment to eliminate lymphatic filariasis, and said it would donate five billion doses of its antiparasitic treatment over the next twenty years. Hewlett-Packard prefers donating computer equipment to schools because it is able to deduct its factoring costs and build goodwill in relationships with future consumers.

• *Excess capacity donations*. This is related to donating products or equipment, but is more linked to service companies that do not have the option to offer physical products. Days Inn has already been mentioned as allowing homeless people to get work and to stay in vacant hotel rooms. In many countries, there is a practice of donating advertising space for free to charitable organizations on a few special days of the year. Advertising on TV is so expensive that few charities find it feasible or worthwhile, even if such profiling could generate new support. Thus, on Christmas and Easter day, for example, the entire day of commercial breaks is reserved for charitable organizations for free.

Extending "Charity" to Customers

Finally, customers are also a group of stakeholders that can be targeted for philanthropic "niceness." Chapter 6 covered extensively what constitutes decent and caring behavior toward your customers, but from a remedial perspective. There are many strategies for keeping customers happy and coming back to buy again and again, such as consistently giving more value for money than others do or than is expected, or treating customers better than they are used to. Fair pricing or even considering a cost recovery or no-profits pricing strategy have already been mentioned, but there are other ways of "being nice" to your customers, either all of them or some that are less fortunate than others:

• Differentiated pricing, a mechanism for allowing customers with special needs to buy the organization's products or services, customers that would otherwise normally not be able to afford to. This is in some ways similar to charitable support, but directed at individuals in need and governed by the organization itself. For example, lawyers often perform pro bono casework for clients who would not be able to afford legal representation otherwise and pharmaceutical companies sell medicines at low cost to people in need. The drawback of such an approach is the danger of cannibalizing the regular markets and thus reducing regular sales.

• Bonus schemes, very often related to loyalty programs, where there are a number of different designs. Loyalty programs have their advantages and disadvantages, disadvantages not in the least linked to customers' perceptions of fairness and the possibility of earning benefits. Very often, such programs have levels of membership, where advancing upward generates more benefits, of course designed to entice customers into spending more money. Some research indicates that for each person happy about advancing up the levels, there are three or four disgruntled over not being able to do any climbing, to the extent that they consider switching suppliers. Some companies have deliberately designed bonus schemes where all customers get a cash-back bonus at the end of the year calculated at a fixed percentage (for all customers) of last year's spending. This has been successfully practiced in many European countries where so-called co-op stores (who call their customers *owners* rather than *customers*) award such a bonus to all members.

• Offering various pricing clauses that give selected customers certain rights and elevate their status among customers. There are various such clauses in use; one of the most widely used is the most favored customer (MFC) clause, where the customer in question obtains the best price quoted to any customer (this clause is used almost exclusively in business-to-business relationships). Price warranties are mostly used in consumer markets, where the seller offers to refund the customer the difference between its selling price and that of a competitor with a lower price, even sometimes with a premium added. A meet the competition (MCC) clause reverses the rights and gives the seller a right to match the best offer of competitors to keep the customer.

• Return- and complaint-handling standards, as has been mentioned before, are an aspect of the purchasing experience that often determines a customer's perception of the seller. Adding additional elements to legally imposed customer rights can often make a good impression; examples include: extended free return periods, extended warranties, service costs included in the price, obliging attitude toward repairs after warranty expiration, and so on.

Finally, many customers appreciate it when organizations they frequently deal with give them the opportunity to support good causes through schemes administered by the organization. The least complicated examples are stores that place collection boxes on the counter and channel any funds generated to charitable organizations. More elaborate schemes allow customers to return products they are discarding, but which are still in working order, so that they can be given to programs that can make good use of them. There are even more advanced ways of facilitating customers' support for good causes (see sidebar).

No matter how the organization facilitates such customer donations, it seems clear that such a practice links the organization and its customers together in a good deed. If competitors offer no such opportunities, this can be a powerful mechanism in tying customers to the organization.

Northwest Airlines operates a program in which passengers are given the opportunity to donate frequent flyer miles to charitable causes. In the first month of the program, St. Jude Children's Research Hospital in Memphis, Tennessee, obtained 120 free tickets. These were used to fly sick children and their families to Memphis for treatment.

And with that, the progression through the business ethics framework is complete. There is no doubt that there are a lot of different detailed approaches to promote an ethical approach to business, and you might be a little overwhelmed, especially if you have been reading the book so far chapter by chapter. However, the framework and all its details are intended to serve more as a menu and source of inspiration than a text you feel you need to know by heart.

IMPLEMENTATION SUMMARY

In this final area of the business ethics framework, covering external philanthropic business practices, the main point is to convert the corresponding policies into specific business practices. And as for earlier operational parts of the framework, the job at hand is refining existing business processes or developing completely new ones, which is a matter of applying business process development tools in a systematic fashion. Which elements to include in these processes will of course vary from organization to organization, but some inspiration can hopefully be found earlier in this chapter. The final chapter will conclude the book by picking up some of the spurs to discussions about negative aspects of business ethics that have occurred several places in the book.

11

Is It All Rosy Red or Do Business Ethics Imply Negative Results As Well?

eing a firm believer that an ethical approach to business will generate a range of benefits for an organization, I have so far done my best to convince you that this is the case. At this final stage of the book, I am certainly not going to renounce this belief of mine. To make my case even more compelling, I could continue piling up all the published and spoken arguments for corporate social responsibility and business ethics. Being "editor" of the arguments to be included in this text, I would be within my rights to do so. However, to live up to the ideal of fairness that this entire book is about, it would be unacceptable of me to conceal the fact that several counter-arguments to CSR have been brought to light. Contrary to supportive statements, quite few of these reservations have been widely published. As I have mentioned already, probably the most extensive critique of CSR was written by David Henderson (2001), commissioned by the New Zealand Business Roundtable. Coupled with a few other sources and my own critical views of some aspects of business ethics, this chapter aims to outline some of the more important potentially negative facets to be aware of.

IS CORPORATE SOCIAL RESPONSIBILITY A BREACH OF THE FUNDAMENTAL CAPITALIST MODEL?

The capitalist economic model, albeit perhaps not as rigidly defined as the term might suggest, forms the basic platform for economic activity in all

Western democracies. Although it has its flaws, it has proven to be a viable model for centuries, and the recent conversion of former communist regimes to a market economy adds support for the model. In the well-functioning capitalist model, private enterprise's main objective is to make profits. This might sound self-centered, egotistical, and showing little concern for society at large. The argument by economists is that enterprises contribute to society through taxes paid of profits made and through people supported by the wages they receive for work performed. Forty years ago, Milton Friedman addressed these issues in his book *Capitalism and Freedom*:

> Few trends could so thoroughly undermine the very foundations of our free society as the acceptance by corporate officials of a social responsibility other than to make as much money for their stockholders as possible. This is a fundamentally subversive doctrine. If businessmen do have a social responsibility other than making maximum profits for stockholders, how are they to know what it is? Can self-selected private individuals decide what the social interest is?

This is of course a perfectly reasonable argument. If private enterprises start pursuing objectives like world peace, fighting poverty, prevention of disease, and so on, and make these their primary objectives, they are no longer operating under the logic that dictates private enterprise. Such objectives are pursued by nonprofit organizations, governments, even individuals. In my view of business ethics, this is perfectly clear—the main responsibility of companies is to make money, money that benefits its employees through wages, its owners through dividends and profits, and the authorities through taxes. Holding true to this objective of course does not preclude a responsibility on the part of businesses for thinking for themselves about what is right or wrong. Laws and regulations can only go so far in describing acceptable behavior in various situations—there will never be laws covering every potential situation—and this requires independent thinking.

From this basic logic, it is possible to build additional considerations. A rational view of the world today is that radical pressure groups, governments, and larger parts of the general population are starting to see eye to eye on industry as not only a positive element in society, but also an element that inflicts damage on the environment, that deceives us with dishonest marketing, that applies unfair business methods to maximize profits, and so on. To avoid negative repercussions in the form of lost sales, tarnished reputation, fines, or legal prosecution, a logical response from enterprises is to clean up their act and avoid behavior that will elicit such repercussions. This is nothing more than staying firmly true to the core objective of making money. CSR in this view is not about taking responsibility for the well-being of the planet or the less fortunate people on it, it is about making a logical response to external pressures in order to avoid negative consequences that could damage profits. One might even say that business has "brought CSR on itself" through years of corporate irresponsibility.

Some go one step further, though, along a line of thinking that, "We make a lot of money from selling our products and services, more money than we could possibly spend wisely anyway. With this excess, why not use some of that profit to improve conditions for one or more groups of less fortunate people or the external environment?" Such organizations still keep their eye firmly on the ball and live up to their promise of being in business to make money, but out of a motivation that goes beyond appeasing potential negative opponents, they also use their profits for a more social objective than filling the pockets of their owners. It is difficult to see why even this more radical approach should be damaging to the basic capitalist model. Concern is in order if enterprises started foregoing profit objectives for the sake of such broader objectives, but very few, if any, such cases have been reported. Henderson frequently cites Shell Oil Company as being radical in their vision and mission statements and portrays the company as virtually being on the brink of disaster from pursuing such alternative objectives. I claim this is still motivated completely from the desire to generate profits, which seems well proven by key financial parameters of Shell: $9.4 billion net income for 2002 and return on average capital employed of 14 percent.

Henderson in his essay goes on to describe CSR as a radical doctrine that, if broadly accepted and implemented, will reduce welfare and undermine the market economy. The claim is that supporters of CSR, if they still see profits as a requirement, view profits not as an objective of its own, but as a means to other ends. This might even be the case—I have not spoken to the most idealistic and ardent believers in CSR, people who perhaps view corporate citizenship as an alternative to capitalism, but such views are primarily found outside businesses. The motivation for promoting business ethics is certainly not linked to such radical views, but has come as a result of a growing realization that such an approach can add to the competitiveness of a company. Based on this thinking, CSR is not harmful, but merely another means to maintain or increase competitive advantage.

Henderson reached the conclusion that CSR is the wrong prescription based on a flawed diagnosis. In an incisive criticism of the concept, Henderson claims CSR would bring far-reaching changes in corporate philosophy and practice, with worrisome implications for the efficient conduct of enterprises. This would lead to increased regulation, limits on competition, and restriction of opportunities and freedom of choice. In the final sentence of the essay, he concludes that the adoption of CSR marks an aberration on the part of many businesses concerned and that its growing hold on general opinion is a matter for concern. Although many share the concern that an abandonment of profit objectives and full-blown pursuit of alternative objectives is incompatible with the traditional way of business, it is difficult to see CSR as such a threat to the fundamental model of capitalism. Henderson even claims that industrial support for CSR is a proof of the poor quality of leadership in industry today. This seems a blatant insult to industrial leaders and their adaptation to novel ways of staying competitive with changing preferences in the population.

CSR IS BUILT ON FALSE PREMISES

These changing preferences are fairly well documented in surveys revealing that large portions of customers use companies' conduct as a buying criterion, that many people will choose a supplier that supports philanthropic causes, and so on. It could, of course, be argued that people have not really changed, that most people know it is politically correct to claim to select products based on such criteria whereas most of us could not care less when we go shopping: "So what if the coat has a fur collar, it looks good and warm so I will buy it, not to mention that the deck chair that would match my old table perfectly is made out of tropical wood. There can only be so much wood in a small chair—it cannot make a difference." If this is true, then enterprises subscribing to corporate citizenship are indeed ahead of demand. Perhaps their pursuit of fair and decent practices makes very little difference to customers and thus only contributes to increased costs and higher prices.

Henderson makes this argument in his essay. In his view, the belief that the world has changed so much in recent decades that business must change as well is false. Rather, the so-called MNEs (multinational enterprises) are the ones that have paved the way for CSR out of a necessity to appease radical groups in society. These MNEs are the most obvious victims of scandalous news reports of corporate wrongdoings through their visibility and the extensiveness of their operations, thus they have had to defend themselves by turning to CSR. However, far from being the general view of the population that MNEs and other industrial enterprises are the big, bad wolves of today, Henderson claims that radical NGOs (nongovernmental organizations) are the bearers of these ideas. These NGOs are radical pressure groups that oppose a free market economy and use all means to fight it. The reason they are allowed to stay on the scene and proclaim their views largely unopposed is that industries and governments alike are afraid to speak out against them for fear of retaliation.

I agree that such organizations exist and that their objectives or means are radical and often nondemocratic. I also support Henderson in the view that CSR has been pioneered by large multinational corporations, but I fail to agree that these are the only premises for the growth of CSR. Again, I see business ethics as a response to wider-reaching changes in awareness, in legislation, and in preferences to adapt business practices to these changes.

CSR WILL LEAD TO GLOBAL SALVATIONISM, INCREASED REGULATION, AND GLOBAL STANDARDS

From the growing number of publications promoting CSR, from the number of organizations formed to host enterprises that subscribe to CSR, and the increasing governmental support for these ideas, it seems clear that an ethical approach to business has a tendency to become the subject of "missionary work. " There is nothing wrong with this per se; this is how all management fads spread so quickly. Companies adopt a new tool, make it a big happening and spend lots of money and time on it, word spreads, management consultants fuel the rage, and soon a new concept has swept the world. The question is, is CSR and business ethics any different from other management concepts in this respect?

Henderson claims that a fundamental trait of CSR is that "new converts" often set out to convert others, usually more fervently than is the case for other concepts. As opposed to say, benchmarking or balanced scorecard, Henderson claims an ethical approach to business inflicts so many negative competitive consequences on its adopters that they need to level the playing field by transferring these to others as well. Originally a concept mainly for MNEs, this has resulted in its adoption also by smaller enterprises. Henderson labels this "movement" *global salvationism* based on a global alarmism and dawnism. At the foundation of this lies a misunderstanding of concepts such as sustainable development and social objectives, concepts which are being used as arguments for CSR, but which are poorly defined and not as linked as many like to think.

This salvationism convinces governments and international organizations of the need for extensive legislation against corporate misdeeds. As legislation is aligned and entities like the United Nations and others take an interest in the topic, global standards seem to emerge in the areas of labor standards, environmental impact, and so on. This has both positive and negative consequences. To the extent that such standards are implementable, they can contribute to improvements in countries where standards have traditionally been lower. However, as was discussed already in chapter 3, such standards can be impractical and expensive, and can result in antiliberal movements that restrict freedom of contract and freedom of choice. In some cases, the definition of minimum standards can actually result in people losing their jobs or fewer new jobs being created. Those companies that are unable to meet such standards are forced to close or will never be established in the first place. For their employees (or future employees), the choice is made on their behalf that they either find work in companies that meet the global standards or they do not work at all. This effect of CSR's propensity to promote such global standards is indeed a problematic aspect.

Henderson also claims that MNEs cannot afford to be the frontrunners in appeasing the population regarding negative industrial effects on society and the environment and carry less-exposed companies as freeloaders. Using their considerable influence, the MNEs will thus fight for more extensive legislation, fees, and so on, that will even out business conditions. As a result, all companies will find themselves facing tougher legislation and more restrictive competitive pressures. This is a thesis many fail to accept. To the extent that legislation has become tougher regarding pollution, fraud, or business practices, this has come as a result of an increasing insight into how various industrial processes do inflict damage and how creative companies manage to circumvent existing rules.

BUSINESS ETHICS RESULT IN A COST DISADVANTAGE

The last, and perhaps to individual companies the most discouraging, piece of criticism voiced by Henderson is that adoption of CSR will lead to increased costs and reduced revenues. To some extent, this is a relevant concern. Henderson lists a number of areas that would drive up costs:

- Adopting policies and practices designed to limit the environmental impact of operations.

- Adopting norms and standards to be applied across national borders in fields of environmental and occupational safety and health.

- Adopting companywide standards for employment and working conditions even when local circumstances are widely different.

- Offering wages, salaries, and terms of employment that are not closely related to market conditions.

- Implementing ambitious targets for diversity in recruitment and promotion.

- Giving preferences to local suppliers and contractors or suppliers with particular characteristics.

- Refusing to buy from firms whose business practices are viewed as unacceptable, or refusing to enter into joint ventures where prospective partners have what are viewed as unacceptably low standards.

Summarized, practices that will drive up costs are grouped under the headings of broader objectives, new reporting systems, and more extensive management tasks. Many of the items listed above concur with practices suggested in the business ethics framework of this book, and I agree that many of these, especially the philanthropic ones, will incur costs for an organization implementing them. When considering which policies and practices to select from the menu the business ethics framework represents, this is an element that must be taken into account.

However, one of the key arguments why an ethical approach is sound is the belief that carrying on "the old way" will also incur extra costs. As customer awareness grows and legislation tightens, companies will experience increased costs related to fees and fines to be paid for breaches, licenses that have to be acquired for discharges and pollution, lost sales from customers turning their backs on unethical suppliers, and so on. Although there exists very little empirical data to support either argument, the studies referred to in chapter 1 seem to provide some proof that this alternative approach is financially sound. There has also been a tendency for mutual funds with an ethical profile to outperform traditional funds. More research is definitely needed to uncover the mechanisms at play, but it seems plausible that any extra costs incurred by ethical business practices will be offset by avoidance of other cost elements and increased sales.

Still, it cannot be denied that many ethical business practices, especially in the philanthropic half of the business ethics framework, will lead to increased costs. In addition to the extra costs, CSR can also introduce increased strain on employees of the organization. Going the extra mile for customers, doing volunteer work, or other aspects that require longer working hours, more efforts, and so on, can all have this effect. I have seen many cases where service companies dedicated to excellent customer care find this to be incompatible with excellent employee care. Employees may work longer hours to complete a delivery only to find that this eats away at their leisure time and introduces some level of fatigue in the organization. This can be a difficult balancing act that can put a strain on the organization and its members.

BUSINESS ETHICS BECOMES A STIFLING STRAIT JACKET THAT LIMITS BUSINESS INITIATIVES

The essay by Henderson does not cover this aspect per se, but in writing this book I certainly am realistic enough to understand that some of the more far-reaching practices suggested here can set limiting boundaries for organizations. There are several issues to consider in this respect. First of all, after it becomes public knowledge among customers, the industry, and media, that a company has changed its strategy and business practices to a more ethical profile, that company becomes highly susceptible to scrutiny and exposure of breaches. The more pronounced this ethical profile is, and probably the larger and more visible the organization, the easier it is to fall victim to journalists or other players deliberately looking for something to make a story out of. This often entails some level of stress and anxiety throughout the organization.

Most of all, though, there have been quite a few examples where the introduction of business ethics into an organization leads to a heightened atmosphere of almost religious zeal. There is a saying along the lines of not having to be more Catholic than the Pope, but in some cases this is exactly what happens. Instead of developing a decent and caring organizational culture that supports one another, the result can be an exacting culture where people are always on the alert for any cases of noncompliance with rules and practices. In such a setting, the entire situation turns into an exercise of covering your back and avoiding doing anything wrong, which is of course not at all the objective of an ethical approach. If ethics lead business to become a stifling minefield of potential wrongdoings, even when acting in the best of faith, it has become a strait jacket that no one truly benefits from. There is also the question of whether to be naïve or simply decent. If trying so hard to "be good" that an organization implements foolishly lax practices toward various stakeholders, this is certainly taking business ethics several notches too far. And in being idealistic in nature, CSR can unfortunately be prone to such a tendency.

So, how to conclude . . . is CSR a fatal blow to the very fundament of capitalism, is it a harmless alternative to ordinary business that will hardly give any benefits, or is it a potentially powerful way of doing business? I guess the jury is still out, and I expect it to stay out for quite some time, as it is difficult to foresee one unified verdict forthcoming. In my personal view, you can go about business ethics for all the wrong reasons and in all the wrong ways and make a complete and utter failure out of it. Equally, I think, partly because I have seen it happen, done right it can represent a powerful source of renewed competitiveness for an organization. All I can do is rest my case and leave the decision up to you. . . .

Bibliography

Akao, Y. (editor). (1990) *Quality Function Deployment: Integrating Customer Requirements into Product Design.* Productivity Press: Cambridge, MA.

American Management Association. (Continuously updated) *AMA Survey on Downsizing and Assistance to Displaced Workers.* American Management Association: New York.

Andersen, B. (1998) *Business Process Improvement Toolbox.* ASQ Quality Press: Milwaukee.

Andersen, B. and T. Fagerhaug. (2001) *Performance Measurement Explained: Designing and Implementing Your State-of-the-Art System.* ASQ Quality Press: Milwaukee.

Aune, A. (2000) *Kvalitetsdrevet ledelse—kvalitetsstyrte bedrifter (Quality Focused Leadership—Quality-Managed Companies).* Gyldendal Akademisk: Oslo.

Bauer, J. E., G. L. Duffy, and R. T. Westcott (editors). (2002) *The Quality Improvement Handbook.* ASQ Quality Press: Milwaukee.

Bennis, W. G., and R. J. Thomas. (2002) *Geeks & Geezers: How Era, Values, and Defining Moments Shape Leaders.* Harvard Business School Press: Boston.

Brandenburger, A. M., and B. J. Nalebuff. (1996) *Co-opetition.* Doubleday: New York.

Brown, Keith T. (2000) *The Interactive Marketplace: Business-to-Business Strategies for Delivering Just-in-Time, Mass-Customized Products.* McGraw-Hill: New York.

Cafferky, M. E. (1995) *Let Your Customers Do the Talking: 301+ Word-of-Mouth Marketing Tactics Guaranteed to Boost Profits.* Upstart Pub Co.: Chicago, IL.

Carroll, A. B. (1991) "The Pyramid of Corporate Social Responsibility: Toward the Moral Management of Organizational Stakeholders." *Business Horizons,* July–August, p. 42.

Cascio, W. F. (1993) "Downsizing: What Do We Know? What Have We Learned?" *Academy of Management Executive* 7, no. 1, pp. 94–104.

Caux Round Table. (1994) "Principles for Business." http://www.cauxroundtable.org/

CNN (2002, updated continuously) "Fraud Inc." http://money.cnn.com/news/specials/corruption/

Collins, J. (2001) *Good to Great: Why Some Companies Make the Leap and Others Don't.* HarperCollins: New York.

Connolly, M. (2002) "What Is CSR?" CSRWire, http://www.csrwire.com/page.cgi/intro.html.

Covey, S. R. (1999) *The Seven Habits of Highly Effective People.* Simon & Schuster: New York.

Covey, S. R. (1998) "Is Your Company's Bottom Line Taking a Hit." PRNewswire, June 4, http://www.prnewswire.com.

Donaldson, T., and L. E. Preston. (1995) "The Stakeholder Theory of the Corporation; Concepts, Evidence, and Implications." *Academy of Management Review* 20, pp. 65–91.

Elkington, J. (1999) "Triple Bottom Line Reporting: Looking for the Balance," Australian CPA 69 (2), pp.18–21.

Fagerhaug, T., and B. Andersen. (1998) "Honest Marketing: A Coherent Approach to Conscientious Business Operation." *The International Journal of Business Transformation* 1, no. 3, pp. 192–98.

Ferrell, O. C., J. Fraedrich, and L. Ferrell. (2000) *Business Ethics: Ethical Decision Making and Cases.* Houghton Mifflin Company: Boston, MA.

Ferrell, L., I. Maignan, and T. Loe. (Unpublished working paper) "The Relationship Between Corporate Citizenship and Competitive Advantage." *Ethics Digest,* http://www.e-businessethics.com/organizational.htm.

Freeman, R. E. (1984) *Strategic Management: A Stakeholder Approach.* Pitman Publishing: Boston, MA.

Galloway, D. (1994) *Mapping Work Processes.* ASQC Quality Press: Milwaukee.

Graves, S. B., and S. A. Waddock. (1993) "Institutional Owners and Corporate Social Performance: Maybe Not So Myopic After All." *Proceedings of the International Association for Business and Society,* San Diego.

Graves, S. B., and S. A. Waddock. (1993) "The Corporate Social Performance–Financial Performance Link." *Strategic Management Journal* 18, pp. 303–19.

Grisham, J. (2003) *The King of Torts.* Doubleday: New York.

Harrington, H. J. (1991) *Business Process Improvement: The Breakthrough Strategy for Total Quality, Productivity, and Competitiveness.* ASQC Quality Press, Milwaukee.

Hartman, M. G. (editor) (2002) *Fundamental Concepts of Quality Improvement.* ASQ Quality Press, Milwaukee.

Hatling, M. (editor) (2001) *Fortellingens fortrylling: Bruk av fortellinger i bedrifters kunnskapsarbeid (The Thrill of the Story: Using Storytelling in the Knowledge Work of a Company).* Fortuna Forlag, Oslo.

Hayes, R. H., and S. C. Wheelwright. (1984) *Restoring Our Competitive Edge: Competing through Manufacturing.* John Wiley & Sons: New York.

Henderson, D. (2001) *Misguided Virtue: False Notions of Corporate Social Responsibility.* New Zealand Business Roundtable: Wllington, New Zealand.

Hochschild, A. R. (1997) *The Time Bind: When Work Becomes Home and Home Becomes Work.* Metropolitan Books: New York.

James, K. E., and P. J. Hensel. (1991) "Negative Advertising: The Malicious Strain of Comparative Advertising." *Journal of Advertising,* June, pp. 1–21.

Johnson, S. (1998) *Who Moved My Cheese?* G. P. Putnam's Sons: New York.

Jones, T. M. (1995) "Instrumental Stakeholder Theory: A Synthesis of Ethics and Economics." *Academy of Management Review,* April, pp. 404–37.

Juran, J. M., and G. Blanton (editors). (1999) *Juran's Quality Handbook, Fifth Edition.* ASQ Quality Press, Milwaukee.

Kano, N. (1984) "Attractive Quality and Must-Be Quality." *The Journal of the Japanese Society for Quality Control,* April, pp. 39–48.

Klein, N. (2000) *No Logo: Taking Aim at the Brand Bullies.* Picador: New York.

Kleiner, A. and G. Roth. (1999) *Car Launch: The Human Side of Managing Change.* Oxford University Press: New York.

Kotler, P. (1988) *Marketing Management: Analysis, Planning, Implementation, and Control.* Prentice-Hall: Englewood Cliffs, NJ.

KPMG Peat Marwick Forensic and Investigation Services. (1994) *The 1994 Fraud Survey.* Washington, DC.

Kurschner, D. (1996) "The 100 Best Corporate Citizens." *Business Ethics* 10, p. 24–35.

Loe, T. W. (1996) "The Role of Ethical Climate in Developing Trust, Market Orientation, and Commitment to Quality." unpublished dissertation, University of Memphis.

Machiavelli, N. (1532) (original publication) *Il Principe* (The Prince).

Maignan, I. (1997) "Antecedents and Benefits of Corporate Citizenship: A Comparison of U.S. and French Businesses." Unpublished dissertation, University of Memphis.

Martin, M. W. (1992) "Whistleblowing: Professionalism and Personal Life." *Business and Professional Ethics Journal* 11, no. 2.

Maslach, C., and S. E. Jackson. (1986) *The Maslach Burnout Inventory Manual* (2nd ed.). Consulting Psychologists Press: Palo Alto.

Maslach, C. and M. P. Leitner. (1997) *The Truth about Burnout: How Organizations Cause Personal Stress and What to Do About It.* Jossey-Bass: San Francisco, CA.

Maslach, C., and W. B. Schaufeli. (1993) "Historical and Conceptual Development of Burnout." In Schaufeli, W. B., C. Maslach, and T. Marek. *Professional Burnout—Recent Developments in Theory and Research.* Taylor & Francis: Washington, DC.

Mentzer, John T. (editor). (2001) *Supply Chain Management.* Sage: Thousand Oaks, CA.

Miethe, T. D. (1999) *Whistleblowing at Work: Tough Choices in Exposing Fraud, Waste, and Abuse on the Job.* Westview: Boulder.

Mintzberg, H. (1987) "Crafting Strategy." *Harvard Business Review,* July–August.

Nash, J. F. Jr. (1950) *Non-Cooperative Games.* Princeton University: Princeton, NJ.

N., Ikujiro, and H. Takeuchi. (1995) *The Knowledge-Creating Company: How Japanese Companies Create the Dynamics of Innovation.* Oxford University Press: New York.

Onsøyen, L. E., L. Andersen, M. Veiseth, B. Andersen, C. C. Røstad, and M. Ranes. (2002) *Arbeidsmiljø og utbrenthet i prosjektorganisasjoner* (Work Environment and Burnout in Project Organizations). Norwegian Center of Project Management: Trondheim.

Pendlebury, J., B. Grouard, and F. Meston. (1998) *The Ten Keys to Successful Change Management,* Wiley: Chichester, England.

Porter, M. E. (1980) *Competitive Strategy: Techniques for Analyzing Industries and Competitors.* The Free Press: New York.

Porter, M. E. (1985) *Competitive Advantage: Creating and Sustaining Superior Performance.* The Free Press: New York.

Porter, M. E. (1990) *The Competitive Advantage of Nations.* The Free Press, New York.

Reicheld, F. (1996) *The Loyalty Effect.* Harvard Business School, Cambridge, Massachussetts.

Reilly, R. R., and E. L. Lewis. (1983) *Educational Psychology: Application for Classroom Learning and Instruction.* Macmillan: New York.

Roness, A. (1995) *Utbrent?—Arbeidsstress og psykiske lidelser hos mennesker i utsatte yrker* (Burnt Out?—Work Stress and Psychiatric Disorders in People in Vulnerable Jobs). Universitetsforlaget: Oslo.

Rousseau, D. M. (1995) *Psychological Contracts in Organizations: Understanding Written and Unwritten Agreements.* Sage Publications: Thousand Oaks, CA.

Ruf, B. M., K. Muralidhar, and K. Paul. (1998) "The Development of a Systematic, Aggregate Measure of Corporate Social Performance." *Journal of Management* 24, pp. 119–33.

Ruf, B. M., K. Muralidhar, R. M. Brown, J. J. Janney, and K. Paul. (2001) "An Empirical Investigation of the Relationship between Change in Corporate Social Performance and Financial Performance: A Stakeholder Theory Perspective." *Journal of Business Ethics* 32, no. 2, pp. 143–56.

Schwartz, N., and T. Smart. (1995) "Giving—And Getting Something Back." *Business Week,* August 28, p. 81.

Sethia, N. K. and M. A. Glinow. (1985) "Arriving at Four Cultures by Managing the Reward System." In Ralph Kilmann et al. (eds.) *Gaining Control of the Corporate Culture.* Jossey-Bass: San Francisco.

Silverman, G. (2001) *The Secrets of Word-of-Mouth Marketing: How to Trigger Exponential Sales through Runaway Word of Mouth.* Amacom: New York.

Skarlicki, D. P. (1996) "What Do We Know About Restructuring and Downsizing?" University of Calgary, http://www.cpa.ca/Psynopsis/restruct.html

Smith, G. F. (1998) *Quality Problem Solving.* ASQ Quality Press: Milwaukee.

Solomon, R. C. (1999) *A Better Way to Think About Business: How Personal Integrity Leads to Corporate Success.* Oxford University Press: New York.

Stamatis, H. (2003) *Failure Mode and Effect Analysis: FMEA from Theory to Execution,* Second Edition. ASQ Quality Press: Milwaukee.

Steiner, G. A., and J. F. Steiner. (1988) *Business, Government, and Society.* McGraw-Hill: New York.

Stewart, T. A. (1999) "Why Leadership Matters." *Fortune,* March 25, p. 2.

Syan, C. S., and U. Menon. (editors) (1994) *Concurrent Engineering: Concepts, Implementation and Practice.* Chapman & Hall: London.

Taylor, G. (1987) *Pride, Shame, and Guilt.* Clarendon: Oxford.

Todd, J. (1995) *World-Class Manufacturing.* McGraw-Hill: New York.

Trischler, W. E. (1996) *Understanding and Applying Value-Added Assessment: Eliminating Business Process Waste.* ASQC Quality Press: Milwaukee.

Tsu, S. (1963) *The Art of War.* Oxford University Press: Oxford.

Vahtera, J., M. Kivimäki, and J. Pentti. (1997) "Effect of Organisational Downsizing on Health of Employees." *Lancet* 350, pp. 1124–28.

Verschoor, C. C. (1998) "A Study of the Link Between a Corporation's Financial Performance and Its Commitment to Ethics." *Journal of Business Ethics,* October, p. 1509.

Index

intermediaries, trusted, 217–18
internal communication, 135–36
International Benchmarking
Clearinghouse, 176, 243
International Committee of the Red
Cross (ICRC), 162
International Institute for Sustainable
Development (IISD), 200
International Labour Organisation,
63, 176
International Organization for
Standardization (ISO), 205
Investor Responsibility Research
Center, 200
ISO 14000 standards, 205

J

JC Penney, 265
just-in-time, 33

K

Kalikå, 294
kanban ordering, 278
Kano model, 40–42
kickbacks, 249
Kmart, 265
knowledge management, 142–44
knowledge worker, 103, 116–17
Kraft Foods, 233

L

lavish organization, 149–51
law-abiding stage, 37, 38, 42
laws and regulations, 139–42
respect for, 60
layoffs, 123
leadership qualities, 104–9
learning, 48, 77–87
on demand, 83
experience-based, 80–83, 89, 91
legislation, formal, 176
Level 5 quality of leadership, 108–9
lifecycle assessments, 205

local community,
actively supporting, 296–98
development programs, 297–98
effects of organization, 245–47
loss leader products, promoting, 229
loyalty programs, 236–37, 306

M

management buyouts, 266–68
management's concern for people
and performance, 107–8
market sharing, 234–35
marketing, 212–20
approaches to, 215–18
cost recovery, 215
image created, 215
warnings, 218–20
marketing uncertainty paradox, 11
markup pricing, 225
Maslow's hierarchy of needs, 269
mass advertising, 214
mass-customization, 217–18
mass tort litigation, 14–15
maternity leave, 112–13
Max Havelaar label, 256
media, 19
media's expectations, 209
media's inherent ethical issues, 209–12
Medicines and Related Substances
Control Amendment Act,
243–44
meet the competition (MCC)
clause, 307
"mercy in business", 302–3
Ministry of Health, 178
Mitsubishi Corporation, 235
monopolies, 234
moral integrity, 53–54
morale, improved, 7–9
most favored customer (MFC)
clause, 307
motivation for change, 42–43
multilevel marketing (MLM)
approach, 219
multinational enterprises (MNEs),
312–14
myths, 83–87